People of the Blue Water

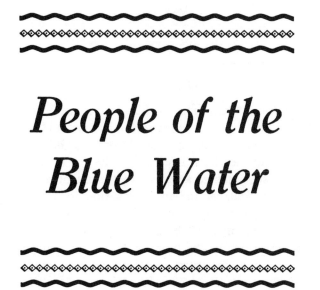

People of the Blue Water

A Record of Life Among the
Walapai and Havasupai Indians

by Flora Gregg Iliff

Foreword by Robert C. Euler

THE UNIVERSITY OF ARIZONA PRESS
Tucson & London

About the Author

FLORA GREGG ILIFF (1882–1959) was born in Iowa and lived as a young girl in Kansas and Oklahoma. After having graduated from the Oklahoma Territory Teachers' Institute at the age of seventeen, she accepted a post as a government teacher on the Walapai Indian Reservation in Truxton (now Valentine), Arizona. She later went on to teach grammar school on the Havasupai Indian Reservation, in the heart of the Grand Canyon. Mrs. Iliff's experiences in Arizona are recounted in her sole book, *People of the Blue Water.*

THE UNIVERSITY OF ARIZONA PRESS
Fourth printing 1993

Library of Congress Cataloging in Publication Data
Iliff, Flora Gregg, 1882–1959.
People of the blue water.

Reprint. Originally published: New York:
Harper, 1954.
1. Hualapai Indians. 2. Havasupai Indians.
3. Iliff, Flora Gregg, 1882–1959. 4. Teachers—
Arizona—Biography. I. Title.
E99.H75144   1985   979.1'00497 [B]   84-24105

ISBN 0-8165-0925-5

TO JOE

Contents

AN EXPLANATION

It would be folly for me to pretend that I remember, for all these years, each date, name and conversation recorded in this book. When I returned home from Truxton, at my mother's death, I found my letters, relating for her sharing the experiences I had so enjoyed, neatly packaged and filed with her other papers. I, too, saved them, little thinking that they would write a book. Others who shared with me these experiences have contributed by bringing to mind incidents that had grown dim in memory. My sister Mabel Davis convinced me that the book should be written, and typed the manuscript; my daughter Christobel Berger shielded me from interruptions, making the writing possible. Leslie Spier made available the material in his "Havasupai Ethnography" (*Anthropological Papers of the American Museum of Natural History*, Vol. 29, 1928, Part III); Little, Brown & Company gave permission for the use of quotations from the books of George Wharton James, *In and Around the Grand Canyon* and *Indians of the Painted Desert Region*. My thanks to all of these for their generous contributions.

Out of deference to those who jealously guard their native customs, the fictitious names Sakawema, Don, Mab, Suja, Tahuta, have been substituted for the Indian names of these persons. Nor is Nina the name of the girl who was employed at the Hackberry Day School, for a brief period.

FLORA GREGG ILIFF

ACKNOWLEDGMENT

I should not like this book to go to press without my most grateful acknowledgment to

HELEN SHAW

whose constructive criticism and pertinent suggestions shine through the words on its pages.

Foreword

When as a young school teacher, Flora Gregg came to the country of the Walapai and Havasupai in 1900, those Indians had been defeated in a war with troops of the United States Army but three decades earlier. Reservations had been established for them for but eight years. Only a handful of Anglo-Americans—soldiers, miners, explorers—had visited them in their homeland.

But government agents already had made inroads, and the aboriginal way of life of these Indians was a thing of the past. No longer could they roam their native homeland. And there were mounting pressures from the domineering Anglos that were playing havoc with the Indians' religion, social structure, and political organization. Flora Gregg, as a teacher and later as agent to the Havasupai, contributed knowingly or unknowingly to these cultural changes that almost brought these native Arizonans to anomie.

To set the scene for the confusing and unstable cultural stage upon which Flora Gregg made her entry at the turn of the century, one must go back some six hundred years. Anthropologists who have studied the Pai—as the combined Walapai and Havasupai are termed—know that they once considered themselves as one tribe. Several political bands owed allegiance to a council of three principal chiefs. They enjoyed this type of polity until the 1880s, when agents of the United States government established two separate reservations and thus, by fiat, created two distinct tribes. These reserves consisted of some 900,000 acres for the Walapai and a mere 516 acres for the Havasupai.

From about A.D. 1300, when the Pai first moved east across the Grand Wash Cliffs to the Colorado Plateau from their earlier homes along the lower Colorado River, until the mid-nineteenth century, they occupied a territory of many millions of acres. They carried on their chosen aboriginal way of life untrammeled by white people. Ranging over the land, they hunted large and small animals and gathered a multitude of edible wild plants. Where there was a reliable supply of water, such as in Havasu Canyon, the springs in Matawidita or Quartermaster canyons, or along the Big Sandy, they farmed the great domestic triad of corn, beans, and squash. As they moved about their territory they lived in simple brush wikiups or in small rock shelters in the cliffs of the canyons. Mostly they were at peace with themselves, although occasionally they suffered raiding parties from the Yavapai to the south or the Paiute from the north across the Grand Canyon.

A few short weeks before America declared its independence from Britain, however, a portent of change appeared on the Pai scene. In June of 1776 there came among them a bearded, brown-robed, white man riding a mule. While the Pai probably had seen Spanish priests during earlier trading visits to their friendly Hopi neighbors to the east, Father Francisco Garcés was the first to visit them in their homeland. Garcés spent a few friendly weeks with the Pai in the uplands as well as in Havasu Canyon before traveling on to a most inhospitable welcome at Oraibi, a principal Hopi town.

Garcés's visit to the Pai had little effect except perhaps to make them aware of strangers in their midst. While during the ensuing eight decades a few more bearded foreigners passed through their country, it was not until the 1850s and 1860s, when prospectors began mining activities, that the Pai came to the realization that their country and their very way of life were threatened.

Then they fought back with a vengeance. They killed every miner they could find and, as one might expect, the United States Army came to subdue them. Troops fresh from the War of the Rebellion, under the command of Lt. Col. William Redwood Price, scoured the country, killing Pai wherever and whenever they could be surprised and burning their camps when the Indians fled. For three years, from 1866 to 1869, the Pai defended their homeland. Finally, they were defeated and marched ignominiously to captivity, first near the present city of Kingman and then to La Paz along the steamy bottomlands of the Colorado River.

The bands we recognize today as the Havasupai escaped much of this holocaust; they were too isolated for army troops to reach them. Those of the Walapai bore the brunt of the Americans' ire. Their numbers were thinned by several hundred during the war.

Later, they slowly drifted back to their own country, only to find it usurped by miners and cattlemen. The Indians hung about the camps and settlements, taking menial jobs, whiskey, and white insults in about equal doses. For example, the year before Flora Gregg arrived in the Walapai country, the Kingman newspaper, *Mohave County Miner,* noted:

A petition from the people of Mohave County to General Miles, asking that the commander at Fort Mohave be instructed to investigate the suspicious actions of the Wallapai [*sic*] Indians, was being circulated in Kingman this week. . . .

"Sheriff Lake daily receives a number of letters from ranch and cattlemen who are alarmed at their strange actions. . . . It is evident that the 'medicine men' have stirred up all the superstitions of which a savage is capable, and if the ways of God are mysterious, the ways of a live Indian are more so.

"Music hath charms to soothe the savage breast. . . .

"And it is said that the most effective is the whistle of a well-directed bullet.

By 1889, realizing that overt hostility had failed them previously, the Pai adopted a great millenarian movement—the Ghost Dance. By following the prescribed ritual they believed that all the hated whites would be driven from the earth and that their ancestors and, indeed, the "good old days" would return.

Three years later, when their utopia failed to appear, disillusionment again set in. It was in this rather demoralized state that Flora Gregg found them in 1900—defeated, subservient, and ready if not willing to accept what the dominant society served them.

Already, since formal Office of Indian Affairs paramilitary schools had been established soon after the reservations, Pai children were regimented and wearing uniforms to class. Adults were thought by Indian agents and teachers alike to be nothing more than "large children" who were to be dissuaded from their "heathen" ways and taught how to be "civilized." White "farmers" were even employed to teach the Pai nineteenth-century agrarian manners, something they had learned for themselves centuries before. Worse were the dictates—both subtle and overt—of the whites: behave like whites (that is, like civilized beings) or else.

Flora Gregg Iliff's book graphically describes her time on both the Walapai and Havasupai reserves. It is a most readable account of those days, colored though it may be by white values. Indeed, if one wishes to understand even a bit about these people today, *People of the Blue Water* is a good beginning.

While not many people visit the Walapai today—Highway 66 through their reservation has been abandoned in favor of the Interstate route miles to the south—more than 25,000 tourists descend to Supai, the Havasupai community in Havasu Canyon, each year. By and large, these visitors come not to see the Havasupai—something for which the Indians are grateful—but to gaze upon the spectacular falls of the "blue water" and to camp in what some writers have called a Shangri-la.

Flora Iliff would be nonplussed if she could see Supai village today. All that remains of her school—flood-ravaged in 1910—are foundations and the school bell. This reminder of the white man's clock was about all that was recovered from that deluge. Until 1983 it hung and tolled from the one-room schoolhouse that served the Havasupai for some seventy years.

Today it is a "figurehead" above a beautiful new school that houses students from kindergarten through the 8th grade. Nearby are tribal offices with telephones and photocopying machines. These are a stone's throw from a new post office—which receives the only mail in the United States still delivered by horseback—a grocery store, and a tribal cafe where weary hikers can buy iced lemonade and fast foods.

Not only would Flora Iliff recognize nothing but the sandstone cliffs behind Supai village today, she would also undoubtedly be concerned with the social issues these canyon Indians face. There is unfortunate political dissension, health problems such as diabetes and alcohol abuse, and general malaise in their canyon world. Yet with promising leadership and a realistic understanding by the dominant society—an understanding which I am constrained to say has not yet materialized—the Pai may prosperously face many more generations.

Read this book with such understanding, be you Anglo or Pai, and profit from its experience.

ROBERT C. EULER

PART ONE

The Walapai:
People of the Tall Pine

CHAPTER ONE

The Lure of a Canyon

⊏⊐ "These Indians are almost completely out of touch with the civilized world," the lecturer explained. "Their village on the floor of the gorge can be reached by either of two trails, both of them steep and both of them dangerous."

I gripped my purse and listened intently.

"The canyon in which they live is so inaccessible that it is difficult to find teachers to work in such isolation. The Havasupai [Hä-vä-sú-pī]—the People of the Blue Water—need you."

I sat very straight in my chair. Would I go? I was practically there!

It was 1900 and I was young and unwilling to weigh consequences. Adventure? Danger? Life was waiting to be lived!

The lecturer at Teachers' Institute where I was supposed to be increasing my ability to teach in the city schools in Oklahoma Territory, must have caught the excitement in my face.

"It's a land of mystery and enchantment where red-angled walls of the canyon hold between them a rollicking stream of sparkling blue water," she continued. "The Indians living there have an intriguing, primitive culture, rich in the lore of their ancestors. This tribe believes that their gods speak to them through rustling trees, flying clouds and running water. Even today, as through past ages, the mythic Bear, Deer and Coyote talk with them and influence all their activities."

The few Indians I had seen had appeared uncommunicative,

stoical and unsocial. Yet under their stern behavior must be hidden this secret religion. Suddenly I wanted to learn at first hand what the Indians of the Colorado River country believed, and how their belief affected their lives.

Such an experience would not mean merely learning to speak a strange tribal language. No! I would be living with people who conversed with unseen forces—wrapped in the mystic wonders of another age. Nobody told me that the Indians in this locality were not far from the days of scalping at the drop of a tomahawk, or that floods, more destructive than earthquakes, could trap a tenderfoot. Or that the trail down was so steep in places that not even a mule, trained in mountain-climbing, could stand on its feet.

But it wouldn't have mattered. Born of pioneers who pushed ever westward in search of space and freedom, the lure of the untried, made more exciting by the thought of life in an Indian village on the floor of an isolated canyon, was a challenge I could not lightly cast aside. Add to that the appeal to help a bewildered people find its place in the social and business world encroaching upon it from all sides, and there was no alternative.

The rest of Teachers' Institute was a total loss to me. The picture of a brown-skinned people whose hopes, whose very existence, depended on a stream of blue water, pushed all thought of any other future away. I wanted to board the first train and start down either of those trails to the canyon floor.

In October, after a preliminary Civil Service test, my appointment came to teach in the Hackberry Day School for the Walapai (Wä-lä-pī) tribe in Arizona. The salary was forty dollars per month.

Mother, my younger sisters, brother and I searched on maps until we located Hackberry, on the Santa Fe Railroad, a town near the school. At a flag station, Truxton*, the conductor could let me off right on the Walapai Reservation. These were not the People of the Blue Water the lecturer had told us about; that disappointment had to be accepted. But the Walapai were related by blood to the People of the Blue Water; the reservations of both tribes

* Now Valentine, Arizona.

were in northern Arizona. This position might be the springboard to my goal, might even prepare me better for work with the Havasupai. I found a teacher who was satisfactory to the city school board; they hired her, promising to release me.

I applied all the psychology I knew to take me through that last day with my class. We talked about Indians and deserts and I promised to write immediately about the little Indians at the new school. That satisfied. The children, too, had itching feet. Vicarious adventure was better than none at all. They trailed off down the stairs with crooked grins on their faces, calling back: "Write us about the papooses. . . . Don't let them scalp you. . . . Good-by, Miss Gregg!"

There was no psychology that could ease the pain of parting from my family. Father had not survived the hard work of putting under cultivation his quarter-section of raw land. After Mother had been granted a patent to the land and we had moved to Edmond, our nearest town, she still was confronted with many family problems. I had been thinking only of myself in the desire to go to Arizona, such is the exuberance of youth. Could she manage without me?

I found her kneeling by the big trunk, carefully packing the dishes and clothing I should need at the school. Gently I asked my question. For a moment her hands were still. Then she smiled at me and her reply was characteristic of the courage with which she met every difficult situation.

"All my life I have wanted to see mountains and an ocean. I never have. This is your chance, also your chance to serve a people who need you. I want you to take it."

Our family made a sad little group waiting on the platform that chilly morning until the train came roaring out of the fog. We quickly said the last-minute good-by that each of us so dreaded, and the moment of parting was gone. Gone, too, was the elation, the feeling that I was starting out on a great adventure. I leaned back on the red plush seat of the coach and looked out on a damp, drab world—a young woman who had traveled little, setting out to civilize Indians.

As the train gathered speed I thought of a trip I had made ten years before, in a covered wagon, from our old home in Kansas to my father's claim in Oklahoma Territory. He had stopped his team in that bright new land of opportunity at an Indian burial ground, and the entire family had scrambled out to gaze in awe at lines stretched from the tops of poles to stakes in the ground. On the lines, like a family wash put out to dry, hung human scalps. The long, silky hair of white women and the short, crisp hair of white men lifted and rippled in the breeze that blew across the prairie.

Even then I knew that the Indians' side of the conflict was not told in the history books.

But where I was going, I might hear at last the Indians' version of the long and bitter struggle between the white men and the red men for possession of the land. I was born with a thirst for adventure; this teaching position would be an adventure in a new field of service.

CHAPTER TWO

Another World

The train left the plateau and began its cautious descent into a wide canyon. I became panicky with the fear that I might get off too soon or not soon enough. How could the conductor or I hope to locate a little Indian school in all that waste of desert, hemmed in by mountains and mesas? I had a vivid picture of myself, dying of thirst and exhaustion, lost out there on the hot sand, where there was not a sign of human habitation.

All too soon the conductor gave the signal, and the train ground to a stop. I stepped down into a deep cut that ran through a shoulder of the mountain. Several young people I had met on the trip followed me to the door, making wisecracks about the savages I thought I could teach.

The conductor made a quick gesture to the left, shouting to be heard above the noise of the train which had started to move again, "The school's over there someplace." Then the train gathered speed, rounded a curve, disappeared behind a red bluff, and I was alone, completely bewildered. The banks, steep and high, shut out all view except of the tracks that ran between them.

For a moment I wished myself safely back with the slate blackboards and the janitor. The sun was dropping in the west; precious minutes were slipping away. Leaving the big trunk standing on end, just as it had been dumped from the train, I took my suitcase and scrambled to the top of the left bank. The view, breath-taking to one who had always lived on the prairie, held me spellbound.

A long, wide canyon, powdered with a golden radiance, throbbed in the heat of the afternoon sun. The sand, flanking the dry wash that ran the length of the canyon, scintillated with gold, red and brown in strong contrast to the dull green of catclaw and sagebrush. The canyon's opposite wall towered high, rising steeply to form mesas and serrated mountains against the vivid blue sky. Outstanding in that stupendous wall was one lone mesa, crowned by a rim of red sandstone. Canyons cut the mesa off from adjoining highlands, so that it stood alone, backed and flanked by mountains and plateaus. Its solid bulk and serenity gave me assurance. It would always be there, silent, unmoved by man's little flurries of defeat or grief. Highlighted by the afternoon sun, it looked old and full of wisdom.

The scent of warm sand added its heaviness to the pungent tang of the gray-green sagebrush that pointed skyward with hard, brittle fingers. This was Truxton Canyon; somewhere within its breadth I would find the school.

I walked along the top of the bank peering into miles of sameness. Suddenly a few Indian wickiups became distinguishable on a distant slope. As my eyes sharpened to the bits of life blending with the landscape, I could identify jerked meat hanging on lines, lean dogs sleeping on the sand. I had stepped from the comforts and conveniences of city life into another world.

A long distance down the wagon road that paralleled the railroad track, I saw a new brick cottage looking out of place in this aged land. Farther on, partly concealed by the almost leafless trees of a small orchard, were rambling old buildings that had merged into their surroundings, taking on the bleak look of the desert. Beyond these was a brick kiln. I hurried to it.

On the way I met an Indian. He didn't look the least bit formidable. His hands were small and plump. His hair, cut raggedly short, made a black frame for his brown, childish face. His blue denim overalls and his checkered shirt were a concession to the white man's influence, but his soft comfortable moccasins were truly

Indian. When he caught sight of me, he tried to escape, but I asked quickly, "Where is Mr. Ewing, the agent?"

He pursed his lips, Indian fashion, and pointing with them said, "*Newe* (There)." At that moment Mr. Ewing, a tall broad-shouldered man with graying hair, came from the far side of the brick kiln where he had been teaching the Indian men to mix and mold the clay.

"We have been expecting you, Miss Gregg. I could have arranged to have you put off at the school and saved you that long walk, had I known your train."

He took my suitcase and we walked toward the old buildings. Now that I had arrived, I was impatient to learn more about the people with whom I should work. "Where are the Indians?" I asked.

He paused to answer. "There are a hundred or so living in wickiups in the village down the wash about half a mile and seven hundred others scattered over our reservation of more than a thousand square miles."

"The man I met up the road understood what I said," I remarked, "and his clothes were mostly civilian. I thought the customs and speech of these people would be entirely native."

"You'll find plenty of the original customs and speech," he replied. "But a few of the men have worked at day labor and learned some English. As to clothes, when deer were plentiful, their garments were of soft buckskin. Now they wear whatever they can get."

"This work is new to me," I said. "I'm afraid I'll make many blunders."

He laughed. "Probably. And you'll find it pretty lonely. Think you'll like it here?"

"Very much," I replied, trying to sound convincing.

We passed a ramshackle building that stood on a patch of bare sand. He nodded toward it and remarked: "That's the school building. Your primary room is on the north end."

"What grades are assigned to me?" I asked. Not just one, as in Edmond, it was evident.

"The first four," he answered, "and an adult primary class of pupils varying in age from twelve to sixteen who have never been in school before."

The shabby, unpainted buildings made me feel that I had traded my pleasant classroom back home for a very questionable future. I was a little scared by the fact that I was a long way from home with only ten dollars in my purse and, at the moment, the fates did not seem propitious. Then in the dry wash nearby I caught sight of a group of little brown children playing with stones. My discouragement vanished. They, not buildings, had brought me here.

On beyond, a creaking old windmill lazily pumped water into a shady pool. Over the pool leaned the orchard trees, their yellow, clinging leaves reflected in the wind-ruffled water—a secluded little scene of enchanting beauty.

We entered the back door of our living quarters, which had once been an old ranch house. It was the rambling building, set in an orchard, that I had seen from the bank of the railroad cut.

I soon learned that everyone used the back door, and that the kitchen was the social gathering place, a custom that sprang from something basic in ranch life. Cooking and baking, bustle and stir made the kitchen the heart of the house, and to its warmth and friendliness all comers gravitated.

The big, low room we entered was both kitchen and dining room for the workers in the Hackberry Day School, as it had been for the family who wrested the land from the desert before it was purchased as a site for the school. Those who built the old Truxton Canyon Ranch had left us more than the work of their hands. Nothing about the place had escaped the impress of their lives: their passion for the soil fruited in orchard and vineyard, in field and garden; the big comfortable barn holding the warmth of their affection for horses, and the spreading old house offering hospitality.

There was no stir and bustle of ranch life in the kitchen now. A small, dark-complexioned girl stood by a wood range, a fork in her hand, turning beefsteak in a square pan. Its appetizing fragrance filled the room.

Mr. Ewing introduced the girl as Nina, then opened the door to an adjoining room. "This will be your room until the buildings across the Santa Fe tracks are finished," he explained. "Those bricks we are burning are for a new school plant, which we hope to have completed by spring."

The size of my room, its proximity to the kitchen, and the small window high in the west wall indicated that this had been the rancher's pantry which someone had converted into living quarters for me. My heart sank at the hopelessness of the rough board walls, browned by age, and the worn, rough boards of the floor, partly covered by a grayish-white wagon sheet, which I carried out and dumped in the backyard. I was so concerned with the appearance of the room that it was several minutes before I glanced up at the ceiling, although had I reached up my hand I could have touched it.

I had thought that the ceiling, like the rest of the room, would be of weathered boards. Instead, a canvas had been stretched across just below the roof, its edges nailed to the four walls. To my dismay, the canvas bagged down under inverted dunes of fine sand. Wind-driven, the sand for years and years had sifted through the roof to accumulate on the upper surface of the canvas ceiling. The fabric, weakened by age, strained under the weight and might split at any moment. If it gave way some night while I was asleep —the thought appalled me! I decided that a good beating might bring the sand through the canvas and end the menace.

Nina was humming a tune as she clattered the dishes on the table for the evening meal, so I appealed to her. "I need help to clean this room. Do you know of anyone I can hire?"

She turned an astonished face to ask, "You think that room dirty?"

"It will stand a good cleaning," I told her.

"Plenty boys walking round in backyard," she said. "You pay boy one quarter, he help you. Maybe you need two. I'll get them."

She went to the back door and called, "Sam, Ted, come here!" When the boys filed into the kitchen, holding their caps uneasily in their hands and glancing about questioningly, she asked, "You want work, earn little money?"

"What work?" Sam asked, a wide grin splitting his narrow face.

He was wiry and thin, his dark eyes alert, the eyes of a mimic, quick to evaluate details and turn them into caricatures. His rather prominent ears gave him a Puckish appearance.

Ted, stolid, heavy-set and rather stern, merely said, "All right."

Each of us, armed with a broom, laid siege to those billows of sand. We beat with quick, hard blows, even though we feared splitting the canvas and bringing its load down on our heads, then we ran choking to the yard for a breath of fresh air. When we returned from one such excursion, Sam grinned at the ceiling and said, "That old sand been there too long, it not coming down, I think."

Sam was right. The sand would not come down except in a soft, thin powder, like flour running through a tightly woven sieve. So we stacked our brooms and I paid the boys their quarters.

They were hurrying to join their companions when Isadore, a young Mexican laborer employed at the school, called to them, "You boys, take the wagon up to the cut and get a trunk that was put off the train."

I dusted the walls, the furniture, and washed the window and the floor. When this was done, the room looked exactly as it had when I first entered it, except the wagon sheet was gone from the floor.

The trunk was dragged, banging and bumping, across the porch and into the kitchen. Nina gave a gasp and exclaimed, "Where you put it? It's too big!"

When I bought the oversize trunk, it had seemed a good idea, for it held so many things; but the charge for excess baggage, and now the question of storage, turned it into a white elephant. It could never be shoved through the narrow doorway to my room. Finally, Nina indicated a big room that opened off the kitchen. It had been the rancher's parlor. Now it was the school workroom where the girls learned to sew on old treadle machines, cut garments on big, heavy tables, and press them with irons heated on a tall stove that bellied out in flat segments against which the flatirons rested.

Nina pointed to a corner and said, "Put the trunk there, boys."

"But those dresses!" I protested. "I don't want my trunk under all those clothes. I'll have to open it frequently to get at my things."

"No other place. Those dresses all been washed and ironed. They won't hurt," Nina said pleasantly and returned to her kitchen.

The boys shoved the trunk under a row of tightly crowded dresses hanging from an iron bar. They were dingy and faded and certainly did not look like clothes that had had the benefit of good suds and hot irons, but there was no other place for the trunk.

A cheerful halloo from the backyard sent us flying out to greet a sturdily built woman with graying hair, who seemed to be in her early forties. She took my hand in a strong, firm clasp making me feel that my arrival at the school was of real importance.

"I am Miss Calfee, the field matron," she said. "I heard that you were here and wanted to meet you. News travels by grapevine on the reservation. Since I work with the adult Indians and you with the children, I think we should get acquainted." She glanced down at her plain dress and stout shoes. "I've been in the village teaching some of the women to make light bread. They had a lot of fun punching the dough, trying to learn when it was light enough."

"It must have been fun for you too," I exclaimed. "I wish I had been there!"

"Well, I came by to ask if you would like to walk up to my house tomorrow afternoon to watch us open a missionary barrel. Quite a number of the Indian women are coming. They love to banter about some of the unusual things that are sent to us, but they're clever in finding a use for everything we receive."

"I'd love to come," I assured her.

She gave me a warm smile. "About two o'clock, then. I live in that brick cottage up the road a bit."

Her pleasant face, the humorous twinkle in her eyes and her cordial manner inspired confidence. I watched her take the path through the vineyard in front of our house, pass through the sagging gate and turn into the sandy road, every line of her body sturdy and strong.

At the employees' mess, we ate dinner that night on a long table by the light of a kerosene lamp. Two of those in the group of six who sat down to dinner charmed me with their quick laughter and witty conversation. One, a vivacious girl whom the Indians had named Chipiya—because, they said, when they looked at her they thought of a little bird—had been temporarily employed in the position to which I had been appointed. We would lose her. We also would lose Sally, a lively girl who had been employed as seamstress for a time, to instruct the girls in making dresses, shirts and underwear for the schoolchildren, and whose work was now completed. Our group would be reduced to four: Mr. Ewing; Nina; Mr. Graham, an Indian employed as principal teacher; and me. With the exception of Mr. Ewing, who had an office and a private room in a cottage set off in the rear of the main building, we were all housed in rooms opening off the kitchen.

The dinner conversation was light, cheerful and confined mostly to relating humorous incidents that had happened in the classrooms. I was secretly studying Mr. Graham. It gave my ego a jolt to discover that here at least was one Indian who did not need my help to gain an education and to acquire the white man's culture. In fact, I would work under his direction. He was from the north, with a smooth olive skin, lighter in color than that of the desert Indians. His flashing eyes, intelligent face and quick movements indicated a forceful personality.

I learned that Mr. Ewing was in charge of both the Walapai

and the Havasupai tribes. This was a chance to get firsthand information of the People of the Blue Water.

At once he disposed of an old myth. Through misinformation, or the story may have been started in jest, the statement had appeared in the press that the Havasupai were a race of giants who kept pygmies as slaves. Mr. Ewing knew these Indians and explained that in stature and general appearance they differed little from the Walapai and that many of their customs were identical with those of their cousin tribe. The superficial differences in their native language indicated that, long ago, both groups had belonged to the same tribe. The canyon in which the people lived was a southern branch of the Grand Canyon of the Colorado.

After dinner, there was nothing for me to do but go to my room. I was sitting in the old bow-back chair, feeling very lonely, when there came a tap on my door. Chipiya, Sally and Nina had come for a visit. They were friendly and full of fun but asked no questions, so I restrained my desire to learn about the school and the work that would fall to me.

All evening, in their quick glances and stifled giggles, I sensed suppressed mirth. Suddenly one of the girls burst out laughing. "You'll never know how queer we felt when you gave this room such a thorough cleaning," she explained. "We had worked and worked, dusting and scrubbing every inch of it. We spread the wagon sheet on the floor to cover the rough boards. We tried to make it look nice and homey."

CHAPTER THREE

Days of the Long Ago

The next day, the unopened barrel of donated clothing stood on the hard-packed sand in front of Miss Calfee's cottage. Women from the Indian village were moving about it with the easy grace of those who live close to nature, talking in low, soft voices among themselves, bubbling with excitement.

The voluminous skirts of their hand-stitched dresses swept the ground. The way they swished when the women walked seemed to symbolize an almost hauty independence. The three or four bands of bright calico, spaced at intervals above the hem, proclaimed their gay outlook on life in general. But there was no accounting for the *sutam* worn by every woman and said by some to be the modesty garment. For this, the women sewed four brightly colored bandannas together in the form of a square. The upper edge was brought about the shoulders, the ends knotted in front, while the lower edge hung free, floating about their knees as they walked.

The older women stood back from the barrel; their bare feet, knotted and scarred by too violent contact with roots and stones, pressed heavily against the earth. The younger ones, occasionally shifting the weight of the babies they carried on their backs, crowded close, eager for clothes for their families. With slender brown hands they pushed aside the thick mane of hair, cut shoulder length with a bang across the forehead, that kept closing in to conceal their faces.

A wizened old man with a skeptical smile seemed strangely out of place. He was wearing flour sack pants, a nondescript fragment of shirt, and beautifully beaded moccasins. But Suja later proved to be the most important person present.

Miss Calfee frequently received boxes and barrels of useful and badly needed supplies from the Massachusetts Indian Association. Opening them was always an exciting event. But this lone barrel came from a different source, sent by a small group of women who had no knowledge of the Indians' needs.

Sam Swaskegame (Swäs-kē'-gä-me), who had helped me attack the sand dunes, stood by the barrel, a hammer in his hand. "Shall I open it?" he asked, his face bright with anticipation.

Miss Calfee nodded. With a few swift blows Sam lifted the head from the barrel, and tore away the newspaper packing. Beneath, lay a wide picture hat with a pink ostrich plume curled about its crown and falling coquettishly over the brim in the back.

The younger women crowded forward. Walapai women did not wear hats, but this useless thing was entrancingly beautiful. Suja's wife pushed the young women aside and edged in for a better view. It took her bewildered mind a moment to comprehend what she saw, then she cried, *"Il-la!"* (their expression of surprise), and reached up a gnarled finger to scratch her tousled head.

Miss Calfee laid the hat on a near-by table and lifted from the barrel a pale blue satin lounging robe, faded in spots and worn, but holding the fragrance of soft living. This, too, was quickly laid aside while more subtantial clothing was unpacked. From the very bottom of the barrel came a pair of blue satin slippers.

While Miss Calfee helped the women select the things they could use, Suja, little, shriveled, but straight as an arrow, approached the table, his speculative glance fixed on the hat. His hair, parted and drawn to either side, hung over his shoulders in two long braids, plaited with strips of gay calico. With a coy glance at Miss Calfee, he set the hat at a cocky angle on his grizzled head, slipped into the robe, and thrust his small moccasined feet into the slippers. Then he danced the slow rhythmic dance of his tribe. Lifting the robe with mock daintiness between thumb and finger, he took a sidestep to the left and began circling the barrel, each movement precise, timed to a cadence.

The incongruity of clothes and man brought shouts of laughter from the young women; the old women grinned appreciatively. He had achieved his purpose. He had shown them the white woman's silliness in finding satisfaction in garments that gave neither warmth nor service. Then, his voice rising to a crescendo, quavering and breaking on the high notes, he admonished his listeners, appealing to the women to return to the ways of their ancestors.

"You are foolish women," he told them. "You looked at the white man's barrel and you thought you saw dresses, coats, clothing to keep you warm when the snow flies and the winds blow. Those things were not there. The white man gives you what he does not want. You forget the old-time things, the Days of the Long Ago, when Coyote and Deer lived with the Walapai. When the god Tochopa taught the people how to grow food and take care of themselves. Live as the gods taught us, sing the old-time songs, work, dance and laugh. Have fun!"

The harangue ended abruptly. The old fellow gasped for breath; his trembling legs threatened to crumple under him.

The women, each clutching her share of the barrel's contents, began to disperse, strolling off along the trails that led to their wickiups. Quickly discarding his finery, Suja accepted, from the few things remaining on the table, a pair of trousers so large that he would be completely lost in them. But he had a solution. Holding up two fingers, he made the gesture of cutting and said, "Make two."

Miss Calfee gave him an affectionate pat on the shoulder and said, "Have your wife bring them here tomorrow, Suja. We'll see if we can make you two pairs out of this one."

Suja had an Indian's appreciation of feathers and an Indian's need. He made the gesture of peeling the barbs from the shaft of the plume, and tying them in a colorful cluster. He envisioned a beautiful addition to his headgear such as no other Indian had. A nod from Miss Calfee, and he trotted off, pink ostrich plume and trousers tucked under his arm.

Grace, the prettiest of the women, carrying her baby boy in his cradleboard on her back, moved to the table. She gently touched the blue robe. "Nice," she said in a vibrant voice, "like baby skin."

"Take it along, Grace," Miss Calfee offered. "It can't keep you warm, but you love pretty things, so you'll find a use for it." A few minutes later, Grace walked swiftly over the rough trail, her baby's dark eyes peeping from the blue satin robe she had draped about his cradleboard.

The Indians had slipped away to their village but they left me with the uneasy feeling that strange gods and mysterious spirits filled the air. I could not forget Suja's tirade.

"Suja did a very nice thing," Miss Calfee remarked later. "There was not much of value in the shipment, and the women were disappointed, but he made them laugh, and reminded them that their ancestors did not need the white man's help."

"But he took the pants," I said. "He seemed glad to get them."

"Yes, he took the pants. He is old and helpless, and he knows that he will be cold this winter. But he is grieved because his people have lost the old way and are confused and troubled and do not know how to shape their lives."

Sam and I helped Miss Calfee clear away the rubbish from her yard, then we walked down the wagon road to the schoolhouse. Suja's imperative voice seemed to follow me as we went. What had the mythic Deer and Coyote taught the Walapai in the ancient days of their proud independence? Finally I asked Sam.

He kept silent for a time as Indians do when questioned about their sacred traditions. Then he said, defensively, "White people having stories, all same Indians. I read about that man Adam in Testament Miss Calfee gave me. That man live with animals all same Kathatkanave."

"I have read about Adam too," I told him. "Was Kathatkanave like him?"

"He first Indian man. My grandfather tell me that," Sam answered. "Kathatkanave live in pine-covered mountains and like walk under trees or sitting by running stream, but his heart feel sad. He got no friends, so he tell Coyote about his trouble. Coyote learn many things; he run fast, go all over world. Coyote tell him make big stone oven, build fire, making plenty hot. He tell Kathatkanave cut many tall rushes and put in oven, lay rows very straight. When Kathatkanave do all these things, he sitting by stream, he dreaming little while, waiting for rushes bake."

Sam continued his story by telling how Kathatkanave went to the oven, but the rushes were not baked. He removed a few, called them White People, and sent them away. He returned to the oven and took out more rushes. They were just right, a reddish-brown color. "Kathatkanave say, 'You my people: Indians,'" Sam added with relish. "But the rest of them rushes burned too done; he call them Black People."

I liked Sam's story, but it had a familiar ring, like something once heard and almost forgotten. So I said, "I think some white man made that tale up just for fun, and your grandfather heard it and thinks it is true."

Sam looked skeptical. "I don't know," he said hesitantly. "My grandfather very old. No talk English."

I didn't know either. I didn't know whether Sam had a grandfather or not, for relationship was loosely classified. He might call any elderly man his grandfather. However, Sam knew other things that only Indians knew, so I asked, "Why do your people call the first Indian man Kathatkanave?"

"My grandfather say that mean 'taught by the Coyote,'" Sam answered.

"Kathatkanave should have left my ancestors in the oven a little longer," I said. "I should have been an Indian. I need Coyote to tell me how to teach the little Walapai who do not understand English."

Sam grinned but made no reply. At my classroom door he said,

"Good night, Miss Gregg. I going down to camp. It getting dark pretty quick."

"Good night, Sam," I answered, and watched him walk briskly toward the Indian village more than half a mile down the canyon on the far side of a projecting arm of the mesa.

I entered the schoolroom in which blue-gray dusk had settled, filling the corners and the spaces beneath the desks. The wide boards of the floor with cracks between, the walls battened to keep out wind, sand and snow, the homemade, splintery desks and benches, all topped by a corrugated iron roof, turned my thoughts back to my Oklahoma school with its central heat, hardwood floors and janitor service. Washington was too far away to function adequately as a local school board.

I walked soberly back to my room.

Dinner the night before had been our last meal as a school mess. Mr. Ewing had warned us that after Chipiya and Sally left, the principal teacher and I must provide for ourselves. Many times I had wondered why a toy cookstove instead of a heater stood in one corner of my room; now I knew. It would both keep me warm and cook my food.

I hurriedly tried out the queer little contraption, topped by lids no larger than a saucer. But the wind and the stove worked in collusion. One swished down the stovepipe while the other, after I had touched a match to the dry wood it contained, puffed out white smoke rings that sailed up to the sand dunes on my ceiling. Then it sucked in its breath and with a whoosh sent the heat up the stovepipe. I could not cook the steak I had bought in town, or even a potato. I ate a cold supper.

That evening I went to the workroom to get some things from my trunk. Tediously edging its way from one end of the canvas covered lid to the other was a slowly moving gray film. Body lice! A migration of them in various stages of injury; some barely with strength to wave one leg; others dragging broken backs to keep up with the procession; many were completely done for, stiff and cold, moving only as the mass moved them.

I called Nina. "You said these dresses had been washed and ironed," I told her. "Look at my trunk!"

She stooped over and gazed at the mass very earnestly. "They are cr-e-e-pled!" she exclaimed, giggling. "Maybe the water was not so hot—maybe the iron too. They look so fun-e-e."

I swept up the mass and disposed of them. Back in my room I sat in troubled silence. Could I handle all the tasks that fell to the lot of the assistant teacher? I was inadequately prepared to teach the little folks who understood no English or those older pupils who had lived the free and easy life of the reservation for too many years and spoke only their native tongue. And I now realized the full extent of my extracurricular duties. Mr. Ewing had instructed me to supervise the preparation of the children's lunch, the work in the sewing room and the washing and ironing of school clothes. I must see to it that the water and the irons were hot. I must intensify our campaign against lice, for these primitive people, who harbored these parasites as unwillingly as I myself would, fought the scourge without benefit of insecticides.

If I failed in all this, I knew exactly what would happen. I was on six months probation; failure would mean dismissal.

In the feeble lamplight, the walls of my room drew in until I felt squeezed and mentally stifled. Outside was air and space. I walked out into the night and stood by the whining windmill. The sharp, staccato yaps of coyotes came across the desert waste. A chill ran up my spine. The ravenous beasts were on the kill; some wild creature was seeking desperate escape. But I had learned by now that it was not this crafty beast, the coyote that I knew, but Coyote Spirit—universal, wise—on which the Walapai and the People of the Blue Water relied for guidance. A desert moon sailed over the mesa's rim, edging the yellowed orchard leaves with quicksilver and flooding the land with a brilliance that made every object stand out sharply. That flood of luminance emphasized the timelessness of mountain and plateau. The coyote voices faded. Our own big mesa seemed wrapped in peaceful slumber. In the thin air, the stars were too big and too near to seem real.

There was comfort in this healing silence and glowing beauty. The god Tochopa must have moved among his people on such nights in the Days of Long Ago.

"The white man gives you what he does not want. You forget the old-time things." Suja had unconsciously thrown me a challenge. I would do my best to meet it in the months ahead.

CHAPTER FOUR

Opening Bell

Monday morning I awoke early. This would be my first day in the classroom!

As I prepared a hurried breakfast, I glanced through the window and saw, in the chilly dawn, a small group of children huddled at the end of the school building. They had come early to see the new teacher. I was equally curious to meet the pupils and learn what the day might bring.

I went to the schoolhouse at seven-thirty, when Patsy, a seven-year-old boy, was scheduled for treatment. Patsy appeared promptly, his head swathed in soiled bandages. My extracurricular chores began. Fanny, one of the older schoolgirls, who had been dressing the child's head for some time, had placed a pan of warm water, a stiff brush and a bar of yellow soap on a table in the yard. Patsy's feet lagged as he approached the table. I helped Fanny unwind the bandages, revealing sores, caused by vermin, that went to the bone. Fanny scrubbed the sores clean with the stiff brush and strong soapsuds while Patsy squirmed and shed a few tears. We applied a healing ointment and bound him up again. Drastic treatment but surprisingly effective; with neither doctor nor nurse available, I could suggest nothing better. Patsy's relief was so great that he gave us a feeble grin as he walked off, his bandaged head looking like a giant puffball on his small shoulders.

In a lean-to washroom, the girls assembled to wash in tin basins, comb their hair and change to clean dresses. We could hear the boys shuffling about, washing, combing and changing in the adjoining shed under the direction of Mr. Graham. Although some of the pupils were neat and clean at all times, these morning ablutions were an established custom at this and other day schools; perhaps with the desire not to embarrass the untidy, it had become a ritual for all.

At the last minute, Mr. Graham came to the classroom to teach me to pronounce the names on my register. "Take this name, Whatapanyege," he said. "The accent falls naturally on the third syllable. If you mispronounce it, the children will think it a joke and call the boy by the mispronounced name. When a child enters school, we help him choose his given name—John, William, whatever name he prefers—but the father's name becomes the boy's family name. That gives the tie-up, child to parent."

A name was not kept for a lifetime by a Walapai, so the tribe bestowed it with astonishing recklessness. Quite often a child would not be named at all until his personal appearance or some incident suggested one, frequently given in ridicule. And the name was his until another incident would cause it to be changed. If a naked brown baby, curled up on a blanket asleep, happened to resemble a ripe watermelon, he would immediately be named Somaja ("Watermelon"). Later, when he was old enough to strut about wearing his father's shirt, his name would be changed to Sack-athut ("Shirt").

An Indian never became too old to have his name changed, if his friends found another that tickled their fancy. An elderly woman who sat, day after day, by the wagon road watching the people who occasionally passed by, was dubbed: "The-old-woman-who-sits-by-the-road-that-people-may-see-her-as-they-pass." A Washington official, recording her name on the tribal roll, wrote one word: "Visible."

The school bell rang at eight-thirty. Ted marched the boys of the primary grades into my classroom while Fanny had charge of the girls' company.

When the children were seated, Ted, taking his official re-sponsibility seriously, stood by his desk looking them over as a distressed parent might survey his flock of unruly youngsters.

Then he settled in his seat. The children transferred their attention to me. They needed to know what this new teacher was like, what they might expect from her, and how far she would let them go.

We had our opening exercises: a few verses from the Bible and a short, get-acquainted talk in which I tried to teach them to pronounce my name, knowing all the time that they would coin one of their own for me. And they did—Hico ("white person"). We discovered that we could sing "Swing Low, Sweet Chariot" with such vigor that the corrugated iron roof actually seemed to clatter. How they loved to sing! Of course they mispronounced many of the words but this was their favorite song. Had I acquiesced, we would have done nothing in the six-hour session but sing "Swing Low."

Their faces fell when I opened my register. Because I felt safe in taking a name in which I had been drilled, I read that of Billy Whatapanyege. Instead of answering "Present," as I had expected, Billy sat as still as a sly mouse, but all the small children in Billy's class sprang to their feet and, pointing at the culprit, shouted lustily, "Bee-lee, Bee-lee"—their pronunciation of his name.

How did one call the roll in an Indian school? I must know each child by name and which seat he should occupy. When a teacher's attention was diverted, the children made a game of slipping about, exchanging seats or leaping through the nearest window. When the latter happened, Ted rose from his seat with great dignity, followed them to the yard, lectured them soundly in their native tongue, and marched them back into the classroom.

Since my public school method of calling the roll had proved unfruitful, I announced: "When I speak a child's name, I want him to lift his hand." Then I asked Ted to tell them in Walapai what I had said.

Ted stood by his desk and barked out instructions. When I spoke a name, he would tell that child to lift his right hand, and explain which hand was the right by saying, "The one that holds your pencil," or "The hand that's in your pocket." I was violating a rule, for this school, like other schools of that period in which we were trying to make white people out of Indians with the greatest possible speed, had ruled that the Indian language should not be spoken on the school ground. But Ted and I got on famously by breaking the rule—until we came to Lily.

It took persuading to bring the little girl's hand above her desk. When it came, it was a twisted claw. She buried her burning face in her sound left arm, while the children pointed and jabbered and laughed. The suffering I had caused the child left me shaken. I was rather severe in restoring order, for my heart ached at the look of humiliation, of abject shame, on Lily's face. When she was a baby her mother had dropped the child in their outdoor fire and her right hand and arm had been severely burned. As long as Lily could remember, that deformed hand had been an object of ridicule. But the unhappy incident gave me an insight into Indian psychology that was helpful in my work among the Walapai and later among the Havasupai.

The next day was to bring another illustration of the Walapai's attitude toward the crippled and deformed. A skeletonlike old man, bent double with rheumatism, hobbled painfully across the school ground. Following him, his posture a duplicate of the old man's, was Sam Swaskegame. Sam was a natural mimic. Each move of a muscle, each backward swing of a crippled arm, was exaggerated. In their wake trailed a grinning string of cheering youngsters. I was shocked and angry.

"Sam," I called to him, "what does this mean?"

Sam slowly straightened up and turned to face me. I can never forget the picture he made, the light of laughter in his thin face giving way to an expression of surprised questioning.

Then, comprehending my disapproval, he replied, "I not hurting that old man. I like to see can I walk like he walk."

Sam flashed an infectious smile in my direction and my anger melted. In the estimation of his schoolmates he had brought mimicry to a high art and the crippled man was a convenient object for study. Sam and I reached an understanding but the incident left me discouraged. I could not forget the look on Lily's face when she lifted her twisted hand above her desk. Sam still lived in his world—I in mine. His world seemed cruel to me; mine, soft and needlessly protected to him.

That first day in the classroom, the children had all seemed to look alike; straight, black hair, dark eyes, and only slight variation in skin coloring made it difficult to identify one child from another. To add to my confusion, the boys' uniforms were alike; the girls' dresses were identical in design and material. When I discovered a mole on the cheek, outstanding ears, anything that I could tie a name to, I felt like celebrating. But before many days I discovered dissimilarities in expressions, in mannerisms and features that were as identifying as green eyes or honey-colored hair. It helped, too, that many of the girls had designs tattooed on their faces. They would have added their native paint, but that was not permitted in the classroom.

At eleven-thirty we hurried to the lean-to to wash up for lunch. The school officers marched the companies to the tables that stood in the yard by our cottage. Mr. Graham "stood tables" to see that each child had plenty of food and to maintain order while the children disposed of the roast beef, stewed dried fruit and homemade bread.

The afternoon session began at one o'clock; at four we were back in the washroom for a change of clothes, and the children scampered off to the village. The first day of my new experience had come to an end, a day of the most intensive education the primary pupils could give a new teacher. My initiation over, we settled down to work. Roll call lost the thrill of the unexpected and became as unexciting as it had always been in the public schools. But the activities in the washroom took on added interest. At first reticent, the girls talked with more freedom when we became better acquainted and I had gained their confidence somewhat. From them I caught hints of the ancient culture that still controlled tribal life, enough to make me realize that down in the Indian village, life was influenced by strange forces—forces that bound these people to the past as their ancestors had been bound for countless generations.

CHAPTER FIVE

Village Life

⊂Ɛ   Saturday afternoon gave me the opportunity to visit the Walapai in their village—an odd assortment of wickiups sprinkled over a sandy slope against the big, flat mesa. The Indians had left their distant homes near mountain meadows, springs in the piny woods or streams, to establish temporary dwellings here so that their children might live at home while attending the day school. Here and there a family group, with traditional craving for space and identity, had set its houses a little apart, grandparents or parents forming the nucleus of a private community, the homes of relatives clustered near by.

Some of the dwellings were of the dugout type, roofed with brush and earth. Others, above ground and rectangular in shape, had walls of wattled brush with dirt-covered brush roofs which were extended to form porches. The less industrious, however, were content with shacks of boards, split-open oil cans and rags, the crevices stuffed with brush. Perhaps the Walapai might have used more imagination and better material in the construction of their houses had they not been people of wind and sun: walls stifled them. Their houses served only as storage rooms and places of retreat during the inclement weather, in addition to sleeping quarters.

The government had erected flimsy board shacks at an expense of fifty dollars each, and the people had tried to live in them but the buildings were cold and drafty, and no Walapai would have boards under his feet when he might have instead the feel of the good familiar earth. However, there was more than that against the cheap little one-room houses. When death occurred in one of them, the government officials refused to allow it to be burned, according to the Walapai custom. So the Indians would have nothing to do with them.

The village, washed in bright sunshine, was filled with color as the women bustled about the cooking fires preparing the evening meal. Tattooed or painted facial designs gave many of the women a piquancy and individuality that was pleasing. Little girls, wearing dresses like their mothers', skirts brushing the sand, ran about on small bare feet or clung to their mothers' dresses, while the small brothers dashed about in their bare skins, teasing the little sisters or camp dogs, impartially.

As I approached one wickiup, a young woman waved her arms and with guttural scolding drove a hungry pony from her corn basket, while the old grandmother sent a thin puppy, investigating a pot of stew, flying heels over head.

Children left their play to take the bread their mothers handed them fresh from the baking stone. Young men rode in on thin ponies, dismounted, squatted on their heels, and began stuffing their mouths with the warm food. Old men, their long hair falling loosely or in braids from their gay headbands, pressed forward for their share. Here and there a family crowded about a pot of stewed rabbit meat and ground wild seeds, dipping it up in their hands and sucking it down with noisy appreciation.

The tantalizing fragrance of paper-thin bread peeled from baking stones filled the air, and I wondered how I could manage to get a taste of it. The Walapai were reticent; they were quietly and unobtrusively on the defensive. I might walk about as I pleased and see the outside of their lives, but an invisible wall protected their inner living. Just then I caught a glimpse of pale blue satin, billowing in the wind; a brown baby face with sparkling black eyes peeped from its folds, and I heard a soft cooing voice. This was Grace's baby. Arms and legs so tightly bound to his sides that they could not move, he looked like a cocoon in his woven cradleboard, propped against the wall of the house. At that moment Grace stepped from the door carrying a basket of parched, shelled corn.

She gave me an indifferent glance, then recognizing me, she smiled shyly, pointing her lips toward her satin-swathed baby. "Nice, you think?"

"Very nice," I assured her, "but not too nice for your beautiful baby."

I squatted in front of him and held up my watch. It turned and sparkled in the sunlight, and his cocoon body jerked convulsively in his eagerness to grasp it, but his arms were too firmly bound.

Grace murmured happily to her baby as she dropped lightly to her knees and began pouring a small quantity of corn into the oblong depression in her grinding stone.

She sat facing me and this offered the opportunity to study her without being too obvious. The faint glow of red in her dark olive skin gave the effect of an inner radiance, heightened by the pin points of fire in her dark eyes. She must have known the pleasing individuality and touch of coquetry the tattooed line from her lower lip to the center of her chin gave her face; and that the circle of red mineral paint she had dabbed over each cheekbone brightened the whole effect. From her pierced ears hung looped strands of garnet-colored beads. About her neck she had wound so many strands of the same small beads that they looked cumbersome, but gorgeous, as they caught and reflected the sunlight. Unlike most of the Walapai women, she was built on slender lines; perhaps the willowy grace with which she moved was not unstudied.

Her grinding stone sat on the ground, tilted slightly forward to make the grinding less difficult. It was rectangular in shape, about thirty inches long by twenty wide, and four inches thick. Grace reached for the mano, a hard-textured, oval stone, dusted it against her skirt, and using one end of it, pounded the corn to break the grains. She was preparing to make bread, so I decided to watch the entire process. Crooning softly, her body swaying as she worked, she reduced the corn to a coarse meal with rolling, crushing motions. As she crushed the grains she swept the meal toward her, and with the side of her hand brushed it into a basket. She lifted the basket, swaying and tossing its contents into the air while she blew lustily and laughed as the chaff flew off in a tiny cloud. But it was not finished: she poured the coarse meal back into the depression and settled down again to her grinding until the meal was fine enough for use.

She stirred the meal into a pail of boiling water until she had a thin mush. And by this time there was a fire going under a large, flat baking stone, which had been polished until smooth, then heated and, while hot, rubbed with gum from the piñon tree to give it a glassy, black surface. With a quick sweep of her hand she scooped up some of the cooled, thin mush and smeared it over the heated stone. She peeled this, paper thin, from the stone just as her five-year-old son, Bela, came running in from play and grabbed it from her hand. His mother gave him a playful slap on his bare rear, and the handsome little chap went galloping back to his companions, wadding the bread into his mouth as he ran.

"He always like that," she said proudly. "Like papa, not care 'bout anything."

She lifted another sheet from the baking stone, rolled it carefully, and held it out to me saying shyly, "You like?"

"Oh, thank you!" I exclaimed. "I've been hoping you'd give me a taste of it." I broke pieces from the crisp sheet, rich as pie crust, but not oily, and they actually melted in my mouth.

"Indians like," she murmured, the corners of her mouth lifting in a secret smile that betrayed her satisfaction at my enjoyment. Again she dipped a handful of the mush and with a swift motion spread it over the stone.

With a loud clatter of hoofs against loose stones, a gay young Indian reined his horse to its haunches at the very door of the small house. He shouted a few words in Walapai, sprang to the ground, hurried to the baby. He lifted a fold of the satin robe and held it across the child's face, then jerked it aside as he barked, "Boo!" and chuckled at the baby's gurgling laughter.

"My man," Grace explained. "Work silver mine; white people." With a toss of her head she indicated the black mountain off to the west.

Still playing with the baby, the man reached out his hand, took the bread his wife offered him, and ate it quickly. Then he sprang to his feet, entered their neat home and reappeared with a tin bowl and a spoon. He filled his dish from the beef and potatoes that simmered in a pail over the cooking fire, then squatted on his heels to enjoy his meal. His clipped hair, blue chambray shirt, blue denim overalls, leather boots, and the sombrero pushed far back on his shining head, gave him a dashing, modern appearance. Both he and Grace had spent their childhod in the vicinity of Hackberry and had learned some English, but he had improved his through work on ranches and at the mine.

A cookstove, the only one I saw in the village, stood in the house, and near it a trunk holding their clothing and extra bedding; but their beds were blanket-covered depressions in the dirt floor, exactly like those of the most backward Indians in the tribe. They depended on the stores in Hackberry for food and clothes, yet when sickness came, they called in the medicine man.

The father paused in his eating long enough to ask, "My boy Dave learning good in school?"

"He is a bright boy," I assured him. "He will be reading stories to you before long."

"Good, good!" he exclaimed. "I got smart boys, even this one." He nodded toward the baby.

Just then Dave came sauntering up from the wash carrying a small lizard in his hand, but he turned it loose and began picking bits of meat from his father's dish. Bela came running home, climbed to the pony's back, dug his bare heels in its sides, and trotted off to a ravine where the horse began eating the sparse grass.

"He likes that spotted pony," the father said proudly. "He gets little bigger, I'll give it to him."

"Do the men at the mine call you by your Indian name, Pu-ut [hat], or did they give you another one?" I asked.

He tossed back his head and laughed. "Indians call me Pu-ut because I'm too proud of this big hat, they say. At the mine I got another name. They call me Boots. The first day I work there, I got stuck in a mudhole. My boots came off. White people, like Indians, give you name for funny things like that." But as he spoke, his face clouded.

"They not want me come home," he added hesitantly, "but this morning Mexican boy put his hand in a machine, and zip, his hand came off. I see it lying on ground. I see fingers move."

His mobile face suddenly looked old and tired. He blew into his open palms, and with a sweeping gesture brushed them down over his face and body, the Walapai's way of ridding himself of a terrifying thought or a bad dream. "I think I work on section gang," he said. "I not going back to that mine."

At Sakawema's camp there was nothing of the modern, nor was there much of the old: no grinding stone, no baking stone; only cold ashes where the cooking fire should have been, and an ash-filled depression in the center of the floor where the family had cooked the last meal within the house. Sakawema's wife was dead; he had no woman to care for his house. He sat on the warm sand of the yard, breaking hunks from a stale loaf of baker's bread and eating them in a grave, disinterested manner.

His fourteen-year-old daughter, Mab, was washing her hair in a pan of clear, sparkling suds which stood on an upended box. She had the plump body, broad, pleasant face and small hands and feet that were typical of the women of the tribe. Mab rinsed her hair, shook it out, and brushed it with the short, handleless brush she had made from the fibers of a yucca plant. Her dark hair shone with a burnished luster.

"Where did you get your soap, Mab?" I asked.

For answer, Mab's toes nudged a cloth sack that lay on the ground. It held the crushed roots of a plant. "It grow up there. I show you," she offered and started walking up the gentle slope west of the camp, motioning for me to follow. She paused by a plant whose swordlike leaves tapered to needle points. "There," she said. "Indians dig that root, pound it, put in water like soap."

That settled the matter of shampoo for me; I had only to go to the mountainside and dig my soap by uprooting several yucca or soapweed plants.

As a rule the Walapai were gentle and kind to children and treated their old people—so long as they remained able-bodied —with respect and reverence. Suja basked in this veneration. Wearing only a loincloth, he sprawled on his back in the sun before his board-and-tin-can shack, dispensing wisdom to a group of the older schoolboys.

He sucked noisily on a pipe that boasted a three-inch stem, happily puffing smoke into the air, until his enthusiasm for the tale he was telling outbalanced his attention to his pipe, and the bowl tipped forward to dust his wrinkled face with ashes. Like a circus clown, Suja went through his performance, clawing, spitting, chattering his annoyance at tobacco and pipe while he brushed away the ash, and his audience howled with glee. Again he was the Suja of the missionary barrel, the wispy old man who would go to any effort to get a laugh or a convert to the philosophy he preached. Suja grinned; the boys appreciated his antics. Then he began reciting an old legend. But the corners of his mouth never lost their humorous quirk, nor his sharp, black eyes their sparkle. Occasionally he flashed an approving glance at his wife, who, her entire face smoothly coated with red paint in true old-woman fashion, squatted by the fire preparing a large chuckwalla (lizard) for the evening meal. The pipe repeated its trick, and Suja his performance many times during an afternoon's telling of the old tales.

The Walapai were open-minded in regard to the white man's innovations, although a little stubborn about which of them they would adopt. Life in this village was not, therefore, wholly of one time or culture. It was a miniature society in transition. And in the ebb and flow of old and new, currents crossed and formed strange patterns. Caught in one of these was a blind old woman.

Life, for her, was limited by the length of a small rope tether, one end of which was tied to her left wrist, the other to a stake in the ground. Her bare feet had grown calloused and crusted with dirt, the toenails broken from hobbling about her picket pin until she had worn a deep circle in the hard ground. When she became too weary for further effort, she crawled into a low, crescent-shaped roofless shelter of woven boughs to rest on her bed of filthy rags. Her seamed face was dark with grime and her grizzled hair hung in matted strands. I had never before seen a human being who showed such utter neglect.

A dull-looking young man was stacking wood and dry roots in a neat rick against the wall of a near-by house.

"Why does the old woman live out here alone?" I asked him.

With a Walapai's indifference to white people, he did not take his attention from his wood-stacking, but pointed with his lips toward a young woman who sat in the doorway, sewing, and mumbled, "Old woman, she's mother."

The face bent over the sewing was that of a woman who spent too much time with her fiber broom, dusting and cleaning, and made housework a burden by her fierce desire for cleanliness, but I put my question.

She answered sharply, "She too old. She got sickness. She live house, little children get a sickness."

The floor of the family's house was hard-packed and cleanly swept. Neatly rolled and suspended from a pole near the ceiling were the blankets for the four beds: hers, her man's and those of their children, a boy and a girl. No one could deny that the old woman, blundering around inside, would disturb the room's neatness. The boy and the girl sat on the floor playing with a sore-eyed, mangy cat. I tried to convince her that the old mother, whom she had turned out of her house, was less of a health menace than the sick cat, but she would have none of it.

She was the only Indian in the tribe, I think, who believed that the cause of sickness was communicable. Their ignorance was their danger. Either curiosity or the desire to be neighborly took them to the sick, whether the ailment was hives, measles or smallpox. So, unwittingly, they spread disease. Neatness and cleanliness were not dominant traits of the Walapai, but Tahuta, when a girl, had worked in a ranch home and had learned their value, and a little, but not enough, about infectious diseases. Since the old woman was a bother, it was convenient to banish her as a cause of disease. But the cat amused their children and the young mother herself laughed at its kitten tricks, so why apply the white man's theory to it?

I followed the worn trail across the desert toward home, but the image of that blind old woman, huddled in her rags against the night's cold, was not a pleasant companion for a walk.

The sun had dropped behind the big black mountain in the west, and the rainbow colors had faded from the sandy floor of the canyon. Out of the gloom, the dim figures of an old man and woman appeared, bent forward against the wind as they made their way toward the village. The woman struggled under a huge load of desert roots and sticks, held by a strap across her forehead. As she stumbled over the rough ground the load on her back jolted from side to side. The man, bent and thin, trotted ahead, scouting, as he had done in his warrior days, until it became necessary for him to drop back to steady her load. He would no more have relieved her of her burden than he would have cut off his long braids. Indian custom had made her the burden bearer that the man might be free to defend his family. Now that he was powerless to fight, he still strode importantly ahead, assisting her only when her back threatened to break under the stack of bleached wood towering above her head. Nor could she have allowed him to carry her burden. Both were bound by traditions and customs that had come down from Those of Old.

I recalled the story Miss Calfee had told me of a young Walapai girl who, orphaned at the age of twelve, had been sent by interested white people to the Indian school at Carlisle, Pennsylvania. Several years later, the girl returned to her people. Her hair, neatly brushed and held by pins; her body, slim and neat in a corset; her clothes, differing from their buckskin garments; and her ornate hat, set the older women jabbering and laughing. But her acquired taste for cleanliness and daintiness aroused ridicule and bitter anger.

"With the tribe against her, the girl had but one choice," Miss Calfee had said.

"What was the sequel?" I had asked.

"She cut her hair Indian fashion, put on moccasins and the *sutam*, and married a tribesman," Miss Calfee had replied. "But, in the back of her mind she cherished the memory of those years at the school; wholesome food served at tables, clean beds, pride in personal appearance, and the satisfaction of mental development had made a lasting impression. So when I came here as a missionary and opened a school, she was the first to enroll her three children."

My talk with Miss Calfee had convinced me that the older Indians would never abandon the tenets of their ancient creed. The men's willingness to place the burdens on the backs of their women, the women's abandonment of babies that might hinder them in fleeing an enemy, the people's sacrifice of their aged and helpless to the ravages of hunger, thirst and exposure were a primitive people's reaction to conditions under which only the fit survive.

Then, too, tribal life must conform to the dictates of the shadowy spirits inherent in all things, animate and inanimate. The spirits of Coyote, Deer, and Bear, Singing Water and Drifting Cloud: these, not teachers nor missionaries, were still the Walapai's true guardians and counselors. If I were to understand these people, I must learn more of their heritage.

CHAPTER SIX

Gods at War

The Walapai's colorful history is preserved in folk tale. I heard Sam's Walapai version of the Story of the Creation of Mankind from other members of the tribe and it varied in the telling, as most legends do. However, there was more to the story than Sam had told. After Kathatkanave had created the Indians from the rushes they multiplied until the land of their origin became crowded. So he gathered his people around him and told them that he would guide them to a more spacious land. He led them to Mattawedita Canyon, a garden spot watered by bountiful springs, a canyon beloved by the Walapai to this day.

Here Tochopa, the Indians' benign god, taught them to fend for themselves in the wilderness, initiated them in the mysteries of shamanism as practiced by their medicine men, taught them to make and use the *toholwa* ("sweat lodge"), instituted the ceremonial dance, and gave them their meaningful but repetitious songs.

Then jealousy entered their Eden.

Tochopa's brother, envious of the popularity of Tochopa, plotted evil. He took charge of one family, the Whajes, teaching them to use bows and arrows; to heat the horns of deer and mold them for daggers, and to make war clubs of stones. In the war that followed, the peaceful families, led by Tochopa, drove the Whajes into the desert.

But the fierce, evil god taught the Whajes to make stone battle-

axes and flint-pointed spears, and led them in an attack for the possession of the canyon. Tochopa and his followers fled to a cave
high up in the canyon wall. Taking their stand in the cave's mam-
moth opening, they defeated the invaders; so the place was called
"Kathatkanave's cave, the place that is impregnable."

When Mattawedita Canyon could no longer accommodate the
many families, Tochopa divided them into family groups, sending
the Mohave west, the Paiutes across the Colorado to the north, the
Havasupai and other tribes to the east. But the Walapai, his chosen
people, he gave the homeland of Mattawedita and the great stretch
of pine-covered mesas and mountains south of the Colorado River.

In this manner, the great Walapai family were established as the
legendary parents of many tribes.

The Walapai gravitated to the springs and streams in their great
domain and planted their beans, corn, melons and other crops. According to their folk tales, they had been an agricultural people
from the beginning, when the gods had given them seed.

Padre Garces, who entered the Walapai country in 1776, is said
to have been the first white man the Indians had seen, but they
offered him friendship and food when he arrived at their settlement, later known as Beale Springs. In his notes Garces stated that
the Walapai wore clothing of antelope skins, but some of the men
wore shirts of cotton, grown by the Hopi and woven into cloth by
them. Garces mentioned speaking to them of God, of whom, he
recorded, they had some knowledge.

Garces saw horses and branded cattle, some bearing several
brands, in the possession of the Indians in this region. He had
reason to suspect that many of them had disappeared from herds
belonging to the missions under his own church, for not all such
animals were come by through legitimate channels. The Walapai
were sly raiders as well as clever traders. While a trade was a social
affair and long-drawn-out, a raid was more to their liking; it
brought something for nothing. It was executed with speed and
cunning, and ended with a good laugh at the victim's expense, followed by a celebration in which each recounted his deeds of daring.

Almost a century after Garces' visit, General Crook, on a mission to the Southwest to quiet Indian disturbances, came to the Walapai country. J. G. Bourke, in writing of this expedition (1870-74), stated that when their party arrived at Beale Springs, they learned that a former agent, Captain Thomas Byrne, had been relieved, and a new man sent to take charge of the tribe. The Indians respected Byrne. He talked straight. But the new agent was an enigma to them.

And he had his handicaps. No reservation had been set aside for the Walapai, so they came and went pretty much as they pleased. However, those who co-operated with the agent in maintaining peaceful relations with white settlers and with neighboring tribes, were rewarded with issues of beef, flour, salt and other needed supplies.

Captain Byrne was at the agency when, without warning, the Indians opened fire on the government buildings. Spurring their horses at a dead run, they headed for their old home, the cave of Kathatkanave, where they could hold off pursuers.

Byrne followed the angry men, demanding an explanation. Their story was that they had lived peaceably in their village but their rations had been reduced until they were getting almost nothing. Byrne persuaded the Indians to return to the agency with him, where they learned that the new agent had departed in great haste. Byrne discovered that for issuing purposes, the scales had been altered to make an eight-hundred-pound steer weigh seventeen hundred pounds. By keeping the record by the altered weights the agent accounted for all the supplies received from the government and had more than half left to sell to ranchers and miners. The profit was his.

This was the Walapai's first experience in defending themselves against an agent sent by Washington to protect them as well as to keep them within bounds. The old, masterful spirit of free men had not yet been conquered; they were still able to turn on an enemy, white or Indian.

Twenty-six years later, I was teaching the Walapai children in the Hackberry Day School. The Indians still had their flare-ups. They were slow to accept the fact that a man could no longer make his own decisions. However, Mr. Ewing had a reservation which set limits to their roaming; he had rations to reward those who complied—and he had a jail, not always empty.

The large reservation of more than a thousand square miles, set aside for the Walapai in 1883 by President Chester A. Arthur, confirmed their ancient claim to the pine-covered mountains and mesas and the precious springs and streams that had long been home to them. The tribe's name, composed of two words of their language, derived from this happy association of man with nature: *hwal*—"tall pine," *pai*—"people," became Hwalpai, "Tall Pine People." The Spaniards changed it to Hualpai, later spelled Walapai, the tribe's present name, although the Spanish form is also used.

Cattlemen and ranchers filtered into the reservation taking possession of the Indians' springs and streams. The Walapai could have handled the situation but the Great Father in Washington no longer permitted them to kill. So the Indians drifted to the towns, the mines, or worked as section hands on the railroad, where white men tempted them with their intoxicating liquor and contaminated them with their diseases. The stern realities by which they had lived had vanished; the Walapai fell victim to the worst the white man had to offer.

The tribe's contact with civilization had shocked and disillusioned them. Their primitive laws prescribed harsh punishment for a tribesman who broke their moral code until the white man nullified their code of behavior. This softening influence prevailed at the time a young Indian murdered several of his tribesmen, and tried to escape. Hotly pursued by the relatives of those he had killed, he committed suicide, taking his pony with him that he might have it to ride in the Other World. In accordance with tribal law, the chief ordered all relatives of the criminal put to death. But white settlers intervened, preventing the execution of the chief's order. This left the Walapai uncertain and confused, their primitive social order completely undermined.

To these scattered and bewildered Indians Miss Calfee came in the year 1894 as missionary and teacher. The Indians had begun to realize that their old way of life was gone; they wanted the white man's school that their children might learn a better way than they knew. Miss Calfee organized in Hackberry a school of fifteen pupils. She persuaded the women, who had become lazy and indifferent, to revive their basket-weaving, the weaving of warm blankets from rabbit skins, and to learn better methods of homemaking.

A year after Miss Calfee's arrival, Mr. Ewing was placed in charge of tribal affairs, later to be appointed agent. Although open warfare was no longer permitted among the tribes, he was confronted with the problem of raids and murders by small wandering bands of Apaches and other enemy tribes. To prevent such atrocities he persuaded the Walapai to invite the Apaches to their Harvest Festival for the purpose of signing a treaty of peace. But the Apaches, remembering the tricks by which they had captured unsuspecting Walapai, feared a trap and refused the invitation. Sporadic raids remained a disturbing element.

Mr. Ewing was successful in forcing the encroaching white settlers off the reservation, and in stopping the destruction, by their livestock, of the Indians' gardens. Later he moved the day school from Hackberry to Truxton Canyon Ranch. Our day school would be changed to a boarding school as soon as the buildings could be erected from the brick the Indians were burning down at the brick kiln.

So at last the Walapai legally possessed the land which had been assigned to them by Tochopa, their favorite god, at the time of the dispersal of the tribes from Mattawedita Canyon.

CHAPTER SEVEN

Mountain-lying-down

November in Arizona can bring the most perfect of all days. On this particular Sunday morning the sunshine was pleasantly warm, the air clear, thin and sparkling. Back home, Sunday was a day of church bells, sermons and big dinners. Here, there was no church within miles and miles; the sermons were locked in rocks and streams to which the Indians held the key; and my dinner would depend on the ability of my stove and me to work together. The children had taken their laughter and play to the village, leaving us a depressing stillness, so after a late breakfast I went out for a leisurely view of my surroundings.

The school grounds formed an oasis of living green nearly four thousand feet above sea level; back of it towered the mesa that I had promised myself to explore. The Indian who coined the word Kaibab ("mountain-lying-down") might easily have had its image in mind, for this mountain had lain down many centuries ago and had not since lifted its head.

Nina came to the back door to give her dishwater a fling, and said, "That old mesa looks like a fat woman's skirt."

I laughed at the comparison but there it was: the rock rim made the broad waistband and from it the skirt flared, voluminous and striped with color, to the canyon floor.

Nina gave her pan a swirl with the dishcloth and disappeared within the kitchen just as Mr. Graham rounded a corner of the house and paused a moment to exchange greetings.

"Does that mesa look to you like a mountain lying down or a woman's skirt?" I asked.

"I'm going to climb it right now. If you'd like to go along, you can decide for yourself which it resembles," he replied. "The view from the top is well worth the climb. I've been up several times and always find something new and interesting."

I wanted the climb and I wanted the view, but found it impossible to keep up with his quick, light step. Every muscle of his slim body co-ordinated perfectly while I felt awkward and blundering until he stopped to coach me in tricks of mountain-climbing. But even then, before we reached the top, my feet dragged like lead, my knees trembled and I gasped for air.

He turned, gave me a quick glance, and said, "If you'll rest on that flat stone, I'd like to scout around a bit."

I sank gratefully on the rock he indicated and replied, "Go ahead. When you come flying back with a mountain lion at your heels, I'll throw a stone at him."

"Between gasps for breath?" he asked with a grin.

"If you value your life, give me a little time before your stir him out," I advised.

While he prowled about turning over stones to send slim lizards skimming, or prodding out those small creatures that build their houses in the ground and leave their doors open, I studied the red rimrock that crowned the mesa. The wall was one hundred forty-eight feet high, I had been told, and it was perpendicular. Finally I asked him how he intended to reach its top.

"It's broken and crumbling on the other side," he explained. "The approach is not difficult there."

When we climbed to the far side of the rim, we found it, as he said, deeply canyoned and broken in places. He led the way to the mouth of a gorge thirty feet deep, half of its close-set walls literally packed with golden honeycomb over which small dark bees worked industriously.

Recovering from astonishment, I exclaimed, "Let's get some of that honey! Oh, look, there are hundreds of pounds of it!" We were on a level with the floor of the gorge. I could have walked right in between those honey-laden walls.

"Go easy," he cautioned, as I crowded in. "Those bees are fighters. We have already disturbed them."

The fact that the bees must have flown many miles across a dreary waste to bring home their loads of nectar was no concern of mine. My Scottish thrift could not bear the sight of honey accumulating there unused. How delicious it would be on breakfast hotcakes or as dessert for supper! I was too excited to remember that we had nothing in which to carry it and kept edging into the mouth of the gorge to get a better view, until a swarm of bees dashed at my head. They swerved and flew away, only to dash madly back to give another warning that the cleft was theirs. I retreated hurriedly. We found a break in the rimrock and climbed to the top.

We were on top of the world. On every side there were jumbled mountains, some sharp-peaked, others with sliced-off tops, tumbling off to the horizon where the farthest etched the skyline. It was a breath-taking experience—and an humbling one—to stand on that wind-swept plateau looking down on a world that had been tossed about and so recklessly scrambled. From other peaks, much higher than our mesa, a gale swooped down, whipping my skirt against my ankles with the sting of a lash, and almost lifting us off our feet. We walked slowly across the top, fascinated by every aspect of the mesa's tortured surface. In looking at it from below, I had thought it flat like a floor, but it had its hillocks and depressions.

On this late fall day its surface was dry and barren. We paused to rest by a lone juniper tree crouched low to the earth, its gnarled and twisted branches turned in the direction of least resistance, away from the fury of the wind. When we reached the east end of the mesa, where we would begin the descent through a deep gorge, I paused for one last ecstatic moment in that high altitude, another breath of that thin, invigorating air and to get the sure impress of space on space, pierced by tawny peaks and red-streaked tablelands.

The descent was precipitous; sliding, clinging to roots or brush, jumping from boulder to boulder, we worked our way to the canyon floor. As we sauntered along in the late afternoon, Mr. Graham suddenly asked, "How would you like a better position? More money?"

"That sounds ominous. What's the bad news?"

"I have been offered an advancement, a place in Washington. As soon as I resign, you had better ask for a promotion." Then he enumerated a long list of duties that fell to the lot of the principal teacher.

Mr. Graham thoroughly understood the Walapai. Their cunning, their shrewdness and their many virtues were made use of in his teaching. His training while a student in a large Indian school enabled him to organize this small school of sixty-six pupils into a smoothly working unit. And by using the system of military training then prescribed for all Indian schools, he had greatly minimized the problem of discipline.

"You haven't mentioned military training," I suggested. "I've watched you drill the companies and you know the right command for each maneuver. I'm afraid I'd be out as your successor."

He laughed. "Don't worry," he said. "You'll have no trouble."

For the rest of the way home my thoughts churned back and forth between the pleasing prospect of a greater salary and the gloomy thought that I would have to discipline grown young men who towered inches above my head.

The matter was settled very quickly. Mr. Graham boarded a Santa Fe train and, with a wave of the hand and a happy laugh, was off for the distant city. I was summoned to Mr. Ewing's office and detailed by him to take over the duties of the position. It was a temporary arrangement, but he insisted that I make written application to the Washington office for the promotion.

He stated his case with a troubled frown: "I don't want the Indian Office to send some Easterner here to find fault and make unfavorable reports on the school to Washington. We are doing the best we can with what we have to work with. Write your application today and I'll forward it with my recommendation."

I wondered how an Easterner would react to my little room with its inverted sand dunes like the sword of Damocles hanging over his head; how he would like the little stove that insisted on having its occasional smoke. Could his brains take the baking the corrugated iron roof on the schoolhouse would give them? And would his nerves stand up under the eerie, clattering noise the metal made when the wind got under its edges and gave it a vigorous shaking? I agreed with Mr. Ewing that a man who had grown accustomed to life in an Eastern city might not like it here. So, with no little apprehension as to what the outcome might be for me, I applied for the position. In the meantime, I took over the principal teacher's duties, and Mr. Ewing employed a local girl for the primary room.

The pupils in the advanced room spent the first few days slyly studying me to learn how much leeway they might expect from this white woman. The Indian principal teacher they had understood. He had made them toe the mark; but the white woman might have a weak spot; if so, school could be fun.

The school, still so new, could not accommodate half of the children on the reservation. The others lived with their parents, thus receiving instruction only in Indian lore and customs. The adult primary class came from this group. They chafed at confinement. Never before in their lives had they sat on hard boards, and our school benches were just that. Why bend over a book to learn "paper talk" when all outdoors was waiting to teach them its secrets! Their unrest drove them to the strange expedients of crouching under desks, hiding under tables or slipping out to roam the hills.

The first day in my new position I managed to give the right commands to the companies at the morning recess and at noon, but after lunch commotion in the primary room demanded attention, and at the afternoon recess my frayed nerves betrayed me. Everything went smoothly until I had the children marching back to the classrooms. With Sam in the lead, the company of large boys, as it happened, marched straight toward the end of the schoolhouse. I saw a roguish smile flash across Sam's face and knew that he and the boy at his side would attempt to climb that wall—unless I stopped them. That would be Walapai humor. Immediately I became confused, my mind groping wildly for the right command. Just as Sam and his companion began clawing at the end of the building, a good, meaningful word popped into my mind and I spoke it with the force of a command: *"Stop!"*

With military precision, Don commanded: "Company, *halt!"*

Every child stood in his tracks. There was a breathless, waiting silence. Don, their captain, turned to me for orders.

"Don, take charge of the lines and march them into the classrooms," I said.

From that day on, until I had mastered all the military terms I should need, my solitary meals were enlivened with such conversation as, "Right *face!* Left *face!* Company *halt!*"

However, I was not finished with the end-of-the-house blunder. It was a long time before I could approach a group of small boys bent over a game of marbles, without seeing them duck their heads to giggle, while one of them exclaimed in a low voice, choked with laughter: "Stop!" To a Walapai a joke was a precious thing, to be told and retold—if it were not on himself.

We teachers dreaded bath day; the children loved it. The girls, supervised by the new primary teacher, crowded into their small washroom; the boys in the adjoining one. Four or five washtubs were lined up near a wall and filled with water from a caldron, tempered with cold water. My duty, as principal teacher, was to supervise the boys' bathroom, but since this would embarrass both the boys and me, I gave Don, our chief officer, charge of the bath and paid him a small sum from my salary. I treated sores and rashes in my classroom and distributed clean clothing to the boys as they went in to bathe. After two or three baths, the tub was upended and the water dumped on the floor. It ran off through the wide cracks but the floor was wet, and steam and heat from the caldrons made the air stifling. The lack of sanitation appalled us, but the best we could do, with our equipment, was to segregate those with sores and rashes and bathe them separately. Regulations required the weekly bath, so we complied.

Bath day was never dull. The children told jokes, laughed and had fun, a pleasant relaxation from classroom study and recitations. In more serious moments, we caught hints of a philosophy forged by a people who had lived with danger, or of the deep-rooted culture which still influenced their lives.

Carl, who was in my advanced class and spoke fair English, had a natural flair for tribal legends and traditions and gave me the benefit of the tales his grandfather told him. Carl's father was dead and he and his mother shared their home with the old man. Carl and his grandfather sat at twilight by the outdoor fire and discussed the tribe's early history as told in myth and legend. After the school children had gone home, Carl would unravel some yarn about the old days, or repeat a legend, explaining why his people clung to certain superstitions. Perhaps the silver dollar I usually handed him at the conclusion of a story had its influence, for to an Indian, at that time, silver had worth, while paper money was regarded with suspicion.

One afternoon Carl lingered after school until the last child had gone, then laid on my desk a buckskin bag tied with a narrow thong. "I brought you some of that red paint like Indians put on their faces," he said.

I untied the thong and spread the square of buckskin open. There was the dull red powder, about a tablespoon of it. This was the red ocher with which old women smeared their entire faces, and young women and girls—even children—used in decorative designs. They spread a circle of it over each cheekbone and made a line of it slanting outward and downward from each corner of the mouth, the red outlined in black and burnt sienna. Girls, gay and giddy, decorated their faces in fanciful designs to make themselves attractive to the village youths.

"Thank you, Carl!" I exclaimed, for this was something I very much wanted, a delightful surprise. "Where did you get it?"

"My uncle got it from a mine. It's hard to get, dangerous. He climbs a high cliff, then crawls on his stomach through a tunnel into the mine where he gets this powder. Some Indian men fell and got killed when they tried to climb up there. I went to that place once, but I did not want to go in. My uncle goes in and gets a little powder in a sack, then he comes out of that hole backward and drags it along with him. All Indians want it, even the Havasupai. They mix the powder with a little fat, any kind they can get, to make it smooth so they can rub it on their faces."

"I've seen old women with their faces smeared all over with it," I told him, "but the young women use other colors, and so do some of the men. I've seen reddish-brown lines and black ones on some faces."

"I know about that too," he boasted in his very serious way and puffed out his chest. "The brown is burned mescal juice we scrape from the stones used in the roasting pit, and we dig the black from a place in the ground the Indians know about. We make it a little wet with water so we can rub it on smooth."

"Not you, Carl!" I exclaimed. "I can't imagine you with paint on your face."

"At dances I paint. I use plenty then, my face just about covered with red, black and white." We both laughed at the thought of very sedate Carl with paint on his face.

"How about tattooing, do they use black earth?" I asked. It paid to get all the information I could while Carl was in the mood.

"No. Indians use charcoal powder. Just a few people do that kind of work. They make a thorn a little wet, then dip it in charcoal powder and prick the skin. Before the place gets well, they rub in more powder. The blue we use is the juice of a plant. White people call it indigo. The white we rub on our faces is roasted gypsum, made into a powder."

His next remark disclosed his reason for so quickly closing the conversation on face-painting. The bag of red powder had been camouflage; Carl had a story in the back of his head and was bursting to tell it.

"Last night my grandfather told me about the flood that came in the old time, like the Bible story," he said.

I settled back to listen, for when Carl launched forth on one of his grandfather's delightful tales, it was worth a hearing.

"My grandfather said that a great flood came to the Walapai country and water covered all the land. The people were frightened and did not know how to save their lives. There was one man, I think he was a giant, who was so big and strong he could move about in the water. He took his big flint knife and the war club he had used to crack his enemies' skulls and walked about in the water until he found the deepest part. Then he stuck his knife into the ground, pushed it back and forth and pounded it down with his club until the earth split open and the water roared into the crack and rushed off to the great place of many waters. The water still runs through that split-open place. The Indians call it Hack-ataia, that means 'roaring noise,' but white people call it the Colorado River. That's the way my grandfather told me the people were saved when the water covered all the land."

"What kept the people from drowning if the water was so deep that only the giant could stand against it?" I asked.

A blank look crossed Carl's face. "I don't know," he stammered. "My grandfather did not tell me that."

"Perhaps they were turned into fish," I suggested. I had heard the legend of the flood as told by another Western tribe, and they accounted for the survival of the people by saying that they were miraculously turned into fish.

"I'll ask my grandfather," Carl said hurriedly, preparing to leave.

But I pressed him with the question, "Do the Walapai eat fish?" although I knew that they did not.

"We never eat that. Long time ago, the Mohave and my people made a treaty. The Mohave said they would eat no rabbits and my people said they would eat no fish; then everyone knew what he could eat, and there would be enough for everybody."

I was convinced that the Walapai's refusal to eat fish was for reasons that Carl did not care to discuss, for I had seen the look of horror on a young man's face when fish was offered him for his lunch. It was not the fear of breaking a treaty that made him recoil from the proffered food, but the fear of food that was taboo. If my surmise were correct, I could appreciate the young man's attitude, for, if by eating fish, one would be eating the flesh of his ancestors, even a white person could lose his appetite for sole and salmon.

I gave Carl a silver dollar. This time it was well earned, for I had learned of a hero who could have taught Noah how to handle a flood; and I had that dab of red paint that had been dragged from a hole in a cliff by a man crawling backward on his stomach. Carl pocketed the dollar with his usual expressions of gratitude and started off for the village.

I locked my classroom door and faced the desert. The looming bulk of the mesa seemed the very symbol of endurance. For centuries it had looked on the comedies and the tragedies of Truxton Canyon. Its composure, its impersonal calmness made me realize that we could change neither this land nor its people in a day nor in a year.

Nevertheless, we would go on trying to help the Walapai find a better way of life.

CHAPTER EIGHT

The Beautiful Intoxication

The "beautiful intoxication" came to the reservation in such an unobtrusive way that none of us who worked at the school would have known of its arrival had not unexpected events revealed its presence.

When I locked my classroom door one day after school, the air was electric with a sparkle and snap that put me in the mood for a long, brisk walk. As I crossed the school ground, I met Mr. Ewing. He remarked that one of the saddle horses had been in the barn for several days and suggested I take him out for exercise.

Isadore brought the horse, a beautiful, impatient bay that pranced and cavorted on long, slender legs, but his prancing and the restless tossing of his head had not prepared me for the bolt of lightning he became the moment I touched the sidesaddle. The road swam beneath his feet and the boulders in the wash skimmed by as he dashed recklessly ahead. My hair came loose and my skirt slapped the pony's flank. Not until his feet plunged into the deep sand on the other side of the wash did the bay settle to a high-spirited walk.

We were passing the fringe of Indian huts on the outskirts of Hackberry when I noticed a white object several rods ahead, crouched under a mesquite bush. It rose to its feet as we approached, and I saw that it was a man wearing white trousers and shirt. He staggered a few steps, then fell to his knees and crawled to a low wickiup, back among the brush. I followed him and found him lying in the shade of the house, exhausted and panting and evidently very nauseated. He was an Indian, but his complexion and features were not those of a Walapai.

A man of middle age, whom I recognized as the father of Bill, one of my schoolboys, sat on the sand outside the house.

"Does that sick man live here?" I asked him.

He did not remove his gaze from a distant mountain peak, but a woman's voice from within the lodge called, "He Kiowa. Ok'ahoma."

"He is sick. Can you take care of him?" I called to her.

"Eh," she answered. "Go away!"

I laughed and sprang to the ground, pinned up my hair, tightened the cinch on the saddle, and took my time doing it. The Walapai's abruptness no longer surprised or offended me. Many of them held to the childish right of acting and talking as they felt; you could like it or not. But I knew this woman had a reason for trying to hurry me off, so I asked, "Why do you want me to leave?"

"He too sick," she said, indicating the Kiowa.

I rode on into town, made my purchases, and returned to the school. When Mr. Ewing came from his office to take the horse, I mentioned the Kiowa from Oklahoma, but visiting Indians frequently stopped for a few days with a family; unless the visit was too prolonged or some harm was done, no one interfered.

One evening, about a week later, I was checking the desks to see if the books were neatly stacked and to remove any pieces of bread or meat that might have been carried from the dining hall when I found a hard, grayish-brown object tucked in among the books. It was more than an inch across and resembled a large, thick button, except that a button does not have a wrinkled appearance or a stiff fuzz on its upper surface.

I had found it in Bill's desk. He was leaning out of a rear window, dusting erasers, laughing and shouting to another boy; each was trying to see who could send the larger cloud of chalk dust into the air.

Even though I knew that the thing I had found was a peyote

button, I walked back to the window and asked, "What is this, Bill?"

He gave it a startled glance, then turned his head aside as his lips stiffened in an embarrassed grin. "Peyote button," he whispered so low that it was only a breath of sound.

"Where did you get it?" I asked, for this was the first peyote I had seen on the reservation, and it was important to learn the source of supply.

With his face still turned aside, he replied scarcely above a whisper, "Kiowa Indian. I buy it last week, one cent."

"I'll give you a penny for this one," I offered.

He turned slowly to face me and his voice had more volume, for this button was a precious and dangerous thing. "They hard to get," he protested. But he accepted the penny, and I owned a peyote button.

"Where is the Kiowa? I saw him at your house last week. Is he still there?"

"He ate too many; he got sick. He went off." He spoke now with excitement. The Kiowa had made Bill's family afraid because he had brought them a secret thing which they could not understand.

I put my arm across the little boy's shoulders and drew him nearer, but he stood rigid and still. "Did you eat the peyote, Billy?" I asked him.

"My father," he whispered, "but they all gone now."

Now I knew why Bill's mother wanted me to go away: she was afraid I would learn of the peyote the Kiowa had brought. And I knew why his father sat staring with unseeing eyes at the distant mountain. He was peyote drunk, enjoying to the full the "beautiful intoxication," the Indians' poetic name for the hallucinations they experience while under the influence of the drug. And the Kiowa had been more than drunk; his system had been in violent revolt against an overdose of peyote.

The "beautiful intoxication" was as Indian as moccasins or wampum. In the dry, hot sands of Mexico the Aztec Indians had found an abundance of the spineless cacti (*Lophophora williamsii*) that produced the ecstasy of colorful and delightful dreams. In shape, the plant resembled a stubby carrot, topped by a rounded buttonlike head, its center bearing a tuft of erect, grayish-white hairs, from which the pale flower issued. It was this tufted head, lopped off and dried for three or four months, that became the peyote button of barter and trade among the Indians. The Aztecs called it *"peyotl,"* said to be their word for caterpillar, because the erect hairs on the button reminded them of those on a caterpillar. In the United States, this dried head of a cactus is generally known as peyote or peyote button, although the term mescal bean has been applied to it. However, it is neither a bean nor mescal, so the term is erroneous.

Peyote had long been an object of worship and a healing agent in Mexico by the time the Spaniards invaded the country, but it formed only a part of the lengthy ceremonial of worship and healing. Its use by the Indians puzzled the early padres, who complained of a plant that intoxicated the Indians like wine. Padre José Oretega, in 1745, wrote a description of a peyote cult meeting he attended, in which he referred to the plant as *"raiz diabolica"* or Devil's root. The padres found a tough antagonist in the cactus, for they had nothing to offer that the Indians considered a fair exchange for their beautiful intoxication.

Primitive Indians examined critically any alien creed or philosophy, accepting only those tenets that met their need. The ritual of the peyote worshipers was incomplete, without prescribed form and definition, so they adopted many of the symbols and much of the ritual of the Christian religion and incorporated these into their own form of peyote worship.

The Apaches of the United States crossed the Rio Grande to visit friends and relatives to the south and brought back with them this form of worship and healing. Since the small cacti thrive on the desert north of the Rio Grande, especially in the region of Laredo, Texas, they had only to gather their drug from the hills. The Kiowa and Comanche tribes in Oklahoma accepted the cult from the Apaches, and from them it spread, like a mild contagion, among the tribes of the central United States and north into Canada. Early in the twentieth century it crossed the Rocky Mountains to complete its conquest on the Pacific Coast.

When it crossed our southern border, the new doctrine fell on a social soil that was conducive to its rapid growth. Students, returning to the reservation from government-operated or mission schools, found no opportunity for leadership, although they had been trained to lead. Ambitious young men seized the opportunity this imported religion offered and became organizers and leaders of the cult.

A government employee who had witnessed the peyote ceremony on an Oklahoma reservation stated that the members of the cult were educated young men and women, yet they donned Indian toggery, painted their faces, decorated themselves with feathers, and some wore the rosary in their hair. These young people brought new vitality to the old ceremony and added new features, such as the reading of the Bible, the confession of sin, repentance and the baptismal service.

The cult was formally organized and legally incorporated in Oklahoma and at least one other state as the Native American Church. As such it became intertribal in scope, a powerful organization for the control of the attitudes and behavior of its members. Permanent churches were built; lacking these, a large tent was erected to accommodate the congregation, or the group met at the home of a member. There was one essential: the door of the meeting place must open to the east so that the worshipers might witness the sunrise after their all-night service.

From these organized groups, messengers or "messiahs" were sent to indoctrinate other tribes, help them organize their church, teach them the arrangement of the altar and the ritual. Following them came the Indian peddlers who bought the buttons at Laredo, Texas, and sold them to the converts for many times their cost.

In some tribes only a minority accepted the new religion; there were those who feared the drug as they feared intoxicating liquor.

In other instances the cult included the greater part of the tribal membership. A nonmember missed the excitement of the all-night session and the great feast that followed; life must have seemed rather drab to him while the worshipers enjoyed their exhiliarating intoxication.

In the well-organized churches meetings were held at stated periods, usually on Saturday night, continuing until late in the day Sunday. However, anyone who could afford the expense of the feast might call a meeting at his convenience, for the purpose of healing the sick or to express gratitude for his own recovery from illness, or for any purpose he might care to name. Since the worshipers came great distances, the peyote feast became important in a social sense. If a large tent was needed, the men worked at it very leisurely all day Saturday. As the day wore on, more members drifted in. Indians loved above all else to visit, share whatever food they had brought with them or their wives prepared while the men worked. They usually arrived long before the stipulated time so that there might be interludes for games; pitching horseshoes was their favorite pastime. The day was spent in laughter, talk, singing and smoking, as well as in work. When the meeting opened, the visiting and easy laughter gave way to seriousness and reverence.

The altar, the focal point, centered in a crescent, built of earth in the center of the floor, its horns pointing eastward. On its top, midway between the horns, lay one sacred peyote. In front of the altar, the sacred fire burned, attended by priests who also attended the door, protecting from evil spirits those who must go out into the night and cleansing them on their return. The leader stood back of the crescent altar, facing the east, with the open Bible in front of him. In some churches, a line was drawn from tip to tip on the altar to represent the Road of Life on which the leader would guide his followers to a higher spiritual plane. An attendant, who burned incense, and a drummer flanked the leader. Gourd rattles, whistles and feather ornaments had their place in the ceremony. However, no description could apply to all altars, or to all ceremonies; these things depended on the whim or the knowledge of the leader.

Each item in the service had its purpose. The fire was used to purify the drinking water. In some cults the purified water was dipped up in the hand and sprinkled on the heads of the worshipers at midnight in a baptismal service. The fire and the colored feather ornaments stimulated the visual nerves to enhance the color hallucinations; the drum, the rattle, the whistle and the songs were the stimuli that gave accent to the sound hallucinations.

The service was opened with prayer by the leader, who also read passages from the Scriptures. Then he was handed a sack of peyote buttons, from which he selected four, plucked the fuzz from their centers and slowly chewed them. He passed the peyote buttons, four to each of the worshipers who were seated on the ground facing the altar, the men in a circle in front of the women. While doing this, he exhorted them to concentrate their thoughts on the sacred peyote that rested on the altar and the god-spirit it represented. Then he seized his gourd rattle and he and his drummer rattled the gourd and beat the drum in perfect rhythm, while they lustily sang the first four songs. These might be Indian songs, or songs composed on the spur of the moment. Quite often they were hymns that the people had learned in the services of the Christian church. The rattle and the drum were passed to the next couple and on around the circle until each couple had sung four songs. Peyote was passed around many times. For the old or sick who were unable to chew the hard buttons, they were steeped in a tea or powdered and filled into capsules that were purchased from a drugstore in the nearest town or city. The singing and the eating of the peyote were interrupted at midnight either by the baptismal ceremony or, in some tribes, by four blasts of a whistle. The latter were given outside the house, one blast to each of the cardinal points, east, west, north and south, to notify all people that the members of the cult were assembled for worship. A second interruption came at sunrise, which was hailed with a special ceremony and the serving of sacred food. This concluded the religious service.

The big dinner, prepared by the women, came later in the day. The afternoon became another social occasion for those not too completely under the influence of the drug, with visiting, smoking and the recital of the experience and the dreams the peyote had brought to each. Some sprawled in sleep, others lay in a stupor, unable to resist the effect of the drug and the exhaustion of a sleepless, exciting night. Those who were new to its use, or whose systems were intolerant of the peyote, reacted with violent nausea, diarrhea and profound intoxication.

Those who had gradually accustomed themselves to the drug claimed that for them the intoxication was a delightful experience; that they entered a state of well-being as soon as they had masticated a few of the buttons. They were content to sit or lie and idly dream. While they were under the influence of the excitant, ordinary noises became a harmonious flow of sound that had the soothing effect of music. Colors were transformed into glowing brilliance that shifted and blended, but flowed on and on in an ever widening circle, a source of enchantment. However, this stage of hallucination was followed by extreme lassitude and depression, which none escaped. It was claimed that peyote addicts allowed their gardens to grow up in weeds, and neglected their homes and their families.

There were some to whom the illusions were frightening, such as the worshiper who saw a snake rise from the heart of the sacred peyote that rested on the altar, and felt his own skin take on the scales of a snake's skin. He denounced the drug and refused to continue its use.

Scientific research as to the effect of peyote on the human body is incomplete, but it has been pronounced a habit-forming narcotic and an intoxicant, which is taken solely for its intoxicating effect. The taste is bitter and unpleasant. The drug has its enemies and its ardent defenders. Battles have been fought in several state legislatures over its sale and its use, but the peyote cult has so confused the Religion of the Cross with the worship of the plant, that any legal act to restrict its use is met with the objection that it would deprive the Indian of his right to freedom of worship.

What would the Walapai do with the plant now that it had come to them? Apparently nothing. It was their great good fortune that the Kiowa who had given Bill's father a dose of the "beautiful intoxication" was not a peyote "messiah" but an ordinary peddler. He had all but exhausted his supply of peyote before he arrived at the village, and had gone, leaving nothing with which to prolong or repeat the experience.

Had a zealous missionary or cult leader brought the plant to them, with his convincing argument as to its godlike and healing qualities, they most certainly would have been converted to its use, for they suffered from all the ills that characterized the tribes that had accepted it. They were disorganized, scattered; they had no strong leaders; their social and religious life had disintegrated. Peyote meetings would restore the old tribal solidarity, give their ambitious young men the opportunity for leadership, and provide the social and religious regeneration for which every Walapai longed.

A missionary would have convinced the Indians that peyote took away the burning desire for whisky in which they indulged so freely. Those who partook of peyote did not commit crimes, so were not arrested by the white man and confined in his jail. In addition to its use in the regular meetings, it could be secretly carried in the pocket and nibbled in the home or wherever one happened to be without arousing the white man's suspicions. Those who were afflicted with chronic ailments, such as tuberculosis, so used it, and found escape from suffering, while they hoped for the miracle of a cure.

However, many cultured and intelligent Indians fully realize that those who waste their time in dreaming peyote dreams cannot cultivate their land nor care for their homes. They are convinced that the drug is a health menace and urge that their tribesmen be protected from its sale and use. An investigation has been conducted that eventually may accomplish just this.

On November 26, 1948, the newspapers carried the report of a committee of eminent physicians, who, after a careful study of the use and the effect of peyote among Indian tribes, recommended to the Secretary of the Interior that peyote be outlawed nationally as a habit-forming drug. The report classed peyote as a narcotic cactus, native to the Rio Grande area. If the committee's recommendation is followed, the time may not be far off when peyote addicts (there are white people who attend the Indians' meetings, worship with them and eat the drug) may no longer enjoy the "beautiful intoxication." If so, the Indian addicts will again be free to enjoy the more beneficial intoxication of self-sufficiency, to feel again the thrill of helping the good earth yield sustenance for their families' needs, as did Those of Old.

CHAPTER NINE

Fishberries for Christmas

⊂⊇ I quite naturally thought that the Christmas vacation in an
Indian school would be the same as that observed in the public
schools, beginning a few days before Christmas and ending with
the first day of the New Year. I based my plans on that supposi-
tion. One of those free days would be spent on Mountain-lying-
down. How cold and serenely beautiful it would be up there
with all the surrounding peaks wearing white nightcaps and the
mesa's top under a deep blanket of snow. I could hardly wait to
make the climb. If the vacation were long enough, I would run
down to Kingman to see what the town was like. It had its cattlemen and miners, as Hackberry had, but it boasted a greater number
of homes and business houses.

One day I mentioned the matter of vacation to Mr. Ewing. He
was deep in plans for occupying the new buildings, and replied
absently, "One day will be enough."

"One day!" I gasped. "Couldn't you give us two, Mr. Ewing?"

"When the children are out of school, they run wild. One day
does more harm than a week in school can counteract."

We had one day.

A cold wind whipped down from the north, blowing right off
the ice. It kept the Indians huddled in their wickiups, and us indoors. We greeted one another with "Merry Christmas!" But
since there were just eight of us at the school, including Miss Calfee, Isadore and his family, each needed to say those empty words

only seven times. We missed the children. Everything seemed to stand still, as if life had taken a holiday. We exchanged the small gifts we had bought from the mail-order houses, then I opened my package from home. The dainty, lovely things sent by my family made Christmas seem real and beautiful.

It was late dusk, but I decided to walk down to the village. How did the Indians spend their evenings? When did they retire? They were up with the dawn, for their lives were governed by nature's timing. The wind that had blown steadily all day had settled; the weather had moderated, and the night was calm, but cold, with stars pricking through the velvet overhead. Christmas meant little to the adults. It was the white man's day, and, although its meaning had been explained to them by Miss Calfee and the teachers, they neither understood nor observed it. But the holiday had given their children another day at home, and the people were in a happy mood. The older Indians, wrapped in their blankets, lounged by their outdoor fires.

Not far from Sakawema's wickiup roared a bonfire of dry roots and brush which the children had gathered for the occasion; near it stood another pile from which they fed the flames. Our schoolboys and girls and the small children from the village were playing an Indian game. Don, a born leader, stood on the woodpile, shouting orders, directing their play. Quick running figures dashed about in the bright firelight, shouts and laughter rose in pitch as excitement mounted, while above the confusion, Don's voice barked sharp commands. The village itself was peaceful, the people relaxed, watching their children play an old game that they themselves had played in their childhood. The leaping flames lighted the beaming faces of old and young. I stood off a short distance, enjoying this glimpse of family solidarity, children and parents sharing the fun, a companionship that the people of my race were on the verge of losing.

The next day, a long-expected Christmas present came, my official appointment to the position of principal teacher of the Hackberry Day School, effective January 1, 1901, salary seven hundred

twenty dollars per annum. Now I could plan my work with confidence; the position was permanently mine, and the increase in
salary boosted my morale.

Mr. Ewing sent the small boy who served as his orderly to
summon me to his office to receive my copy of the order. He congratulated me on my promotion, then reached into his desk, drew
out a canvas bag and handed it to me.

"These fishberries were sent here for us to try. I'll have to make
a report on them," he explained. "Steep them and have the children wash their hair in the tea, and report the result to me."

"Fishberries for Christmas!" I exclaimed amused at the incongruity. "But why does the Great Father in Washington want the
children to wash their hair in fishberry tea?" There came a soft
rustling sound from within the bag, and I could feel the light
berries sliding over one another.

"To kill vermin," he said.

"But we use kerosene once a week. Nothing could be better.
It kills instantly; even the nits shrivel up and die. And the children
think it is good for their hair."

"Give this a trial, make out your report on it and hand it to
me," he said impatiently.

I had been in the Service long enough to know that an order
from a bureau in Washington called for action. The bag contained
only a small quantity of the berries, so there would not be much tea.
I decided to ask a few of the older boys and girls to try it out,
make my report, and be done with the matter. On the following
bath day, I had the infusion ready, but dreaded to make the test,
for our children were very suspicious of any change from the
accustomed routine.

Fanny, Mab and Emma agreed to try the experiment. They
were reluctant at first, for they kept their hair brushed and shining, but when I explained to them that we were to use it only once,
and that they might wash it off immediately, they complied,
laughing and exchanging remarks about the liquid with caustic
humor.

I entered the boys' washroom to find Sam disdainfully viewing the concoction in the pan that sat on the bench. "I not wanting my hair brown like that," he declared.

"My hair is brown," I said. "What's wrong with brown hair?"

"It not look strong like black hair."

"Then what do you think of yellow hair and blue eyes?" I asked. I knew that the Walapai considered Indians superior to all other races. Could this be the clue?

"All Indians say they too weak. They not like them."

"So black hair, black eyes and brown skin belong to a strong people. Is that what you mean?"

"All Indians say that," Sam affirmed.

"Well, let's talk about fishberries," I said. "The tea will not change the color of your hair. How would you like to be a guinea pig, just this once?"

Sam gave me a feeble grin. He was recalling the accounts we had read of heroic men who had offered themselves for experimentation that humanity might benefit. He stooped and dipped his hair in the liquid, but immediately washed it off in a good suds. Seth, Don and Jim, who had been cautious observers, said, "We'll be guinea pigs too," and laughing, followed Sam's example.

My report on the fishberry infusion did not mention the casualties it had caused in the insect world, for of that I was profoundly ignorant. I stated that the children were unwilling to use it, that kerosene was entirely satisfactory for our purpose and was greatly preferred. This seemed to end the matter, for no more fishberries were sent to us, and we never learned the motive that prompted the one shipment.

CHAPTER TEN

Coyote Medicine

On April first the Hackberry Day School moved its scanty furniture across the railroad track and settled in the new buildings. This was the occasion on which we were expected to expand into a fully equipped boarding school, but our supplies had not arrived. We had no beds, not enough dishes, not enough of anything; so we would remain a day school until after the summer vacation, and the parents would continue to care for the children when they were not in school.

In contrast to our former quarters, the new buildings seemed splendid indeed. The children's immense dining hall was so shining clean with varnished woodwork and white, hard-finished walls that it was almost as beautiful as the blue sky under which their meals had been served. The kitchen, bright and shining too, would delight any cook.

The west wing of the two-story building housed the boys, with my classroom on the lower floor. It was as complete as the one I had had in the Edmond school: slate blackboards, hardwood floor and heat from a furnace in the basement. I soon learned that the furnace, stoked by schoolboys, added another duty to my full day. Cold water turned into a dry, hot boiler would cause an explosion, so I took time out to read gauges until the weather moderated and the furnace was no longer needed. There was no janitor to drag in his mops and brooms at four o'clock and drive me from the classroom. Cleaning was my job, with the help of the school children.

The east wing of the building was occupied by the girls, the primary classroom being on the east end.

Each of us teachers had a private room in a new two-story brick building. It, too, had a pleasant dining room, a small bright kitchen and two bathrooms, one for the men and one for the women. Everything seemed perfect until we discovered that our water supply came to the new buildings through pipes that lay too near the surface of the hot sand, and was warm and unpalatable. Then someone produced an artistically decorated olla, made by the Pueblos. We wrapped it in burlap and suspended it from the ceiling of the front porch. By keeping the olla full of water, and the burlap wrapping wet, we had cool water all summer, and on hot dry days it was so cold it made our teeth ache.

Nina had gone the way of all maids—to the marriage altar. Isadore had taken his family to Mexico. The employees' club was re-established, and Frances came from Los Angeles to cook for us. But there was no one to manage the children's kitchen, so the primary teacher and I assumed that too, with the help of some of the older boys and girls. We took turns, dashing in between classes to make sure that the meat or the beans did not burn, that the light bread did not rise too long, and to keep things running smoothly. So it was not too many cooks, but the lack of one cook, that spoiled the beans.

I had dismissed my pupils at eleven-thirty, then hurried to the kitchen to help the girls dish up the food. The food looked good: navy beans baked with plenty of salt pork, home-baked bread and tender, sweet prunes. It happened to be my turn to stand in the dining hall to keep order and to see that plenty of food was served to all of the tables.

The companies were marched into the dining hall by their officers and the children stood while they said grace, with their quaint mispronunciation of certain words:

"Lord, we thank Thee for this fu-ud
And Thy many blessings good:
Give us each a thankful heart,

May we ne'er from thee depart. Amen."

Their mingled voices made a dull roar, but as the fragrance of the food took effect, the tempo increased; they raced through the last lines with unseemly speed. Scarcely were they seated before every bread plate was empty and being waved vigorously above some child's head, with the polite request, "More bread, please! More bread!" The girls who waited tables filled those bread plates many times during a meal.

On this particular day, the children disposed of their food as usual, except the bowl of beans that sat at each plate; these were untouched. This called for an investigation. Jim Johnson, a slender, attractive lad, gifted with a brilliant mind, came out with the truth.

"The little girls tell us these beans have coyote medicine in them," he said.

I went to the kitchen to trace the matter. There I learned that one of the girls had spilled a lump or two of sal soda in the beans while they were being washed. The lumps had been removed immediately and the beans washed through several waters before being cooked. Our little boys and girls were the ears and the eyes of the school. They saw everything, heard everything, told everything. A few of the small girls had slipped into the kitchen to get advance information as to what would be served for lunch that day, in order that they might spread the news. They had seen the washing soda fall into the pan, and had run out to warn the other children that a white powder had been put into their beans. To a Walapai, a white powder is coyote medicine, and coyote medicine is poison.

I returned to the dining room and gave the true version of the "coyote medicine." Without a moment's hesitation Jim said, "I'll eat my beans, Miss Gregg." He stood up—to impress his schoolmates—held his bowl in his hand and ate every bean. Then he asked for and disposed of another bowl, the children stolidly watching every move, expecting him to drop dead any moment. Not another bean was eaten that meal, but the next time we served them, they were devoured as usual. Jim won a warm place in our hearts by defying the Indians' superstition and, in this instance, the children's suspicion of us.

I learned to use our small talebearers to good purpose after I had served a cornstarch pudding that no child would touch. We threw out about two hundred sauce dishes of it. The small girls had broadcast that it was made of a white powder—coyote medicine, of course! A few weeks later I called our small folk into the kitchen, boys and girls. They helped open the cartons of cornstarch, helped measure and stir, and we tasted as we cooked, and had a delightful time. Then I sent them out to play. At lunch that day, the cornstarch pudding was eaten first, the rice, meat and bread later. After that, we could introduce new foods with the certainty that there would be no waste.

Had we been in the old buildings across the track, I doubt if the bean incident would have happened, for the children felt completely at home there, and they had confidence in us. The newness and the strangeness of things confused them. The white hard finish on the walls aroused suspicion; they had never seen walls so glittering white, and were alert for danger. The bathroom showers, that made the weekly bath so simple for us, frightened them out of their wits. When we tried to get a girl to enter a cubicle that had warm water spouting from the wall, she shook with terror. The little folks clung to our skirts and wailed at the thought of entering the showers, so we sponged them off and hoped for the children's speedy adjustment to their new surroundings.

For weeks the showers were unpopular, then quite suddenly, some of the older pupils asked for midweek baths, and within a short time they were bathing daily.

The necessity of using a toilet instead of dodging behind a bush, was not of their choosing, and the swift rush of water was so disconcerting that they could not attend to their needful chores. The radiators, unlike a campfire, showed no flame, but when one touched them they burned like fire, and their pipes rattled and banged terrifyingly in the early morning hours. It was a good thing, especially for the little ones, that for lack of equipment we had to let them go home at night. Had they been compelled to sleep on high bedsteads with mattresses, pillows and bedding instead of on fur robes or Indian blankets on the dirt floor, the night as well as the day would have been one long nightmare.

The village must move across the Santa Fe track so that the children might live at home, and the Indians made a gala day of it. The women ran about, packing their few household possessions with much excitement and chatter. The men worked at the wickiups, tearing them down and moving them to the new location, where they would be hastily thrown together again. Wagons that groaned on wobbly wheels, loaded with family possessions and drawn by thin ponies, made their way to a wide pass between a low hill and high, red bluffs. It was a sandy patch of rough ground, separated from the school by the low hill, a desolate spot for a home. The wind had a clear sweep through the pass, and the miserable shelters the Indians were able to build gave little protection against its fierce blast.

It was a strange and colorful procession that moved from the old village to the new, and strange were the things the Indians carried on their backs, in their arms or piled in wagons. Old weapons, ceremonial headdresses, charms, buckskin clothing, relics of past splendor, were brought from secret places, carried to the new home and stored again.

Old Suja, whimsical and stubborn, refused to have these relics hauled in a neighbor's wagon, and contrived his own mode of transportation. Selecting two stout, slender poles, he placed them a short distance apart and joined them with a woven fiber saddle. With scraps of old rope and buckskin, he hitched his dog between the shafts, and lashed his treasures to the saddle. As usual, the boys gathered about the old man. Sam led his dog, while two boys steadied the load, and with much giggling, helped him gather up and replace articles that bounced off. While the old man ranted at the dog, the sled and the roughness of the ground, and boys laughed hilariously.

When he changed his theme to decry the fact that the Walapai no longer planted the seeds the gods had given them, but lived on barren ground; when he told them how Coyote had taught Kathatkanave to make fire that the Indians might live more comfortably, they listened in profound silence that not a word might be missed. Deep within the heart of each schoolboy was the conviction that the old ways were best, and no truth could be truer than the stories old Suja told of the days when animals taught men the secrets that only the wild creatures knew.

The villagers soon lost their joyousness, for the mesa no longer reached out her arms to shield them from the cutting wind, nor did she hold them close to her voluminous skirt when summer's sun grew hot. Their houses, hastily put together, were less substantial than before; they stood on rocky soil, barren of bush or tree. The wind that blew through the shallow pass was laden with sand; nowhere in the village was there comfort or joy. Grace and Boots had built their house against a bluff, a little apart from the others, a little more sheltered. Suja's shack was in the heart of the village; here he could sprawl on the sand, smoke his pipe and be assured of an audience. Sakawema's house had been carefully put together. Don and Mab had taken the heavy end of the work, making it tight and snug. There were no windows, only a roof vent through which the smoke from the indoor fire might escape, and a doorway, closed by a tightly woven blanket. The dull young man, and his wife, Tahuta, had rebuilt their house as neat and solid as it had been in the old village, but the blind old woman and her crude brush shelter still cluttered their yard. The family had no sooner settled in their new home than the husband died. Now that Tahuta had the full responsibility of the home, we expected her to become even more worried with her added cares. But summer, the season when the Indians held their great mourning ceremony, the Nemitiawak, was yet to come. At the Nemitiawak, sullen, industrious Tahuta, courted by a handsome man, blossomed like a young girl.

This great annual celebration was yet another link in the chain that bound the Walapai to their remote past. It would afford us a further glimpse into the background of these people whose lives we were attempting to mold on an alien pattern.

We had seen the caution and suspicion of Those of Old reflected in the Walapai's unconscious cruelty and fear of coyote medicine. Now, in this ceremony of faith and dignity we were to witness a more positive side of their heritage. The Nemitiawak was to prove a revelation to those of us who did not yet understand the primitive culture of these people.

CHAPTER ELEVEN

Nemitiawak (Meet to Cry)

⊂⊒   The spring day was pleasantly warm and every window in my classroom was thrown wide to admit the stimulating air loaded with the tang of growing things. Tiny fernlike plants spread a quick carpet over the desert, lifting a sheen of pink flowers above the greenness. And restlessness pervaded my classroom. The bright, warm weather, after a winter of cold and snow, quickened pulses, whipped the red blood into the children's cheeks, and put a sparkle of expectancy in their eyes.

During the last period of the afternoon, I had a spelling class. While hearing recitations, I liked to walk in the aisles: it seemed to bring me closer to the children. I think they liked it too. As I paused near Sam's desk, I noticed his foot turned back against the iron support of the seat, his sockless heel pulled free from his low shoe; Sam had broken a rule by not wearing socks. I was not concerned with rules at the moment. The whimsical thought ran through my mind: "The Indian's heel trying to escape the white man's shoe," and I smiled. Sam glanced up. Encouraged by my smile, he grinned broadly. World War I was to prove that his heel could not escape, but neither of us suspected then what the white man might do to Sam.

A moment later, neither of us felt like grinning.

The spelling class stood in line. I had pronounced a word and Bill was spelling it, when from outside the room a thin, quavering sound cut through the stillness. Bill closed his lips in a grim, tight line and every child in the room froze to a motionless silence. I felt my own muscles tighten, for although I could not understand its message, the very tone was a portent of disaster. Again and again it rose and hung in the air like a broken note; something more than grief, for it had terror in it, and despair.

I felt as if I were standing on the brink of an unknown world when I spoke in a low voice to my class, "You may be seated." Noiseless, tense with listening, they moved to their seats.

I walked to the rear window and looked down on the sand beneath, from which the sound came. An old woman huddled there, her back pressed against the brick wall of the building, gray hair matted on her bent head, bare feet protruding from soiled, voluminous skirts. Her *sutam*-covered shoulders heaved convulsively as her body shook with sobs. The haunting cry rose and fell at spaced intervals, and had in it all the agony of a mortally wounded animal. Recitations were impossible; not a child would speak. At four o'clock the old woman scrambled to her feet and wandered slowly off to the village.

For ten minutes, in awed silence, we had listened to her voice, and her departure left a lingering sadness. The children were quiet and subdued, for many times in their lives they had listened to that ancient chant. Its meaning was clear to them. From the Days of Old an elderly one of the tribe had passed on news in this peculiar Walapai fashion. But I was completely puzzled as to the cause of her coming or why she had shed tears so copiously.

When I dismissed school, there were no volunteers for janitor work, but Don and Seth remained when I asked them to sweep the floor and dust. Bill lingered to clean the erasers, a task that fascinated him. Don and Seth worked in gloomy silence and soon finished, but Bill continued to beat his erasers.

I went back to him and asked, "Why did the old woman come to the school building? What did she want?"

Bill cleared his throat before he replied in an awed voice, "Little boy die in camp today. That old woman crying." He placed his erasers meticulously on the blackboard ledge and went softly from the room.

I wanted to learn what child had died, for I had heard of no sickness in the village, but I had not asked Bill. One did not speak the name of the dead.

When the soul leaves the body, it lingers only a few feet above the earth, hesitating between its longing to remain with the people and the places it loves and the necessity of embarking on that long journey to the beautiful, ethereal land far to the northwest, a land of joy and abundance, its people forever young. To speak the name of the dead child would have the effect of calling him back, and, since he had started, there must be no return.

I received the information from another source. Grace's small son, Bela, had died of pneumonia that day. Instead of reporting the child's illness to the school, Grace and Boots had called in the medicine man, but his efforts had failed to save the child's life.

For a time I worked on my lesson plans, then as early dusk laid a thin shadow over the land, strange sounds from the outside took me again to the classroom window. A slow procession moved up from the village, followed a trail that paralleled the railroad, and crossed the track, the Indians walking in single file. I could hear the professional mourners, women's voices, lifted in wailing, "Oi-oi-oi," they chanted on a sharp, high note, then dropping to a lower note, "Oi-oi." On and on it went in doleful repetition, "Oi-oi-oi—oi-oi." It was the funeral dirge of the Walapai. It was heartbreaking, especially when I saw Bela's small, limp body dressed in the best garments the family could procure and lovingly wrapped in their choicest blanket, strapped, face down, on the spotted pony his father had promised him when "he gets little bigger." The procession filed across the wash and followed its bank to the mouth of the canyon separating old Mountain-lying-down from the highland to the east. They were taking Bela up the gorge to some lonely, sun-drenched spot to bury him beneath a pile of stones.

All his little boy treasures accompanied him on this last ride; no tie must be left that would hold his soul to the earth. His playthings and all of his belongings would be burned at his grave so that their spirits might join him in the spirit world. The spotted pony, too, must go with him that he might mount it and ride, wild and free as the mountain wind. The pony would die slowly, with a wet buckskin thong tied about his neck that would tighten as it dried, until not a vestige of air could reach his tortured lungs. He would stagger on trembling legs until he fell near the spot where his young master lay beneath the stones; vultures and coyotes would pick the flesh from his bones.

That night from our cottage porch we looked across the low hill to the west at the reflection in the sky of the deep-red flames that consumed the neat house Grace and Boots had built for their home, the house in which their son had died. With it were burned many of their household possessions. The burning of these familiar things would help free their son's wandering soul from earth ties. The family must move to a place unfamiliar to Bela, or he would seek and find them and hover near. And a Walapai feared nothing else as he feared the spirit of a departed loved one.

I went to my room, but was too depressed to read, so got out a mail-order catalogue and indulged in an orgy of buying. Fishnet curtains for my windows, a green rug for the floor, a bright runner for the table and a spread for the bed; inexpensive things, but I took satisfaction in anticipating how gay my room would look when they were in place. Then I wrote letters home, and eventually recovered from the gloom that had held me from the moment I had listened to that weird crying beneath the classroom window, a gloom that had deepened with the unfolding of the afternoon's tragic events. I longed to go to Grace and Boots to express my sympathy, but death came to the Walapai wrapped in so many taboos that I might easily offend when I had hoped to comfort.

Their custom of burying the dead had but recently been substituted for cremation. No Indian seemed to know why they had cremated or when the practice originated, but they knew why they had discontinued it. They had learned of a Paiute shaman who claimed to have made a journey to the land of the dead and there learned that the dead would return to live again on earth. A delegation of Walapai and Havasupai men paid a visit to the shaman and became his disciples. Returning, they converted their tribesmen to his creed. A corpse could arise with greater ease from beneath a pile of stones than from ashes scattered by wind and rain.

Grace and Boots with their two sons settled in the new home across the village from the one they had destroyed. With nothing to remind them of the child they had lost, Bela seemed to have been forgotten. Not until later did I learn that they would mourn for him at the Nemitiawak, an assemblage of the people for social pleasure and general mourning, conducted according to an established ritual.

As the spring advanced, we noticed a quickening of village activities, a heartening bustle and stir. The word Nemitiawak ("Meet to Cry") was on every tongue. Messengers were riding off to notify tribesmen in the scattered settlements on the reservation, while others were making the longer journey to the Havasupai and other friendly tribes to the east, and to the Mohave on the west. Each messenger carried a knotted cord. The knots stood for the number of days that would elapse before the Meet to Cry took place. By untying or clipping off one knot for each sun, the invited guest knew the exact day the ceremony would begin.

A hard winter had brought exposure and sickness. There had been many deaths; families would assemble to mourn their dead publicly, and to enjoy the accompanying festivities. The presence of friends from neighboring tribes added to the dignity and social importance of the occasion, and contributed to the merrymaking.

Poles and boughs were brought in from the hills to erect an open arbor on a space that had been leveled near the center of the village. The call went out for food. There would be three days of feasting. No animal was too old to make savory stew in the pot; sheep, cattle, mountain sheep and rabbits contributed their quota to the feast. Canned tomatoes, crackers, coffee and other "store" foods added variety to roasted mescal, piñon nuts, Mormon tea and the Indians' garden-grown vegetables and fruits.

The last knot was cut from the counting cord; the great day had dawned. To accommodate the visitors, brush wickiups mushroomed among the permanent dwellings of the village. The food was assembled at the pavilion to be prepared for serving. The size of an individual's contribution did not limit the amount of food he might consume.

At each end of the open pavilion, women worked in groups over the cooking fires. Blackened kettles and cans simmered and bubbled, filling the air with appetizing odors. Toasting baskets were brought out and sunflower seed, corn and wild seeds were toasted with live coals to a golden brown. Grinding stones and baking stones were in use. Paper-thin bread and that made from thick dough and baked like fat pancakes on the heated stone added their fragrance to that of simmering coffee; a feast was in the making.

Old men sought one another, lounging on the sand and smoking their pipes, while they exchanged news of friends and tribal doings, talked longingly of the Old Days, or dispiritedly of their vanishing hunting grounds. Young men were noisy at their games of chance, gambling their cash, their possessions, even their ponies. Children ran about on bare feet, the boys clad in shirts that were inches too short or wearing no clothing at all. The little girls, hair cut in the fashion of their mothers, faces daubed with native paints, swished about in long calico dresses. Teen-age girls walked through the crowd, juggling little green watermelons or anything that could be tossed into the air and caught, keeping three or four objects going without allowing one to touch the ground. Laughter, shouts and the babble of mixed tongues made a strange confusion, for each tribe spoke its own language. Off to one side, a parade was forming for the opening event.

Young men, decked out in their most gorgeous finery, faces concealed by bizarre masks, sat their ponies awaiting the start. Their ponies, gaily caparisoned with silver-mounted bridles and saddles and adorned from ears to tails with long streamers of bright cloth and greasewood boughs, caught the excitement; even tired old nags managed to prance and toss their heads. Old warriors had brought from hiding their ancient, feathered war bonnets, which they wore with great dignity. The parade moved off, colors flashing, gay decorations reflecting the June sunlight.

Bridles jingled, silver ornaments clinked and homemade noise-makers rattled and banged. The commotion brought cooks and fire tenders from their cooking pots and gamblers from their games to applaud the spectacle.

At frequent intervals the parade disintegrated; old men clambered down from their horses to smoke and rest rheumatic legs; the young men indulged in pranks. One, using his quirt, sent his horse on the dead run toward a favored maiden who, clutching her long skirts and screaming, scampered to the protection of the older women. He was choosing his woman, publicly.

During one such interlude, Van, a young Havasupai, sprang to his feet and danced, clad only in loincloth and moccasins. The features of his handsome face remained immobile while he pranced, twisted his body from side to side, plunged, stamped and cavorted in fancy steps, the muscles of his strong body rippling under his oiled bronze skin. He glanced neither to the right nor to the left, but the young woman for whom he performed stood a little to one side, her covert glances missing not one movement of his lithe body, her lips curved in an approving smile. She was Tahuta, the widow of the dull young man.

After each intermission, men remounted, the parade continued.

During the morning, the men of each visiting tribe had held themselves aloof, mingling with other tribes to visit, but not too freely; taking part in some of the games, but betting with restraint. At noon, all gravitated to the arbor where the air was redolent with the aroma of food; each tribal group, with the exception of the Havasupai, who were cousins, sat by itself. This was a custom that still held from the days of recent warfare and treachery, when a tribe resorted to trickery in order to snare an enemy. Many of the old men had fought in bloody battles against the very tribes whose representatives now partook of the feast. Cunning and shrewdness flowed in their blood and they had long memories.

Cans were opened, stew dished from steaming kettles, boiling coffee poured into tin cups and, according to old custom, visitors were served first. Eating and drinking together, suspicion thawed, the members of the several tribes mingled freely, laughing, jesting and visiting.

The last crumb of the feast disposed of, pans and kettles were whisked aside, and the Indians sadly and silently filled the cleared space, forming a circle that faced the center of the pavilion. They squatted on their heels or sat on the ground with outstretched legs while Puchilowa—known to us as Jim Fielding—harangued the women and children as to proper conduct during the Nemitiawak. His words carried weight, for he was employed at the agency as Indian policeman, at a salary of ten dollars per month, and kept his policeman's badge polished to an eye-dazzling brightness. There was the rustle of several hundred people settling themselves to give attention, with undertone admonitions to restless children and slaps and scoldings for slinking dogs. Puchilowa sternly demanded order, "Sit still! Do not talk!" he shouted.

Chief Wilatouse rose with dignity, walked to the center of the pavilion and with upraised hand, commanded instant attention. "It is good to meet here to mourn for those who have gone to that far-off place," he intoned in a high chanting voice. "Our hearts are lonely. We meet to cry." Then he launched into the death song for a recently departed chief. "Our leader is gone to that far place. We hear his voice no more. We send him warm clothes. We send him many things. We send him our tears." As his voice flowed on in a rising crescendo, his old wife began gently swaying her body and crooning a weird melody that was immediately taken up by the entire audience. The voices, low and soft, held a savage undercurrent of grief that mounted and swelled, while a wild hysteria took possession of the mourners.

Flanked by her two children, Tahuta sat well to the front of the circle, her face distorted by weeping. Her widow's weeds, prescribed by Walapai tradition, were peculiarly becoming to her. The clinging dress of red flannel added a soft glow to her pale face, and the peaked cap of the same violent red sat jauntily on her smoothly brushed black hair. Her moans and wails and copious tears for the dull young husband who had been laid beneath the rocks could not conceal the fact that she was young and vibrantly alive. Van, the Havasupai who had danced for her with such fierce abandon, sat rigidly on the outer edge of the circle, arms tightly folded, eyes straight ahead.

Grace and Boots sat shoulder to shoulder, clinging tenderly to each other, their faces twisted by the agony of their grief, while their tears flowed unrestrained. In a low crooning voice, Grace recited the many good qualities of their little Bela. "His body was straight and strong; his face like the morning sun; his feet light and fleet as the western wind," she moaned, rocking her body gently. Then she talked of their great love for him. Boot's strong hands held hers in a crushing grip as he rocked back and forth, his body shaken by sobs. He endorsed his wife's eulogy of their son by repeating, *"Hanaga! Hanaga!* (Good! Good!)"

The Havasupai, the Navaho and the Mohave moaned and wept as loudly as any, but not for their own dead; the Meet to Cry was a Walapai ceremony and for their hosts' dead the visitors lifted their voices.

In accordance with the old-woman custom, Suja's aged wife, thin and grizzled, clambered to her feet and rushed to the open space in the center of the circle. With hands lifted above her head, palms outward, she declaimed in staccato phrases the virtues of a brother whose body had been carried to the burial ground that winter. The tears from her red-rimmed eyes washed her withered cheeks, while her body shook with the violence of her weeping. In the mounting ecstasy of her grief, sobbing and screaming, each hysterical outburst bent her body lower and lower until she fell, a disheveled heap, her head resting on the sand. Tender hands lifted the old creature and carried her to the outskirts of the circle, where she lay, groaning loudly. Her wild demonstration had whipped the audience into a greater fervor; moans, wails and shrieks filled the pavilion.

Puchilowa took charge. He admonished them to dry their tears and gave them a brief outline of coming events. The death song was stilled on quivering lips; tears were wiped away; the young people and the children sprang to their feet but the cramped muscles of the elderly made them slow in rising. Quick laughter chased away grief. Everyone began preparing for the races and games that would follow. They were as eager as children; not a tear, not a laugh, nor the excitement of the races would any of them willingly miss.

Horse racing was first in order. Each had his favorite horse and he would bet on it almost to the limit of his possessions. Even the children contributed to the hubbub by staking whatever they owned on the horses. Suja's wife had made a speedy recovery and was helping her man assemble the clothing and household articles they would wager. Visiting Indians ran their horses and bet heavily but the Walapai were gamblers of long experience and horse racing was their favorite pastime, so many good Navaho blankets, silver bracelets, ponies and saddles fell into their hands.

The foot races were less exciting on this particular day; the bets placed were low.

Early in the afternoon, everyone drifted back to the pavilion where food was apportioned to the visiting men, then to the men of the tribe, the women and children taking what was left.

Indian games, horseshoe pitching and games of chance occupied the time until, just before the evening meal, all were summoned to the pavilion to mourn again for their dead. This session was a repetition of the first. There was the same hysteria, the crooning of the death song, moans and shrieks until the mourners were again engulfed in an emotional orgy. Then, like a desert storm, the Big Cry ended abruptly and supper was served. Again kettles and pans were whisked aside, great bonfires lighted the evening sky, drums throbbed, dancing and fun filled the night.

The song leader took his stand by the drummer and urged the people to form a circle and dance, but the younger generation, especially the young folks who had attended school, held back, abashed. The leader read the lines of the dance song, either an old-time song or one of his own improvising; the audience repeated them until they were able to join him in singing. But the ceremony aroused little interest until the chief's wife, with a sweeping motion of her hands, inviting others to follow, joined the dancers. Soon the circle was filled, even children taking part. The dancers moved to the left with slow shuffling steps, bodies swaying slightly to the rhythm, all singing lustily.

For three days laughter and tears followed each other in quick succession, then the Meet to Cry ended in a big dance. But even the dance had interludes for oratory, exhortation and tearful tributes to the dead. Then came the last sacred rite of the ceremonial. The great pavilion was brought crashing to the ground for a monstrous bonfire on which new clothing and other precious belongings were sacrificed to the flames—the Walapai's way of sending gifts for the comfort of friends and relatives who had gone that year to the spirit world. Thus ended the Meet to Cry, where tribesmen and friends annually assembled to visit, to feast, to laugh, to weep, to dance and to sing to the point of exhaustion. And to philander a little.

The visitors departed for their homes—all except one. Van moved in with Tahuta and her children. Marriage to the Walapai, and I supposed, to the Havasupai was uncomplicated by ceremony, and was consummated, as they so aptly expressed it, "When a man loves a woman, and the woman loves the man, and their needs are the same."

Also, marriage to a widow called for no bargaining for the woman's hand. A young girl was a commodity for whom the parents required a suitor to pay in blankets, ponies, food or cash. A widow had been bought by one man, and that transaction had terminated parental authority. He who won her had only her wishes to consult. Very simply and comfortably Van settled into the scheme of things, undisturbed by the old woman staked out near the house.

We at the school were shocked at the blind old woman's apparent neglect, but had we given her a room in one of the buildings and taken over her care, she would have died of homesickness and the longing for accustomed foods and the sound of familiar voices. She may have felt grateful for the crumbs of comfort that came her way, for most certainly she had witnessed, in their recent wars with other tribes, the Walapai's abandonment of the old and helpless to die of hunger, thirst and exposure that the fit, unhampered by these, might survive; the sacrifice of the few for the good of many seemed logical and right. In her younger days, she herself may have sacrificed her parents in this same heartless manner.

The Walapai had had three great, exciting days, which left them a little flustered, but they quickly settled down and became the self-disciplined people to whom we had grown accustomed. They had exercised their old initiative in carrying out the Nemitiawak wanting no white man's help. Soon they were again trusting, dependent, bringing to us their every problem—from the need for a dose of physic to a request for help in ousting white intruders.

When the Havasupai rode away in the bright June sunlight, I did not expect to see them again until they returned for another visit with the Walapai, but within a few days I followed them to their canyon home.

PART TWO

The Havasupai: People of the Blue Water

CHAPTER TWELVE

Mule Train and
Canyon Walls

Vacation schedules had been posted, and through the last hot weeks of June the school hummed with preparations for summer closing.

The village had already begun to break up. And with school's dismissal, families piled their possessions and their children into creaking wagons and drove away to visit relatives or to spend the summer in a former home.

My vacation was scheduled for July. This first hard year in a small Indian school had left me completely discouraged. The duties of too many other positions had been assigned to the teachers to permit efficient work. I had rosy memories of my uncrowded classroom back home with its eager children competing for the privilege of reciting; no study hour at night; duty only six hours a day, five days a week. My trunk was nearly packed. I would submit my resignation before leaving.

One pleasant evening late in June, a few days before my departure, I sat on the front porch of our cottage and watched the pale glow of the rising moon brighten the sky above the mesa. But even the magic of mountain and highland outlined in silver could not hold my straying thoughts. I was back in my home, enjoying once again the loving congeniality of a family dinner—rich with its talk and laughter. How I had missed that warmth and understanding. Absorbed in my thoughts, I had not noticed a small Indian boy's approach, until he spoke from the shadow at the foot of the steps, "They want you at office."

At his desk, Mr. Ewing looked up worriedly. "I'm sorry, Miss Gregg," he said, "but some of the employees on whom I had depended to help me through the summer have resigned and gone to Los Angeles. The superintendent of the Havasupai has been granted a leave of absence. I'll have to ask you to take charge of the affairs of this tribe until he returns." He glanced at my face and added hastily, "He'll be away for only one month. But before you decide, I want you to understand that you will be completely cut off from the outside—except for mail twice a week. You will supervise the work of three white employees, have charge of two hundred and fifty Indians, and teach a school of something like seventy pupils."

I had promised myself that some day I would go to the home of the Havasupai, the People of the Blue Water. This might well be the only opportunity I would ever have. My experiences with their cousin tribe had only sharpened the urge to work among this completely primitive people, to learn something of the unseen forces that influenced their lives. The decision was not an easy one, but my incurable thirst for adventure permitted just one answer.

"When do you want me to go?" I asked.

"You will meet the outgoing superintendent in Seligman July first. I'll go up to Seligman with you. I want to talk to him, and to Mr. Burnett, who will drive you out to the canyon."

Back in my room I repacked my trunk. Many of the things I had planned to take home could now be left in my room. The square of buckskin with the red paint Carl had given me, a little beaded purse made by one of my schoolgirls, gifts from those who had so little to give, brought me face to face with new values. These children needed me. I would go to the Havasupai during my school vacation, but the fall would find me back with the Walapai.

I dashed off a note to Mother explaining the change in plans and stressing the importance of the salary of seventy-five dollars a month I would receive as temporary superintendent. I did not tell her that I would be on duty from daylight until long after dark. Nor did I admit my doubt as to my ability to handle situations that might arise, although I had been told that, on one occasion, the Havasupai men had terrorized the man in charge with knives and guns until he reversed his previous decision. How, I wondered, could I hope to control grown men—the chief, for instance, or the medicine men? But on July first, Mr. Ewing and I boarded the train.

The town of Seligman, bleak with dust and desert heat, looked as if it had been blown in on a dry wind and stranded. My interview with the departing Havasupai superintendent was scarcely more heartening. He told me that he was not coming back to the reservation. "I'll *never* bring my family into that hole!" he stated with emphasis. The tales he told of the hardship, deprivation, isolation and actual danger to life in the canyon were disillusioning. Regardless of his discouraging remarks, I was determined to go on to Supai, the name assigned to the post office and accepted as that of the Havasupai village.

Immediately after breakfast the following morning, I went to the trader's store to buy food for the two meals Mr. Burnett and I would need for the seventy-mile drive across the plateau. Following that, we would have an eight-mile climb down the wall of the Walapai Canyon, a western arm of the canyon in which the People of the Blue Water lived.

I made my purchases and returned to the hotel where I had spent the night. Mr. Ewing and Mr. Burnett, who would act as farmer at the school, were waiting, the wagon loaded with supplies. The mules took a steady gait, following the dim wagon road that lazily rounded hillocks and depressions. We might have lost it completely had it not been for the winding swath it cut through the desert growth. The heat, reflected by the sand, became almost unbearable. Sand clung to the wagon wheels and lifted to fill the dry, hot air. A few venturesome rabbits hopped out from the scraggy brush to stare at us, then retreated quickly to the shelter of their hideouts.

We stopped at noon to build a fire under a wind-twisted evergreen. I made coffee and spread the lunch on newspapers while Mr. Burnett fed the mules and watered them from the keg in the wagon. As far as we could see, in every direction, there was the monotony of sand and red bluffs with a scattering of pine, cedar and piñon trees. We were soon on our way again. Before the dinner hour, we must reach Halfway House, a sheep ranch well known in that section of Arizona for the hospitality of the young couple who owned it.

Mrs. Rose came out to the wagon to greet us. She was slender and pretty, her windblown hair and sparkling eyes made her look like a little schoolgirl. "Oh, come in! It's wonderful to talk to another woman!" she exclaimed. It was as wonderful for me too.

The sun's rays had lifted from the wide stretch of desert in which the house stood, but gold was still lingering on the encircling hills when we heard the sheep coming in. Bathed in that light, a shining, living mass topped the low hills, spilling down the shady slopes until we could distinguish individual sheep, noses outthrust, gray bodies swaying on dainty feet. Mr. Rose, tall, lean, hardened by wind and sun, was everywhere, helping the herders pen the sheep for the night. In this vast, desolate expanse, I marveled that so much life could be sustained.

The next morning as we were starting to leave, Mr. Rose, with typical generosity of people living in isolation, laid the half of a freshly killed lamb in the back of the wagon, a gift to his overnight guests.

The day was a repetition of the previous one, except that the terrain grew rougher. Mr. Burnett pointed out old landmarks and water holes. He had hauled freight, a few times, from Seligman to Hilltop, the name given the storehouse at the head of the trail, so he knew the country we were traveling, but he had never gone down to Supai. I suggested, tactfully, that we would have to make better time if we were to arrive at the school that night.

"Climb down that trail tonight! Impossible!" he exclaimed.

The remark shocked me, for no one had suggested that the trip from Halfway House to the school could not be made in one day. I had been told only that the road wound around boulders and bluffs and dipped into gorges, ending at the shack called Hilltop, where the trail down began. My determination to reach the school that night, even if I had to climb down the trail alone, increased as we made the descent into rugged Walapai Canyon, approaching Hilltop. Otherwise, I would have to make camp at the shack with this stranger. We rounded a cliff, and there lay a sheltered basin. At its lower edge stood the shack. The soft twilight, which would turn so quickly into darkness, and the wild, rough terrain, convinced me this would end the day's journey for Mr. Burnett, and that I'd better find the beginning of the trail and start walking. Then, in front of the shack, as if in answer to my need, I saw the flash of a campfire. A light breeze brought the aroma of coffee and frying bacon. Two figures, bent over the fire, straightened to wave a welcome to us, and I recognized one of them.

"Frances! Frances!" I shouted with such vehemence that she dropped the fork she held and started for the wagon. The mules were jerked to a halt. I sprang over the wheel and ran to catch her in an embrace that took her breath. Then I let her go and we both laughed, for we realized that my exuberance was due more to my relief in finding her here, than to the renewal of our casual acquaintance. She had been mess cook for a short time at the Hackberry Day School, and had been sent to Supai to teach the girls cooking and to supervise the preparation of the children's noon lunch.

She introduced her companion, Miss Goenawein, the housekeeper at the school, who taught the girls sewing, laundering and homemaking. They had climbed eight miles of dangerous trail to meet us, bringing food and extra pack horses.

"We knew you couldn't go down that trail tonight. Anyway, it's fun to get out of that dreary old canyon and have supper and breakfast up here where you can see more than just a scrap of the sky," Frances said, and turned to flip the bacon over in the pan.

Supper was almost ready but I walked over and stood on the rim of the inner gorge that cut deeply through the red sandstone in an easterly direction. I looked down into a giant bowl that was hundreds of feet across and so deep that I could barely see the shadow-shrouded bottom—typical Colorado River country. Above the red sandstone formation that held the bowl, the white limestone of the outer gorge rose three thousand feet in broken, tumbled walls, fashioned by wind, rain and frost into pinnacles, towers and mellowed old castles from which knights might have ridden, their colors flying. In the lingering daylight, glowing pinks, soft grays and cool blues tinted the white limestone and contrasted strangely with the darkness that filled the somber inner gorge. Nothing moved; the absolute stillness was appalling. Clinging to the south rim of the bowl lay a thin white thread—the trail we would follow the next morning! It started out on smooth, firm ground but somewhere it descended that sheer, red wall.

Frances hallooed from the campfire, "Supper! Last call!"

I retraced my steps, grateful for companionship in this place of such frightening vastness and silence. The food was placed on a large box from the wareroom; boxes were our seats. Never before had bacon and eggs, bread and coffee tasted so delicious.

Night settled in the basin, and we began discussing the safest place to make our beds. There were rattlers in abundance, wildcats and mountain lions, so we three women slept in the wagon bed. However, as the stars grew dim, our hard bed could be endured no longer, so we slipped into our dresses, stockings and shoes and climbed out to stretch our stiff muscles. None of us knew where the Englishman made his bed, but he emerged the next morning, washed and combed and very businesslike. He remarked to me, "If the folks hadn't met us, I planned to fix a place for you to sleep in the storehouse, but when I opened the door just now, a big, fat blacksnake slid over the bales of hay and disappeared among the supplies."

While the girls cooked breakfast, I unpacked my trunk by lantern light. Mr. Burnett and I fitted its contents into the clumsy packsaddles that were strapped on the burros. He assured me that the trunk would be banged to kindling wood if we attempted to take it down the trail. But the more convincing argument was that the trunk would bump the burro off the trail and into the gorge.

After breakfast, while Mr. Burnett packed the remaining supplies, Frances walked off a short distance on the road that led to Seligman. I followed, for I had seen the wistful sadness in her face. She stood in the early morning twilight, her blue eyes and graying blond hair hinting of her vanished youth.

"I'd like to start walking and not stop until I reach Los Angeles," she said pensively. "I want to see a train. I want to wear a dinner dress, dine by candlelight, and see people laugh and have fun. Those walls down there hold one like a grave."

"For over a year I've been thinking that life down there would be exciting," I told her. "I intend to get acquainted with the people and prowl around to see what's in that fabulous canyon of theirs."

Her face brightened. "I'll prowl with you," she offered. "I've been there only a few weeks, and have stayed pretty close to the school. The Indian village is farther down the canyon; maybe the people do interesting things. We'll see."

Mr. Burnett called, "Well, let's get going!" so we walked back to Hilltop.

This was my first venture on a really dangerous trail, so they took the trouble to coach me. "When we are on the edge of a chasm, don't lean over to look below or you'll overbalance your mule," they advised. And added, "When the going gets tough and we dismount, walk in front of your mule or he will go on down to the school and leave you on foot."

Since no animal could negotiate the angles on the trail with a sidesaddle on his back, I rode astride for the first time in my life, on a big gray mule. I objected to the mule. I knew that I would be uncomfortable riding the ungainly beast; I preferred a neat burro that sat closer to the earth or one of the horses. But they insisted that the mule had traveled the trail for years and knew exactly where a misstep would be fatal, for he had been present when another mule had crashed to the bottom of the gorge—when they found the unfortunate animal, not even his hide had been worth salvaging. My mule was "trail conscious" and placed his feet with care, so I climbed on his back.

We followed the trail as it half-circled the bowl, then I dropped to the rear and brought my mule to a halt, craning my neck to gaze at those mystic rocky towers and castles looming against the brightening sky. A pale blue haze clung to their sides, deepening at their bases to a dark blue-gray. As I watched from the narrow trail, the sun's first rays flashed golden on the distant peaks, and long bars of light flowed down through the haze, changing it to orchid, then to a deep rose, startling in its beauty. An instant of this, then the towers stood clear in the light of a summer morning.

My mule had become impatient and was stepping gingerly ahead to join the train which was descending the almost perpendicular wall of the inner gorge in countless steep switchbacks.

We had climbed down to a shelf on which the mule jogged along at the end of the train, when I glanced up and saw a flash of crimson against a background of blue sky—an Indian standing on a white cliff, with face uplifted to the morning sun. His knee-length red blanket, tossed back, revealed strong, brown shoulders and statuesque body. His long black hair, bound in a knot at the nape of his neck with strips of gay calico, and his moccasins and bright headband made a colorful picture against the clear blue. This was a man of the Havasupai, paying homage to the rising Sun. To a Havasupai, the Sun is more than the god of warmth and light; the Sun is the forefather of his tribe.

Proud and straight the Indian stood, communing with his legendary ancestor. I felt a strong desire to climb to a lonely peak and lose myself in adoration, but my mule turned an angle of the wall, reminding me that the pack train was zigzagging its way down the trail. I hurried the mule on; I would feel safer when I got back to my old place somewhere between the lead horse and the end of the train.

The steep and dangerous descent continued. Had the mule stepped too near the crumbling edge of the gorge, or had he slipped, we would have gone bouncing and crashing to the canyon bed far below. Sometime in the dim past, the Havasupai had worked their way up this canyon wall, establishing a path wherever they could find a foothold, until they reached the outside. When the early explorers descended, they too followed the crude path that satisfied an Indian's need. Men who were employed at the school and must travel it often, spent much time repairing it, trying to make it safe, but each quick flood washed out their man-made trail leaving the rugged walls as nature had formed them.

The narrow path, crowded by jutting walls, forced us to dismount frequently, but once, when we approached a treacherous spot, I was told not to dismount. Before I realized what was happening, my mule bunched his feet, settled back on his tail, and slid down the glassy surface of an inclined slab of stone. Constant use kept the surface smooth and hard; the incline was so steep that no animal dared lift its feet to walk. I hung on for dear life, too surprised and frightened to do anything but cling to the saddle and lean over the mule's head to keep from sitting on his tail. At the lower edge, the mule lifted his weight from his nether end and ambled off on a safe stretch of trail. This experience was commonplace, however, compared to the danger of Tenderfoot's Delight.

Frances had tried, for my benefit, to describe Tenderfoot's Delight, a choice bit of the trail that struck terror to the hearts of newcomers. This fact suggested to old-timers its appropriate name. She had crossed it at least twice, and did not hesitate to express the wish that it were on some far-off mountain instead of suspended on our canyon wall. We were making our way over a tricky descent when, immediately ahead, a high bluff loomed on the lip of the gorge. Apparently our trail ended in mid-air. Frances and Miss Goenawein were in the lead, while Mr. Burnett brought up the rear with the pack burros. I watched, my heart pounding, as the girls dismounted, faced the cliff, fitted their fingers into handholds and eased their way over the inches-wide trail, so narrow I had failed to see it. They stood out, clean-cut silhouettes, empty space on one side, the cliff on the other. I followed, using all their caution on that slight ledge that half-circled the bluff, then turned to watch my mule place his small feet with surprising care, curving his body to make the turn. This was the turn that pack animals sometimes failed to make.

I paused to view with disbelief the scene ahead. On our left, yawned a great red sandstone bowl that looked to be thousands of feet deep, its walls precipitous. On our right, confining to a narrow ribbon the trail that followed the circular rim of the chasm, rose angled walls. This was Tenderfoot's Delight! I am one of those unfortunate persons who cannot cross a railroad bridge without getting so dizzy that I am forced to crawl. They told me of a young man who, dizzy and frightened, had crawled the entire length of Tenderfoot's Delight, complaining bitterly as hands and knees were cut and torn. But when they told it, they laughed. Tenderfeet were not admired in Arizona. So I walked that long harrowing stretch of trail, knowing that if my mule, who kept his nose against my shoulder, stumbled, he'd take me with him over the rim.

Occasionally during the morning the sun's rays reached in to warm our stiff muscles, but the walls narrowed and again threw us in deep shade. At last we reached the floor of the canyon, which brought us to a drop of about thirty feet.

The Havasupai at first had spanned this drop with a crude ladder of poles, held together with buckskin thongs. But this could accommodate only those who traveled on foot; the Indians had ponies to ride. So they built a log and wattle cage against the face of the drop, sloping it from the ground below to the top of the low precipice. The cage was filled with stones, on which they built a corduroy road of short logs. This was known as the Corduroy Bridge. A sharp turn to the right put us on the bridge over which the animals clattered to the ground below. They scuffed through deep sand to the mouth of Walapai Canyon at its juncture with the Havasu Canyon.

I had arrived! This was the land of the People of the Blue Water—the home of a tribe which, it is estimated, has lived for six hundred years beside a mysterious, almost mythical stream. Their cousin tribe, the Walapai, had named them "Havasupai," a combination of *aha*—"water," *vasu*—"blue," *pai*—"people," words of their own language meaning the "People of the Blue Water." However, each neighboring tribe has its special name for these canyon dwellers. One, noting the Havasupai's manner of clubbing their firewood from living trees, named them *Kohunina*, "Wood Killers." To this Indian word we trace the present name of Coconino Forest and Coconino County, in Arizona. But the friendly Zuñi affectionately call the Havasupai "Younger Brother."

The Havasu Canyon cuts across the high plateau of north-central Arizona from Bill Williams' Mountain on the south to the Grand Canyon on the north, forming a part of that great system of canyons. The perpendicular red sandstone walls, from three to six hundred feet high, resemble those of the canyon we had just descended and, like them, shut out our view of all but a narrow strip of sky. Above the rim of the red inner gorge rises the outer canyon, a tumbled wilderness of white limestone, mounting higher and higher until it merges with the plateau.

To eyes that had grown weary of gazing at stone, the lush verdure of Havasu Canyon, overshadowed by tall cottonwoods and old willows, seemed straight out of some fantasy. There was greenness and life and growth and I could hear the purling of restless water. Shrubs and bushes outlined the stream and spread across the canyon from wall to wall.

A short distance ahead, within a barbed wire enclosure, we saw a crude stone house; Government House, some called it. It was the house in which Frances, Miss Goenawein and I would live. In its main room, Miss Goenawein conducted her classes in homemaking. This room was also our kitchen, dining room and living room. A stone chimney indicated that the house had a fireplace. But what was that little outhouse off to the right? It didn't take long to guess.

A few Indians stood about; they had come up from the village to be the first to see what the new woman was like. If they were to bow their proud heads to outside authority, that authority, in their opinion, should be vested in a man. No white woman had ever held this position, and they were gravely concerned as to how one would use her power to grant or deny their requests. The village was aquiver for the news they would pass on when they returned. The two Indian policemen stepped forward, and Frances introduced them. The older, leaner man was Vesnor. The young, handsome chap was Lanoman.

The policemen offered to help carry my things into the room that I would share with Frances. This room boasted the fireplace, so I could forgive its low ceiling, lack of sufficient windows and other shortcomings. Miss Goenawein had a small room in the rear of the house; opening off the main room was a small storage space for government supplies.

I put my things away and went out to view our domain, while the Indians lounged about, hoping to add a few bits to the news they would circulate in the village. An old Indian woman curled her shriveled body about the roots of the enormous cottonwood that stood near the front door of our cottage. Later I was to know her as Gentle Annie. Her mate lay on the sand, dozing in the sunshine.

A small stone house with drug-filled shelves contained a desk and a swivel chair, converting it into an office for the superintendent. The farmer's small cottage sat off by itself. A wide, low building, with its back pressed against the base of the canyon wall, was the schoolhouse.

Everywhere I heard the gurgle and splash of running water. I knew that the stream had its real source up on the mesa near Williams, but it sank into the desert and, gathering reinforcements on its way, flowed through underground channels to an outlet in the Havasu Canyon. I found this outlet, hidden in a deep thicket, guarded by wide-spreading willows and tall cottonwoods. The stream bubbled in a thousand whirling springs through a bed of fine sand only a few yards from our house. Clear, but of a lively blue, it formed a wide pool from which it dashed off over cataracts and scenic falls to join the Colorado, six miles below. We used it for drinking water and for every household purpose, although we had been warned that the mineral it carried would coat the intestinal tract with stone. At the village the Indians too used it in their homes and to irrigate their gardens and orchards. After the day grew warm, adults and children dived into the pools for a cool swim. One would expect fish to be plentiful in this clear, lively water, but I saw none and the Indians said there were no fish in the stream.

That night I decided to go to bed early. Every muscle was sore from the ride down the trail; my neck ached from hours of peering at the astounding stone formations on the walls. I had tossed back the covers and was about to crawl in, when Frances spoke sharply, "Wait! Wait a minute!" She brushed by me and whisked everything from the bed down to the mattress, shook each cover fiercely until a yellow scorpion, its tail upcurled, flipped out and was promptly crushed.

"We always strip the bed before we turn in," she explained. "They crawl out of that old, damp fireplace."

"I'll make a fire and scorch their toes," I said.

"Isn't this room hot enough?" she asked. "If you're chilly, look at the thermometer."

The room was hot enough—the thermometer still hovered around one hundred. I tumbled into bed and rode a big gray mule all night over a hair-raising trail.

CHAPTER THIRTEEN

Report for the Great Father in Washington

◆ I hopped out of bed at five o'clock the next morning, forgetting the little scorpions whose toes I had promised to singe. I faced many problems, but my immediate concern was to form a mess. That was solved when Frances offered to do the cooking and Miss Goenawein, Mr. Burnett and I agreed to buy the groceries.

"What were the other superintendent's duties?" I asked at breakfast. I was determined to keep the school up to its former standard during the month I would be in charge.

"Teaching seventy-two children," Frances said, grinning, doubtless expecting this information to floor me.

"Mr. Ewing told me about the seventy-two pupils," I answered.

"Issuing drugs to sick Indians," she continued.

"I am neither a pharmacist nor an M.D.," I objected.

"Also settling the Indians' disputes." She hesitated a moment, then laughed and added, "Oh, I almost forgot one important duty. You climb the big cottonwood east of the house to take readings from a government thermometer and mail them to Washington."

"Tree-climbing too!" I exclaimed. "I've *really* been promoted. At the day school I was delouser, manager of the bath, cook, engineer and principal teacher; salary, sixty dollars per month. Now, for fifteen extra, I am doctor, judge, teacher, superintendent, weather reporter and tree climber. Six positions for the salary of one!"

Later, I went out to have a look at the cottonwood tree that held the thermometer. It hugged the wall of the house, spreading heavy branches over the roof. A few years afterward, this tree became very important to one of my successors. He and his wife saved their lives by climbing as high as its creaking limbs would allow while a flood raged below.

A short ladder leaned against the gnarled trunk. By standing with one foot on its top rung, the other on a stout limb, I would be able to read the thermometer that was enclosed in a rectangular box, nailed to the tree's trunk. I had played in trees in my childhood; tree climbing had always been fun. But now, when I tried to picture myself in my ankle-length skirts perched on a rung of the ladder and a limb of the tree, peering into that box, I couldn't bring the picture into focus; I didn't want to. But that didn't keep me from taking the readings and sending the reports to Washington. The canyon's temperature, I learned, varied by ten degrees from that of the mesa, winter or summer. Even nature applied a special law to the land of the People of the Blue Water.

Mr. Ewing had been right about our isolation. I was soon hungry for news from the outside. Our mail was brought by Indian carrier from Seligman, and this was "mail day." We were so eager for letters that by the time the sun's rays had left the canyon at three o'clock, we were already watching the trail, hoping the carrier had made a faster trip than usual. However, we had lighted the lamps before Spoonhead came riding in with the mail-sack thrown across his saddle.

It was the first time I had seen Spoonhead, but I did not need to speculate as to the origin of his name; just as the Indians declared, his head was shaped like the bowl of a spoon.

Miss Goenawein kept the post office in one corner of her room. She sorted the mail while we waited. Among my letters was one from Mr. Ewing, asking me to prepare an annual report for the Commissioner of Indian Affairs covering conditions on the reservation for the past year, a duty neglected by my predecessor. It was long overdue, and he urged that I submit it immediately. Although

I had not been at the school long enough to acquire the needed information, it was evident that I should have to submit a report of some kind.

To learn the form and material embodied in such accounts, I studied the reports on file, beginning with the one drawn up in 1895 by the teacher who had established the school. He and his farmer, with the help of the Indians, had hauled the stone and put up the buildings in which we now lived. When he arrived in the canyon, after the drive from Seligman and the descent of a far more primitive trail than we had traveled, he found no shelter for himself and wife, nothing to work with, nothing to work for except the Indians, whose children he described as "wearing a covering of grease, mescal juice, and filth, fearfully and wonderfully combined." After he knew them better and had recovered from the shock of that first impression, he wrote of them as "sturdy, simple mountaineers, who simply asked to be let alone." When he reported: "Death by perishing from thirst on the desert is the punishment to women for promiscuous amours," I knew that the Havasupai were stark realists, daring and stoical, and I would not have a dull moment.

I also came across an order for one thousand eight hundred pounds of dried peaches which I must purchase from the Indians and ship to other Indian schools for use on the children's tables, and an order for twenty cords of wood to be bought and shipped. I learned, too, that the superintendent must co-operate with the officials of the Grand Canyon Forest Reserve, who controlled the plateau region surrounding the small Havasupai Reservation. There were many infringements of law by the Indians, who claimed the reserve as their age-old hunting ground, and the officials made occasional trips to the school to request an investigation.

Among the orders was one prohibiting polygamy. The busy, contented Havasupai seemed so free from the evils afflicting the Walapai that I was convinced that no man in the tribe claimed two wives, although I knew that some of the older Walapai men had two or more. These Indians apparently had no knowledge of peyote. There was no intoxicating liquor of any kind on the reservation. I was beginning to realize that, on the surface, life in this canyon might be like living among children, except when savage tempers were aroused—and then? Well, I had asked for adventure.

I still did not know what to write in that annual report.

The school session had been interrupted by the departure of the former superintendent. Vacation, at this school, came in the fall, when the entire tribe made an exodus to the mesa to hunt game and to gather wild seeds and plants, so I planned to open school on Monday morning, asking Vesnor to notify the people in the village. The following Saturday I would be free to take a census of the tribe and determine the acreage under cultivation. So far, I had no basis whatever from which to work out the report Mr. Ewing wanted. But by verifying the statement of a former teacher that there were two hundred fifty Indians in the tribe and three hundred fifty acres in gardens and orchards, I could incorporate his figures in my report to Washington.

Even in summer, the sun did not rise in our part of the canyon until after nine o'clock, so it was still gloomy and damp when I crossed the grounds to the school building Monday morning. The school plant stood at the head of the stream, the dividing line between the upper, desert end of the canyon and the lower section, a jungle of greenness. Immediately behind our schoolhouse stood a column of stone about three hundred feet high, partly detached from the wall by rain and frost. If it fell, it would bury the schoolhouse beneath tons of rock. The danger seemed imminent as I gazed at the upper end of the column, standing straight and free. Later, I learned that such columns topple over only after a flood.

I had rung the warning bell, and it was time for school, but no children had appeared. Then the bushes parted violently and dozens of little Indians burst through on the run. Behind them, maneuvering his well-trained pony with all the skill of a cattleman rounding up strays, rode Vesnor. The older pupils followed more leisurely; Vesnor did not drive those who came of their own volition. Nevertheless, this method of bringing children to school seemed wholly unnecessary, if not cruel.

"Why do you drive them?" I protested. "They should come to school without that."

"I no bring, swim in creek all day. I got no time to fool," came his indignant answer.

Vesnor's method of maintaining an average attendance of seventy-one out of an enrollment of seventy-two doubtless had been instituted by a former teacher, and must have grown out of necessity. I decided not to change it until I became better acquainted with conditions governing school attendance.

The children were timid, but wholesome and obedient and gifted with a pleasing native charm for they had come in contact with almost no white people except those employed at the school. Their complexions were light, because most of their day was without sunshine. They came to school with faces cleanly scrubbed, hair sleek and often still dripping wet, and wearing clean uniforms. They had that beautiful stream, while the Walapai had only the water the women carried a long distance in cans or in woven bottles suspended from straps across their foreheads. Very noticeable, too, was the effect of their permanent homes compared to the temporary shacks in which their cousin tribe lived. We allowed these children to wear their school uniforms home, where they folded them neatly and laid them over a pole near the ceiling of the house before they dashed out to play in the stream. What a relief it was—no faces to wash, no hair to comb, no sores to treat, no bath day!

Finally seventy-one children had crowded into the room (built to accommodate forty-six!). All—except Lucy. There was a suspicious silence when I called her name. The children stared at me with their honest eyes, but refused to explain her absence. So I read them a story and we sang songs until the room was light enough for study.

Recess gave us a breath of fresh air out under the trees. And how we needed it! The air in the room was thick with the smell of sweating bodies and campfire smoke. I kept wondering why Lucy was not in school that day, so asked Sue, her sister. Sue was an intelligent girl of thirteen, and quite unhappy about Lucy. She told me that her father had sold her sister to an elderly widower because he offered more blankets and corn than the boy with whom Lucy was in love could pay. I wondered if I should rescue Lucy from the old widower's clutches, and argued the matter with myself until the task of trying to teach seventy-one pupils in that hot room drove all thought of her thwarted romance from my mind.

Shortly before the noon recess, the room grew dark, except for occasional flashes of lightning. Heavy rolls of thunder reverberated up and down the canyon. Rain was pouring at dismissal time, so we sang songs until the quick summer shower had passed. Unless Frances and her detail of boys and girls had the food cooked before the rain came, there would be no hot lunch for the children, since the cooking was done out of doors. The dining tables stood under the big tree in front of our cottage.

The officers marched their companies to the tables, which had been hastily wiped off and set after the shower. There were dishes of stew and cooked dried fruit on each table. I tapped the bell for silence, and the children said grace, yanked the stools from under the tables and began filling their plates. The habit of eating hurriedly was their heritage from the days in the not distant past, when too many meals had been interrupted by enemy raids.

As a special honor, and also because we needed their help, we seated an older boy at one end of every table and an older girl at the opposite end, each an officer. They served the smaller children, then usually got too busy with their own meal to give further attention. So I supervised the serving of the food, giving help where needed and encouraging correct table manners.

The waiters brought plates of hot biscuits; they were emptied as they touched the tables but when the biscuits were broken open, the inside was soft dough. The shrub, under which the range stood, had been too meager a protection; the rain had put out the fire, leaving the biscuits half baked.

In the warehouse, we had stacks of wooden boxes filled with hardtack—hard, saltless crackers. We opened one of these boxes and served the hardtack, but not one was touched by the children. Frances, who understood the situation, called me aside and laughing, explained.

"It happened a few weeks before you came and we've joked about it ever since," she said. "The Indian women were hired to pack the hardtack down the trail on their burros. One of the burros bumped a case against an outjutting ledge, breaking it open. We suspected that the women had a hand in the accident—gave the burro a shove, maybe—for they are always ready to eat. They gorged themselves, then climbed down to a spring and drank all the water they wanted. Believe me, they were sick! When they finally staggered down to the village, they branded the hardtack 'bad medicine,' saying over and over, '*Hanatoopega!* (No good).' Since then the children will not touch hardtack."

Unless the children could be persuaded to eat the crackers, they would leave the table hungry; also our entire supply would be wasted. I had used experiments many times to intrigue the interest of my public school pupils; a very simple one might do the trick now. I held up one of the hardtack for them to see, calling attention to its size. I laid it in a dish of water and in almost breathless silence they watched it swell and swell. I explained that their mothers had eaten too many crackers and drunk too much water, making their stomachs too full. That was why they suffered.

The children caught the picture of the women's greed causing their pain, and laughed. Like all people who live precariously, the Havasupai found relief from hardship and danger in a ready sense of humor. The discomfiture of even one's own mother was funny, except in cases of illness or severe suffering. But the experiment had restored hardtack to its rightful place as a food. They ate it with their former relish.

When I dismissed school that evening, we had no need of

Vesnor and his horse. The children scampered off through the brush on the trail that led to the village. At home there would be food, the kind they were accustomed to and for which they hungered in a way no white man's viands could satisfy. Perhaps it would be the delicious corn bread their mothers made by crushing grains of new corn to a pulp, molding it into elongated shapes which were fitted into the husks of green corn and baked in the ashes. The bread would be rich and sweet and more delicious than any hardtack ever made. Or if it were the season for little green squashes, there would be another treat. The squash, cooked, mashed and mixed with the cooked grains of new corn, was a delicacy so enjoyed that the thought of it could start the children's feet running toward home. There would be food at every house they passed on the trail, and a Havasupai shared as generously as our own ancestors did before we measured our sustenance by its cost in dollars and cents.

That week another letter came from Mr. Ewing demanding that I submit the annual report immediately. He added the important news that the Hackberry Day School would open in the fall as the Truxton Canyon Training School. This would be the fulfillment of the promise he had made to the Walapai that he would establish a boarding school for their children.

Early Saturday morning I started to the Indian village to get additional information to incorporate in the annual report. The trail hugged the foot of the west wall. I had passed scattered wickiups, tucked back among the willows, before I came to a high, precipitous section of the wall that narrowed the passage. Bob, one of the tribe's medicine men, had told me that the god-spirit lived in two columns of stone on the rim of this inthrust section. The Indians had discovered these at the time they had settled in the canyon.

I had an excellent view of the two great pillars of red sandstone, as tranquil and aloof as images of Buddha. Neither white man nor Indian could fail to be impressed by them. What force placed them in that exposed position? How had they stood through the ages, battered by gales and floods which had brought down sections of the wall itself? The Indians must have asked themselves these questions many times. The wise men of the tribe gave them a satisfying answer: the indestructible god-spirit lived there to watch over and protect the people in their new home. The Indians spoke of these gods with the naturalness with which one mentions a neighbor or a friend.

"Our gods make gardens grow good. They watch over the people," they told me confidently.

And in a sense, I was indebted to their gods for this greatest adventure of my life. The Indians' well-being depended on these god-spirits, so they had refused to leave the canyon. When the Indian Office considered establishing a school for the Havasupai children, pressure was brought to induce the Indians to move to the plateau. It would be simpler for them to move out of the canyon than for the government to freight equipment for the school across the desert and down the precipitous trail. But the Indians became bewildered and frightened. "If we leave our gods, we die!" they cried. So the school came down to them. Yet the officials located it a little too far up the gorge for the gods to guard it with a watchful eye, which may account for the fact that, later on, it was destroyed by a flood.

Just beyond the gods, the walls swung apart. The broad, level floor between was occupied by the village. Spaciousness of land and sky inspired a sense of freedom. The cultivated acres were laid out like a checkerboard, in somewhat irregular squares, each displaying the mixed greenery of gardens and orchards. A fence of brush or poles enclosed each square, emphasizing the mosaic effect. The Indians had not completely removed the wilderness from the canyon; the stream could be traced by the tangle of wild vegetation lining its banks, and dense thickets claimed too much of the land. Old willow trees and cottonwoods dominated the scene.

The houses sat cosily near the gardens, or were connected with them by tree-shaded lanes. There were several half-dugouts, but most of the houses were rectangular or dome-shaped. Their construction involved no expense. A man needed only poles, brush and dirt; by exchanging work with neighbors, his shelter was soon completed. There were no windows; the low doorways were closed with a blanket or a rough board door, hung on leather hinges.

Everywhere men, women and children were working in their gardens, stirring the soil, planting the seed, irrigating, weeding and cultivating the growing plants, although the sun's rays would not reach them for hours. They boasted that they worked in their gardens and orchards when it was "little light"; then the canyon was cool, the soil soft and pliable.

The fascination of watching them grow their food, preserve it and store it far outweighed my interest in gathering dry statistics, but Mr. Ewing wanted facts and figures. I knew I would encounter difficulties in getting the necessary information, especially from the older people who spoke no English.

At Chickapanyegi's home I watched the family at work on their small plot of ground. Chickapanyegi was irrigating his patch of corn. When he heard me approach, he turned, a quizzical, batlike expression puckering his countenance. The Indians must have noted that same expression, for his name, Chickapanyegi, meant "bat."

Here, again, the people appealed to those benevolent, unseen forces, especially in the first planting of their corn. The planter knelt on the ground, struck a wedge-shaped stick deep into the earth to loosen the soil, then offered a prayer that his corn might grow well, and dropped the seed into the place he had prepared. This done, he made an offering to two white blotches on the wall of the gorge—the first mythical ears of corn given to the people by their gods—by blowing toward them one grain of corn. At the conclusion of this sacred rite, the planting of the remaining ground was done in the usual manner.

Chickapanyegi's wife was weeding the plot, while his son, Jess, one of my pupils, was stirring the ground with a shaped piece of wood which he pushed through the soil like a small plow.

Their garden was lush with corn, beans, pumpkins, watermelons and sunflowers that grew large seed heads. Purple figs and red-cheeked peaches grew at one end of the plot.

Chickapanyegi worked unhurriedly, pushing the dirt aside with his bare toes to open the floodgates, letting the water gush through to fill the ditches that ran between his rows of vegetables. Toes did the work of fingers, opening ditches or packing the soil to close them, picking up sticks and stones and piling them ready to be removed. Here was a way of life new to me and very intriguing. The Walapai that I knew lived in idleness on bare sand, accepting government rations, a few working at odd jobs. These people produced and stored food, not only for the immediate future, but for years ahead. At one time, the Walapai, too, had been self-supporting and self-sufficient; then agents of the government had come, using rations as a buying power, and had established controls that crushed initiative.

The Havasupai had devised their own garden tools, even making a spade by fashioning the blade and handle from a long, flat piece of wood. They used the shoulder blades of horses or anything they could get that would loosen the soil or chop weeds. Obviously they were greatly handicapped by these primitive tools; sticks, bones and toes were poor substitutes for spades, hoes and rakes. The Indians themselves restricted production by refusing to till inherited land until it had lain fallow for a year or more. The spirit of the dead might at any time return to its former home, so they would not make immediate use of such land, partly through fear, but also to show respect to the former owner. Thus many acres of fertile soil lay fallow, necessitating more intensive cultivation of the land in use.

Tending their crops and preserving their food was the main object in life for the people of this village. Always the crop was divided into portions: some for eating, some held for an emergency, but the best kept for seed.

Chickapanyegi's rectangular house stood near his garden. The flat, brush-covered roof, topped with earth, and the sides, thatched with heavy boughs still fully leafed, kept the interior cool. An open porch sheltered the doorway. When his wife wiped the soil from her hands and entered the house, I intended to follow, but hesitated as I caught the odor of cooking meat. It came from a lard pail, propped on stones over an outdoor fire. She turned and motioned for me to lift the lid; she was pleased that they had fresh meat, for it was far from plentiful. Curious to know what she was cooking for the family dinner, I uncovered the pail.

Two large glassy eyes stared at me from above the boiling water, and made the cooking rabbit seem alive. The hairy ears stood erect increasing the impression. The skinned body had been crammed into the bucket, but the head had refused to remain submerged. The lid dropped, clattering from my hand. Since then I have not cared to eat rabbit!

The interior of Chickapanyegi's house was arranged like all well-kept Havasupai homes: rolled bedding in the depressions in the floor where the family slept; personal possessions tied in a cloth and hung above the bed; and the inevitable pole, just below the ceiling, loaded with rabbit skin blankets, fiber mats, Navaho blankets and clothing not in use. Poles supported drying ears of corn and spirals of squash that brushed the head and shoulders as one moved about within the house.

I wanted next to see Gentle Annie's home. Her house would not be neat and spotless if Gentle Annie was the housekeeper. She was old and tired from the wars she had survived and the hardships life had dealt her. I found her standing at the door of her dome-shaped wickiup. Her wrinkled face and bright black eyes held friendliness. That may have been why she was known to Indians and to whites as Gentle Annie, the only name I ever heard for her.

A brand-new bedroom chamber, pink roses painted on its yellow side, stood on a box near by—filled with delicately browned navy beans.

With toil-worn hands Gentle Annie reached up to the lintel, took down a hard, dry slab about twelve inches wide by sixteen long, folded back the cloth in which it was wrapped and breaking off a small chunk, handed it to me saying, "Eat!" How long it had lain there, growing harder and drier with age, I had no way of knowing, but to refuse her hospitality would give offense. I took a bite. At first it tasted like dried sweet potato, but the mass grew bigger and bigger until my mouth was full of coarse, hard fibers. I made an excuse for leaving, that I might get rid of it without hurting Gentle Annie's pride. I learned later that the Indians dried mescal in sheets and stored it as this slab had been stored, so I may have had my first and only taste of mescal.

When I arrived at Little Jim's home, his wife E-e was leaving to empty and clean her storehouse. I accompanied her for I wanted to learn more of their ancient and peculiar method of storing food. The small stone granary, with a round opening for the insertion or removal of food, was built in a crevice in the canyon wall. The hard stratum beneath made a solid floor that rodents could not penetrate. Neither could they work their way through the stone walls, plastered with a hard cement of native manufacture from material available in the canyon. There was a never-ending fight against rodents. The numerous rats, mice and chipmunks, when winter reduced their food supply of growing plants, raided any storehouse into which they could gnaw their way.

The opening in E-e's storehouse was closed with a flat stone, sealed in place with cement in which the family's mark of identification had been placed. If anyone helped himself to her stores, a break in this seal would warn her of the theft. She dug away the mortar, set the stone aside, then lifted out the few stores that were left.

Crawling through the opening, she brushed up the floor, then began storing the food she had brought with her: ears of seed corn in one place; shelled corn in another; strings of dried squash and pumpkin necessitating special care to prevent spoilage, by themselves. With amusing gestures, when I failed to understand her native tongue, she showed me how she tied the dried seed of sunflowers, squash, melons and pumpkins in a cloth and packed them in this dry, safe place.

Through generations of experimenting the women had developed safe methods of preparing food for storage. Mold and decay must be fought or there would be famine. Beans, corn, sunflower seed, figs and peaches were dried in the usual manner, but it took an Indian's ingenuity to develop a method of drying squash and pumpkin so they would make good eating in the winter. The women first cut off the rind and allowed the squash or pumpkin to dry somewhat on the outside. They next removed the seeds, which were dried for food and for planting, then cleaned and partly dried the inside. This partly dried flesh was cut in one long spiral and hung over a pole until dry enough for storing. Many homes were so filled with drying spirals that there was little room for the family. The dried pumpkin or squash was cooked with water and served as a vegetable. I was sure it would be tender and sweet but I did not get a taste.

I had seen peaches spread to dry on the sandy ground, fly-covered, dogs romping over them, ponies nibbling them. So when I saw two laughing gossiping women laying their halved peaches on the clean floor of a crevice in the canyon wall in which a family had set up housekeeping, I climbed up for a better view.

When I reached their level, to my surprise—and to his—I saw a naked old man sprawled on the floor, taking a sun bath. He gave me a startled glance, bounded up and scampered away among the rocks where he hid until I left the place. The women, their fat bodies shaking with laughter, jabbered and pointed. The old fellow would have thought nothing of his nudeness had a woman of the tribe appeared. It was the privilege of old men and young boys to follow the dictates of comfort in discarding clothes. But a white woman! He couldn't figure out what she might think, or say, or do.

I wanted a picture of the women and their drying peaches, so focused my camera. The women threw their *sutams* over their heads and ran screaming to hide behind the rocks. It was the camera they feared, so leaving it in a shady spot, I went over to where they crouched behind a boulder and asked them why they ran. With much excited sputtering they made me understand that if I took a picture of them, their souls would go into the picture. One could not live without a soul. They illustrated with exaggerated gestures how dead they would be when their souls left their bodies.

I retrieved my camera and opening and focusing it, tucked it out of sight under my arm. When they returned, talking and laughing, I snapped the picture without their knowledge.

Families who owned large plots of ground had several storehouses, some as many as five. Regardless of how the land had been distributed when the People of the Blue Water settled in the canyon, through inheritance some individuals had acquired more land than they could till, and it was loaned or rented to friends or relatives. There were a few whose plots were no larger than the floor of a room, but every family had at least one storehouse tucked away in a crevice in the wall.

It was late afternoon when I returned to the school and wrote my report. I had been so intent on learning how the people raised their food and preserved it that I had not measured a foot of ground, nor counted the members of the tribe. Besides, what the Commissioner must know, I finally decided, was that the Havasupai needed garden tools; that the school children ate out of doors in all kinds of weather, and that their food was cooked on a range protected only by a bush. These things he could do something about. Here is my report, as it appeared in the *Annual Report* of the Department of the Interior for the year 1901:

SIR: I have the honor to submit the annual report of the Havasupai tribe and school for the fiscal year ending June 30, 1901.

Havasupai Tribe—The Havasupai is entirely self-supporting. He depends on the products of his farm for his livelihood. He is proud of his gardens and his orchards, but prouder still of the fact that he labors. Living on the banks of a clear, sparkling stream, he is never troubled by crop failure. He utilizes the water of the stream for ir-

rigating purposes and an abundant crop is assured him. The almost perpendicular walls of the canyon, which he has made his home, are
lined with storehouses which in the autumn he fills with corn, beans, and
other products of his labor.

The most discouraging feature at present to the Havasupai is the
fact that many of them have no farming implements. The farmer often
loans them plows and hoes, which are always promptly returned. When
unable to borrow implements, they laboriously loosen the soil with
sticks. If farming implements were furnished them, they could easily
cultivate all the land to which they have access. Much labor and time
would thus be saved, and what is still more important, their surplus
products thus gained could be marketed, which would enable them
to provide themselves with warm clothing for the winter months.

All of the Indians of this tribe dress in part in citizens' clothes, and
most of them are quite willing to adopt the ways of the white man.
They depend very little on the professed abilities of the medicine
man. . . . As they come in contact with very few white people, except
those employed at the school, very few of them speak enough English
to make themselves understood.

Havasupai Day School—This school has a capacity of 46, but has
been crowded beyond its proper limit, having an average attendance
of 71.

We have a good stone school building, but it is not large enough to
accommodate the school. The pupils' lunch is served under a cottonwood tree, which fails to protect them from the heavy summer rains we
are now having. . . . As there is an abundance of stone in the canyon
it would cost but little to build a dining room with a wareroom attached,
where the supplies could be safely stored.

Work in the laundry and sewing room is ably conducted. Both boys
and girls are detailed to assist in cooking the noonday lunch, and,
under the supervision of the cook, do excellent work.

I trust that either 20 of the largest boys and girls will be transferred
to the Truxton Canyon Training School when it opens September 1,
or a kindergarten department will be added to this school, as it is impossible for one teacher to instruct 71 pupils in a creditable manner.

Permit me to express my appreciation of your support and encourage-
ment.

Very respectfully,

FLORA J. GREGG, *Superintendent*

At last Mr. Ewing had the report, months late. But neither he nor the Commissioner of Indian Affairs would ever know what a good time I had had collecting information that never went into it.

We were led to believe that such reports were never read by the officials in Washington. This one was read. It brought results. The Havasupai enjoyed the nearest thing to Christmas they had ever known when a large shipment of gardening tools arrived for them.

CHAPTER FOURTEEN

"I Too Mad"

◼︎ Lanoman, the son of Sinyella, was the younger of the reservation's two policemen. According to his father's estimate of his age, he was in his early thirties. Taller than many of the men, and stockily built, his regular features and light complexion gave him a handsome appearance, which somewhat justified his vanity. He had mastered enough English to meet his needs but his courtly manners were his greatest asset. "Lanoman, the gentleman," he was dubbed by a visiting tourist, for all who met him were impressed by his graciousness.

No one seemed to know Vesnor's age. Counted in years, it might have been forty or fifty, but the dark wisdom in his gloomy eyes made one feel that he had witnessed savage cruelty and lived with danger until he no longer knew the meaning of fear. He was thin and wiry, his muscles taut springs, his skin dark and wrinkled, but there was a sureness and swiftness about him that inspired confidence. Whenever I was in my office, Vesnor was there, ready to jump astride his pony to bring in a bad Indian at a moment's notice. Occasionally, when not too pressed for time, I laid aside my work and we talked, sometimes quite frankly. Vesnor's questions sprang from whatever thought was uppermost in his mind, and he probed into my personal affairs with native simplicity—as if he were with one of his tribesmen. He wanted the straight truth, even though the Havasupai themselves delighted in making false statements to an inquisitive white person. One afternoon when the office became unbearably hot and stuffy, I took my work to the shade of the cottonwood in front of our cottage, while Vesnor sat in the hammock until needed. I was aware that he was regarding me with a puzzled expression, but was unprepared for the question he asked, "You got man?"

"No."

"Why you no catch 'em?"

"Too busy. I've never had time."

"Um-m-m," he murmured. He couldn't figure it out. There were so many more Havasupai men than women that the latter were at a premium. When a girl reached the age of fourteen or fifteen there were such numbers of suitors pressing their claims that to remain single was unthinkable. Yet here was a white woman who did not want a man. It was beyond Vesnor's understanding.

I took my turn at questioning, wanting a glimpse of his past. What put those deep lines in his face and that somber look in his eyes? No doubt he had witnessed the bloody deeds of the old chief Navaho, who had recently died; deeds that had won the acclaim of the people and made him their head chief. But Vesnor had no thought of revealing his past and knew exactly when to quit answering questions and substitute, "No savvy." So weeks slipped by without my learning much of what went on in his mind, until one day he lifted a corner of the veil—and left me more puzzled than I had been before.

The thermometer in the shaded center of the cottonwood registered one hundred and seventeen degrees that afternoon while I worked in my office. Vesnor, comfortable and at ease, occupied his usual chair near the door. His eyes shone with a new eagerness, and his countenance brightened with a thought that, sooner or later, I knew he would express.

Suddenly he asked his question, "You savvy Jesus?"

"Yes," I said, "I savvy Him."

"Long time I sick. Think maybe die. Indians come, look, say pretty quick die. No eat. No sleep. Just sick—plenty!"

For a long moment he sat there, his somber eyes on space, but his mind was fumbling for words. "One day Jesus come. Stand by bed. All white. Dress, everything all white. Shine like sun. He say pretty quick get well. He go 'way. I get well quick."

That was all. Vesnor had no more to tell. Perhaps he saw the astonishment in my face, for his thoughts recoiled and tucked themselves away in a secret place back of his inscrutable eyes. My imagination conjured up the scene: a sick Indian lying on his blanket on the dirt floor of his home, by his side a Shining Presence. Vesnor, an untutored Indian, had experienced the miracle of healing much as John G. Whittier had so beautifully written of it:

> The healing of His seamless dress
> Is by our beds of pain:
> We touch Him in life's throng and press,
> And we are whole again.

Vesnor's story left me awed and puzzled. From what source had come his concept of Jesus the Healer? No missionary had ever worked among these people. Long ago, a Mormon official, while a fugitive from justice, had lived for a time in the canyon. In our Sunday service and at each opportunity we explained our Christian faith, as former teachers had done. But Vesnor, his mind still ruled by the edicts of the medicine man, strange spirits and his gods, had had that very personal revelation.

The Indians respected and obeyed Vesnor. His background and experience made him a valuable policeman. Lanoman, however, gently sidestepped any errand that might involve ruffled feelings or bring unpleasant repercussions. If word must be sent to the men of the village that we had a load of freight at Hilltop, and would pay cash to the packers who brought it down, Lanoman was the man to send. He could escort tourists or forest rangers to any part of the canyon, and win their hearts while doing it. Everyone liked gentlemanly Lanoman. It was hard to believe that he had no white blood, or had never been taught the white man's social customs. Yet under that suave exterior was a mind steeped in the traditions and superstitions of his people. He had been healed, dramatically, by the medicine man. Leslie Spier, in his "Havasupai Ethnography," relates the story as told to him by Sinyella, Lanoman's father.

"Once about 1885, when Lanoman, my oldest son, was about seventeen years old, he was pretty sick." He then explained that he had appealed to a Walapai shaman who decided that the illness was too difficult for him to heal. Sinyella continued:

Then I took him over to Coconino Basin; other Havasupai went there, too. I found many Navaho there; I asked who was a shaman. They said, "One who is here is a good shaman," and they showed him to me. I asked him to cure my boy: "If you cure him, I will give you two dollars," and I gave it to him. He sang for the boy two nights; he had two women with him who also sang. He had four stone arrowpoints, and he stuck one in the ground at the head and one at the foot and one on each side of the boy as he lay there. He stopped after two nights and said that the boy would not get well.

Next, Sinyella appealed to a shaman of his own tribe. His verdict was: "It is pretty hard to cure that sickness." The shaman proved his point by declaring that Sinyella's grandfather, now deceased, who had been a shaman, had sent his spirit to take Lanoman to the spirit world. However, he recommended his younger brother A'mal, also a shaman, for whom Sinyella sent a messenger. Sinyella related what followed:

The night he arrived, he began; he sang all night very loud, and sucked. His spirit brought out all kinds of things, hail (it looked like hail), lightning, clouds, snow, and something relating to a wolf. He brought out all the things that made the boy sick and showed them to us in his hand. . . . He showed us the hail, but he told us about the lightning, clouds, snow, and wolves: "I got these, but they cannot be readily seen. My spirit can see them perfectly, however. I will just show you the hail, so you can see it is all right." When he sucked out the wolf, he staggered around and ran out into the darkness. We heard the wolf howl. The hailstone was round and white; it loked like hail. He also sucked out my grandfather's spirit, which he showed us; a little white man, with a head but no limbs. He did this two nights. Then the boy said he wanted to eat more, and got up and walked; he said he was a little better. The shaman made him well quickly.

A'mal's pay would be scorned by a medical doctor. Sinyella gave him a blanket and a buckskin. Some of his friends, who had returned from a successful hunt, gave A'mal so much venison that he was forced to borrow an extra horse to carry the load.

In some ways Lanoman was less progressive than the other men of his generation. Even though cremation had been abandoned by his tribe in favor of burial, he had insisted, when his young wife died, on the time-honored ritual of the funeral pyre. Custom decreed that a relative preside at this ceremony, placing the wood about and on the body, laying thereon the girl's possessions, setting the torch to the pile and waiting until all was consumed. I wondered if this had been Lanoman's task.

For the cremation, he chose the deep, shady gorge below Mooney Falls, a wilderness of ferns, shrubs and trees surrounding a turbulent pool. In one immense column of water, the Havasu River poured into this pool from a cliff more than two hundred feet high. To reach the burial place, the body was lowered by a frail ladder into the gorge. After the conclusion of the service, when the mourners had climbed to the rim, the ladder was made unusable. Lanoman wanted no invasion of this secluded spot of supernal beauty, sacred now to the memory of his wife.

Here at the foot of the "Mother of the Waters," the Indians' poetic name for the majestic falls, he left his wife's ashes to be lifted by vagrant winds and carried across the green jungle to the Blue Water. The "Mother of the Waters" would woo the girl's wandering spirit into its rainbow-colored mists, where, occasionally, her spirit, with those of the other dead, would later be seen rising and falling through the heavy spray.

The girl's favorite pony must go with her but the Indians' ingenuity was not equal to the task of lowering a live horse over the wall of the gorge that its spirit might take its departure at the pyre. So another expedient was tried. The animal was led to the very brink of the chasm. Following their tribal custom, a strip of wet buckskin was tied about its neck, which slowly tightened, in drying, until the pony gasped for breath and staggered helplessly; a shove sent the animal crashing over the rim. It bounced from ledge to ledge, then, caught on a projecting point, lay there to decay, far above its intended destination.

In the village, peach trees were cut to free their spirits that they might bear their sweet, luscious fruit in the new home of the beloved wife. The house was burned; the girl's name must never again be spoken.

Indeed no biographies could be more fascinating than those of our two policemen, if the author delved into the forces that made each man what he was: the cloak of courtliness concealing Lano-man, the Indian of primitive culture; Vesnor, the stern, forceful Indian of the warpath, healed by the Christians' Savior. By apportioning duties according to the merits of the man, we had an efficient police force.

When a feud broke out resulting in the destruction of growing corn, I called on Vesnor. It might mean a quarrel that would stir the tribe to the boiling point, or it might be child's play, but I wanted the help of a fearless man.

Late one Saturday afternoon Little Jim entered my office. He wore the Indians' comfortable moccasins, but his hair was cut short, white-man fashion. Faded blue jeans and a torn red shirt clung to his damp body, for the canyon walls still reflected the heat.

"Um-m," he began with embarrassment, "Me got corn. Little grow." He reached his hand down to about twelve inches above the floor to indicate his corn's tallness. "Last night, womans walk on corn. Break down. No good."

I went with him to his corn patch down in the village. It was a small plot, about fifteen feet square. The corn on one corner was broken and trampled into the ground, and everywhere were the imprints of small, bare feet.

"Whose footprints are these?" I asked, for a smart Indian like Little Jim couldn't be fooled on the imprint of a tribesman's foot.

He stooped and carefully examined the earth, "Maybe woman's," he volunteered.

"Yes, you said in the beginning that women had destroyed your corn. You will have to tell me their names."

He frowned deeply as he viewed the broken stalks, but finally admitted, "I think two womans: Billy squaw; Prince squaw."

"I'll have Vesnor warn them not to bother your corn," I assured him. "I'll also investigate this myself. They must have a reason for destroying your crop."

I took my departure, and Little Jim joined his family, his wife E-e and two small sons. They formed a circle about the food for the evening meal—burned squash, cold and unpalatable. E-e broke off hunks of the sodden stuff and handed them to the children who devoured them hungrily while she and Little Jim shared the unappetizing fare. E-e was an indifferent housekeeper and one of the poorest cooks in the village, but she was a good-natured wife and her cheerful companionship pleased Little Jim.

Vesnor was waiting for me at the office as usual, so I sent him to instruct Prince and Billy that their wives destroy no more gardens. I also told him to bring the two women to my office on Monday evening for a hearing.

School had not yet convened Monday morning when Billy appeared at the building, carrying in his hand seven stalks of newly cut corn. He held them out for me to see.

"That my corn," he said angrily. "E-e cut with knife."

I examined the seven stalks. They were cleanly cut. "What has happened in the village that causes the women to destroy one another's gardens?" I asked Billy.

"No un'erstan'," he said, still angry.

"You know that your wife walked on Little Jim's corn. He has a family and needs all the food he can raise. Did you tell her to leave his garden alone?"

"Vesnor say. She hear." Billy looked chagrined. It was a different story when blame fell on his own household.

"Did Vesnor tell your wife to come to my office this evening?

We are going to put a stop to this destruction of food, and I am going to learn the reason back of it."

"He say. She hear."

"I'll have E-e brought up too," I told him. "We'll find out why she got into this feud."

Billy turned and walked slowly home, carrying the wilted corn in his hand.

I was so eager to get at the trial and learn why these complacent, childish women were determinedly destroying one another's food, that I forgot this was a school day until the bushes parted. The little folks came through at a comfortable walk and entered the classroom. Vesnor had learned to restrain his impatience, but experience had convinced me by now that if he and his pony were absent, the children would spend the day playing in the creek.

Vesnor, Little Jim, Billy, Prince and the three women were waiting at my office when school was dismissed. I unlocked the door, and they filed in, the women abashed by the formality and frightened by Vesnor's disapproving mien. They had been accustomed to indulging their love of trickery until the time came for physical combat; the victory then went to the one who could scratch and pull hair faster than her antagonist. A hearing in the superintendent's office was something new and quite disturbing.

Since Little Jim was one of the plaintiffs, he was the first to testify. He stated his case briefly: "I go work corn. Little light. Sun no come up. I see Billy squaw, Prince squaw in corn. Make walk on stalk, break down. I see run in bushes. Run to camp." Little Jim sat down, his troubled face creased by an angry frown.

At that moment a woman, her *sutam* floating behind her, breezed through the door and eased her plump body into a chair. She was Vesnor's wife, a giggling woman, much younger than he, whose ears were attuned to gossip. She had come to gather news, first hand, so that she might gleefully dispense it later to an eager audience. This feud had been going on for some time, possibly years, and interest was keen, for word of the trial had swept through the village.

Billy's wife testified in her own defense. She rose from her chair and moved to the center of the floor with the grace of a shy wild animal. She was slender and lovely, with the clear brown skin, small shapely hands and feet that distinguish the elite. The long bang above her piquant face, the neat, bobbed hair, the colorful *sutam* over the clean, gay dress made her a picture that would attract attention anywhere. Her face had been artistically decorated for the occasion: a round spot of red paint glowed dully over each cheekbone; a line of burnt sienna extended from the middle of her lower lip to the center of her chin. But most bewitching were the delicate blue shadows beneath her eyes. These were achieved by daintily applying a paint made from the wild indigo plant. Her bracelets, necklace and ear ornaments of blue beads added to her natural charm. She spoke in her native language, Vesnor interpreting, and told her story with such eloquence that I wished with all my heart that I knew enough of the tribe's language to understand her softly spoken words.

She was explaining to me, and her every word and gesture were for my benefit as she said: "Long time ago Little Jim marry my sister. She good woman. She cook. She work, make clean house. He no work. No buy dress. He no buy things eat. She hungry all time. She get sick. She die. Little Jim marry E-e. He happy all time. He work. He no lazy. He buy dress. He buy everythings. I too mad. I walk. I walk on trail. I see Little Jim corn. It little grow (not very tall). I think. E-e like corn. I get plenty mad. I walk, maybe five, maybe ten stalk, break down on ground. I too mad."

Like an angry princess she swept to her seat, and I knew that I was not the right judge for this case, for I was ready to defend her for her courage, her beauty and her loyalty to her dead sister. Yet I admired the straightforwardness and sincerity of Little Jim.

Prince's wife took the floor. The women were sisters, but Billy had chosen the more picturesque, the more charming of the two. This woman's story was less dramatic, but differed little from that of her sister. Little Jim's first wife was her sister, she said. He neglected her, and she died. "Now he good to E-e. I mad. I want to make go hungry. I walk thirty stalks his corn. I plenty mad." She gave E-e a glance loaded with malice and hesitantly took her seat.

Billy stepped forward and voiced his complaint. E-e had cut seven stalks of his corn. He found the stalks lying in the field. He explained that he needed the corn for food for his family. He would not have seed, he could not fill his storehouse, if his crop were destroyed. His face had lost its jovial expression and was puckered with concern.

E-e, the accused, came forward reluctantly. The look of lazy contentment had drained from her face; there was fear in her dark eyes. She spoke haltingly, with many gestures. "I pick up brush." Her quick fingers went through the motions of gathering and piling brush. "I dry. I want fire. Billy's squaw throw brush. Scatter everywhere." Again her fingers spoke, making the gesture of tossing brush to the winds. "I no find. No make fire. No cook bread. She break Little Jim corn. She make brush scatter. I plenty mad. I walk little on corn. I cut little. I too mad."

I managed to keep a straight face, but was chuckling inside. Those precious, mischievous women. They refused to submit to the deadly monotony of their lives, and added a touch of excitement by playing sly tricks, each striving to be more cunning than the other. I wanted to pat them on their plump shoulders and send them happily home, but when a garden is no larger than the floor of a room, and a family depends on it for food, it must not be the pawn in a game.

We discussed their crimes with great seriousness. They were quick to agree that the destruction of food must stop, and they expected to be penalized, but I hadn't the heart to levy against their pitiful possessions. So I asked them, individually, if they would drop the feud and never revive it, if allowed to go unpunished.

They all shouted in their eagerness, *"Eh! Eh, mi!* (Yes! Yes, you say it!)"

The case was dismissed. I heard of no more such pranks, but

their love of excitement undoubtedly would prompt them to find some other way to keep the village astir and themselves interested.

Long after the dispute was settled, Billy's wife's reiteration, "I too mad," stayed with me. It helped me to appreciate the basic honesty of these children of nature: no soft words covered angry thoughts; no smile hid a broken heart. They expressed their emotions, with zest and energy and, if the occasion required, with violence, as did the Bear, the Coyote and the Deer who, from the Days of Old, had taught the Havasupai the wisdom they themselves had gleaned from the wilderness when time was young.

CHAPTER FIFTEEN

To the Mouth of the Havasu

Late one evening Frances and I were lingering at the supper table talking over the events of the day, when there came a sharp knock on the door. This was surprising as a Havasupai did not knock. He framed his face with his hands and looked in through the window or threw the door open and stalked in, accustomed to latchless doors. Also, after darkness fell he stayed close to his own campfire and the living, for the ghosts of the dead walked at night. The person outside our door was not an Indian.

Frances and I were the only white people in the canyon. Miss Goenawein and Mr. Burnett had driven to Seligman on business. The night was dark, and neither of us felt too brave when we opened the door to a stranger, since we were completely alone, the policeman being at home a mile farther down the canyon.

George Wharton James, author of several books on Indians of the Southwest, introduced himself.

Mr. James had established his headquarters at the home of a village Indian whose friendship he had won on previous visits to the tribe. This time he had come prepared for a trip he believed no white person had ever made—the descent of the Havasu Canyon to its junction with the Grand Canyon. He had engaged Ute, a very old Indian, blind in one eye, as guide. He suggested that the ride might be interesting for us.

We couldn't miss this adventure! I had determined that I would not leave the school until I had followed the Havasu stream from its turbulent source to its end, where it tumbled into the mighty Colorado. So when Mr. James returned to his camp, Frances and I began assembling the supplies we should need for the two-day journey.

Early the next morning the supervisor of the Grand Canyon Forest Reserve and a ranger arrived at the house. They had come to investigate conditions at Mooney Falls. Our trail would lead by the falls, so we invited them to ride with us that far.

Frances planned to ride the only trustworthy burro in our herd, a quick-stepping, sturdy animal. I intended to hire a horse in the village, so went down early to select one that could travel rough country. When the Indians learned that we were attempting the route to the Grand Canyon, trailless below Mooney, they shook their heads, declaring that no horse could make it. I suspected this was a buildup for bargaining as to price, so reminded them that old Ute had scouted out the way in order to serve Mr. James as guide. They admitted, "Maybe one, two Indians go; maybe horse break leg on rocks." As usual, a crowd had gathered to consider, craftily, whether or not the venture was feasible. As the leisurely discussion continued, the price asked for a horse soared until it almost equaled the value of the animal.

Then Walapai Bill, a square-shouldered man of middle age, spoke, "You take my horse. I bring your house pretty quick." He and I made a bargain, while the crowd murmured at his reasonable price of five dollars, which I quickly accepted.

When we were ready to start, I put Vesnor in charge of the school property until Mr. Burnett returned later that morning. Then I thrust my foot into the stirrup and sprang to the back of Walapai Bill's big, bony horse—only to discover that I was not being a lady! Ladies were assisted in mounting, I remembered, too late, when I glanced down at the cupped hand of the gallant young ranger and saw the surprised look on his face.

As we followed the trail through the village, the Indians were free with their comments. It was common knowledge that an Indian could endure hunger, thirst, and exposure. But Hicos were soft. They joked, hilariously mimicking the picture we would make on our return—wilted as a squash vine severed from its root.

We jogged on until we came to the mile-long strip the Indians used as a race course. Without an instant's warning, my horse took the bit in his teeth and ran like the wind. At the mile's end, he stopped, heaving and gasping for air. He was, I discovered later, Walapai Bill's best race horse.

Our party of three and the two men from the forest reserve followed old Ute along the widening stream, which was so highly charged with minerals that every root, branch or leaf obstructing its flow was coated with solid stone. I gathered some of these leaves from the stream; each tiny vein and serrated edge was plainly marked in the stone coating. The debris along the banks had been transformed into a filigree of great beauty, concealing hollow places and deep caverns that became a danger when one walked too near the edge.

We passed Navaho Falls, so concealed in its jungle of tangled growth that we could not see it, but only heard its roar as it dashed over cliffs and boulders. This was the first large falls, and by some considered the most beautiful, perhaps because of its isolation.

The stream dropped rapidly, but we continued at the same level, traveling on a wide shelf that flanked the chasm. On the rim above Bridal Veil Falls we halted and looked down on the impressive scene two hundred feet below. Here the canyon formed a bowl or amphitheater, centering attention on the falls. The river spread across a high, wide cliff, dropping like a wind-tossed, gossamer veil into a deep blue pool. Thick mysterious folds of mist churned up from the pool, curtaining the gnomelike caves. Weird mineral formations, deposited by the water on shrubs and vines, covered the canyon walls on either side. Shaded by tall trees, the floor of the bowl was a tangle of bright green grass, climbing clematis, mosses, ferns and columbine.

In the past weeks we had visited this amphitheater several times and entered the caves back of the falls, finding giant stalactites and stalagmites and long stone-coated tendrils of maidenhair fern, fragile as old lace. Branches of trees, roots and trailing vines, heavily encrusted with mineral, hung over and almost concealed the entrances to the caves. We broke off some of these and found the wood, in some instances, still green and alive underneath.

As we continued down the trail we rode to the rim again and again, unable to resist the wild beauty of our river, roaring with such violence through its narrow gorge.

We passed Crematory Gulch, a western branch of our canyon where the Indians had cremated their dead before accepting the practice of burying in a canyon nearer the school. A former employee once told me that he had visited Crematory Gulch and was surprised to find large Navaho blankets, undamaged by fire, medicine gourds, saddles and, most gruesome of all, the partly burned club of a man's graying hair. He fully realized the danger of desecrating an Indian cemetery, but slipped away with a shaman's gourd rattle. At the time he told me of his venture, he was hoping for an opportunity for a second visit, but whenever he made the attempt, an Indian appeared with disconcerting suddenness, and stood, watching, until he gave up the quest.

We rode to the brink to look down on Mooney Falls where the river roared in a solid column over a ledge higher than Niagara. The noise of its crash into the foaming pool below was deafening; the picture it made, hundreds of feet below us, was like a bit of toyland. Mineral accretions were plastered, like the halves of umbrellas, against the sides of the precipice. I knew that just below our feet were the dangling remains of the frail Indian ladder down which Lanoman and his friends had tenderly lowered his young wife to her funeral pyre. There, too, rested the bones of James Mooney, a sailor turned prospector, who with a few companions had tried to descend below the falls to locate abandoned mines, about which he had heard such fantastic tales. The rope they lowered over the precipice had been too short, and Mooney, the first to make the descent, fell to his death. As a tribute to his memory, white people gave the falls his name, but the Indians continued to use "Mother of the Waters." I thought of those two, resting there in the shadowy gorge, where nature rioted and roared; and yet, in the cool, protected place where they slept, there was an inner quietness and soul-resting peace. Reluctantly we turned our mounts back to the trail, leaving the park officials to make their observations at the falls. We did not suspect it then, but later we had reason to believe that their visit resulted in an invasion of the canyon that filled the Indians with terror.

The sun's rays had by now reached us. And the parching waves of heat which the walls reflected filled us with almost unbearable thirst. A large fat dog that we had not been able to prevent following us, crept under bushes or ledges of rock for one precious moment of shade, then ran, panting, to catch up with us. Finally he crawled under a rock and his pitiful moans told us that for him the journey had ended. On our return, we found his body huddled far back under a shelf of stone.

Beaver Canyon, a narrow crack in the terrain over which we were traveling, cut across our path. A short bridge would have spanned it, but when we peered into its depths it seemed bottomless; we made the twenty-mile detour around it. We had had no food since our early breakfast, so after rounding the canyon's head at four o'clock, we dismounted and prepared supper. Ute slid over a steep incline into the gorge, and filled two canteens from a spring. Our fried chicken, hard-boiled eggs, green beans, peaches and cocoa disappeared so rapidly that we were appalled when we discovered that Ute, who had agreed to bring his own food, had only a green watermelon (which he declined to cut) and a few peaches. We shared with him, and he was quite pleased with our contribution. We had yet to learn that an Indian carries a minimum of food and travels long stretches without water.

When we had finally completed the long detour around Beaver Canyon, Ute led us to a "rain tank" and the horses had their first drink since we had left home. Then darkness settled down rapidly and it was time to make camp. While we ate a hasty lunch from a shelf of stone, Ute cut his green watermelon and devoured it noisily in addition to the food we gave to him. He held himself aloof in true old-Indian fashion. A younger Havasupai would have made himself one of the party and pointed out places that had made tribal history, but Ute wrapped himself in profound silence. Later, when mosquitoes, gnats and flies came from out of nowhere to torment us, he built a fire and tended it all night to keep them at a distance. Frances and I spread our blankets near a boulder, and I slept until the dazzling moonlight awakened me. The night was too gorgeous to waste in sleep. I lay awake for hours on the hard sand, under the deep blue desert sky, watching the brilliant stars and a majestic moon riding the heavens.

We ate breakfast by moonlight, and packed the burros for an early start. The day would bring heat and burning sand, and we had only one canteen of water left. There was no trail now. Frequently we forced our horses up banks and over boulders, while we walked to make the climb possible for them. Old Ute led the way, and I kept close to his horse's heels. His one good eye was quick in locating landmarks and in finding the faint imprints of his horse's hoofs, made on his scouting trip. When we approached a rough stretch, he motioned for us to dismount. This passed, he would give an upward fling of his hand as a signal for us to climb on our horses. Once when he gave the signal to remount, he turned to me and his wrinkled face broke in a grin as he spoke the Havasupai word for mounting a horse. Before that, he had been just an elderly guide, unkempt and uncommunicative. The friendly gesture and his willingness to teach the Hicos changed his status— old Ute became human and likable.

I brought my horse as close to his as the rough ground would permit, and repeated the word. He made me say it over and over until he approved accent and pronunciation, then he asked, *"Hico, caviu?* (White people say what?)" I told him, "Mount horse." He jogged along, repeating "Mount hoss, mount hoss," until he had the words memorized. We took other words, the names of plants, animals and land formations, which he taught me, then I gave him the English equivalent, each of us playing the game with relish.

Mr. James and Frances brought up the rear, taking turns in releasing the young pack burro from the catclaw bushes into which she repeatedly rammed her way—packsaddle and all—in order to thrust her head into the cooling shade. Occasionally I interrupted my lesson with old Ute to take my turn at extricating the animal from a thorn bush.

About eleven o'clock that morning, old Ute pointed ahead and shouted excitedly, "Hackataia! Hackataia! (Roaring noise!)"—the Colorado River. In the distance we saw the red north wall of the Grand Canyon. We rode on as far as the horses could travel then tied them to some bushes and climbed a mile to a point where Havasu Canyon joined the Grand Canyon.

I had promised myself that I would not leave the school until I had traced the Blue Water from its source to its mouth. This was the end of the stream. In one of his books, Mr. James had expressed the hope that he might make this trip we had just completed; so he too had realized an ambition.

So far as we were able to learn, no white person had ever before stood on this point—two thousand feet above the rivers and several thousand feet below the upper rim of the canyon. We could neither climb down the precipitous wall to the water nor make our way over the canyoned white limestone to the plateau, but must return by the route we had come.

The Colorado—two thousand feet down—was no more than a brown ribbon, twisting, and threshing its way through a crooked gorge. At this point it made a turn, and into the apex of the curve the Havasu River poured its torrent of blue, sparkling water. Its clear, strong current could be traced for a long distance before it disappeared in the muddy water of the larger river. Havasu Canyon was filled from wall to wall with a dense, green jungle, forming a vivid contrast to the bed of sand and stone through which the Colorado roars.

I took my camera and went to the rim. Below were outjutting rocks from which I could get a picture of the junction of the two rivers. I eased my way down but the heat curled the film, making it useless. The rocks were scorching hot, the canyon terrifyingly deep; I became so dizzy that I crawled back to the rim with great difficulty.

After lunch we started home. The heat increased; we suffered with thirst, for both canteens were empty. After several miles, Ute led us to a "rain tank" in a side gulch, to which we could not take the horses. We lay flat on the ground and drank our fill of the stagnant rain water that had collected in the concave surface of a layer of stone. Then we noticed a half-dozen lizards, white stomachs turned to the sky, floating on its surface. Within a few minutes I developed a blinding headache and could not sit in the saddle. I lay in the shade of a mesquite while Frances bathed my face with some of the water which we had reluctantly poured into the canteens, and massaged the tight cords in the back of my neck until I was able to ride again. This was as near sunstroke as I ever wish to be.

Late that afternoon we returned to the pool where we had watered the horses the previous day. They were wild for water. Ute's horse reached it first, and drank until he began to bloat and groan in agony; so Frances and I took ours away before they could satisfy their thirst. We urged the horses on, conscious of that long detour around Beaver Canyon. Finally we arrived at our quarters, tired, hungry and dirty, but filled with a vision that time cannot erase of angry waters fighting their way through stone walls.

CHAPTER SIXTEEN

Havasupai Home Life

I had discovered by this time that there were polygamous marriages among the Havasupai, and often wondered how much they disturbed the serenity of the homes involved. And then one day during a visit to the village, Head Chief Manakadja led me to one of two brush wickiups set in the same yard. Entering, with me, he pointed to an elderly woman sitting in a corner, shelling corn, and said laconically, "Old wife." Returning to the yard, we entered the second wickiup. A woman much younger than the "old wife" sat within, weaving a basket. In the same matter-of-fact fashion Manakadja pointed to her and remarked, "Young wife," then hurried through the low doorway to identify, by name, his children playing in the yard, several of whom were enrolled in school.

The innocent way in which he had called my attention to his two households made it difficult for me to break the news which surely would be a staggering blow to him. But I could not ignore the Commissioner's order to field officials regarding polygamous relations without taking a chance of being called to account. So I explained, "The Great Father in Washington made a paper talk; he said an Indian may have one wife, only one. You have two."

Manakadja stood for a bewildered moment just staring at me, then he asked, "What they do, wife, chillen, I no keep? Where go?"

That was one phase of the situation the Great Father had not thought out; neither had I. The old wife and her children would be the ones to go, and she had borne her share of trouble. I told him to keep both families, and give them equal care. I did not report his case to Washington, nor did I seek advice as to the best method for disposing of surplus wives and children.

The Indians said that Manakadja had first married the older woman, a member of his tribe. Years later, while camped on a mesa, he met a young Paiute woman whom he wanted for his wife. Whether the Paiute girl objected to sharing his affections with another or whether he had tired of the "old wife," he discarded her. Later, they were reconciled and he established homes for the two women in the same dooryard.

Leslie Spier relates a story,* told him by Sinyella, the elderly tribesman, which helped me realize that not all broken marriages involved the heartache I had imagined.

While hunting on the mesa, Sinyella's father met a young Navaho woman, living in a brush shelter of her own contriving. She must have been a venturesome girl to have walked across the snow-covered desert from "away back there" to her camp site, searching for Navaho relatives whom she had heard were camped in this region. The girl had anticipated her need for a campfire by carrying the Indian's "slow match." This was made by rubbing cedar bark until soft and pliable, binding it with yucca leaves into a slender rope, and igniting one end. The rope was carried in a loose coil. By blowing on the smoldering end, fire could easily be lighted.

Sinyella's father wanted the girl and took her to his home as his wife. Years later, some Hopi men came into the canyon to trade. The woman slipped away to the Hopi village and became the wife of one of the visiting men. Her Havasupai husband followed, demanding her return. When the Hopi man refused to let the woman go, Sinyella's father stated his alternative: "You must give me something; then you can have her." The "some-

---

* *Havasupai Ethnography*, American Museum of Natural History.

thing" was a good-sized blanket—accepted as a fair exchange for a young and daring wife.

Marriage came early to the young people of this tribe. Those who had established homes were spoken of as "husband" and "wife." The formality of divorce was unknown, and separations were unusual. Was it the very sacredness of the marriage ceremony that thus secured the stability of the home? I knew that almost every act of a Havasupai's life was performed according to a prescribed formula. Since marriage was the basis on which the home existed, and tribal government was dedicated to family welfare, the ceremony uniting man and wife should be most impressive.

On Bob's next visit to the school, I had my explanation. "Man, woman, love, they marry—that all. Coyote tell Indians that. Coyote not un'erstand paper marry, like white man. He tell us all he know. Coyote our father. People do like he say."

There it was again, "Coyote is our father," an expression that made me question how Coyote differed from Deer and Bear. Sometimes a man would say, "Coyote taught us." Coyote's unique leadership gave me the feeling that in some way, the animal was a member of the tribe. Other tribes had gens or clans, each designated by the name of a wild animal. This leads to the thought that when the tribes separated, one clan, the Coyote, may have become the Havasupai people.

Among a people so dominated by ritual, it was surprising to learn that marriage here was often consummated by a sort of hit-or-miss procedure. The boy might take his chance by slipping into the wickiup of the girl's parents at night. If he were not welcome, the women of the lodge chased him out, and if he were not too fleet of foot, gave him a beating that discouraged any thought of return. But if he were accepted by the girl and her family, he presented his gifts to the parents and moved into the family home.

Not all marriages were arranged in this manner. In the small village of Supai, each individual knew every other person intimately, so when two young people fell in love, with the parents' consent they set up housekeeping, usually with the girl's family.

Like Jacob of old, the boy became a member of the household, serving or working with his father-in-law. With the arrival of children, the young couple established their own home, unless the girl's parents were old and needed their help.

Life in a Havasupai home with its unfathomable undercurrents was even more interesting than the mysteries hidden in the canyon walls. These people lived close to the earth; the soil was warm and friendly, giving life to the sustenance by which they survived. It was the table from which they ate, the chairs on which they lounged; on it they built their cooking fires. They liked the feel of the familiar earth beneath their feet as they walked, and under their bodies at night. To it, as to the stones and water, they ascribed a living force. Just why they paid tribute to inanimate things instead of to the power that created them, I failed to understand. But I had no difficulty in understanding why they hedged themselves about with superstitions. Hadn't I, when a child, broken a mirror and been told that certainly bad luck would follow? Why had my race become subservient to this and other superstitions as senseless as those that dominated the lives of the Indians? I have never learned the answer. But I was reminded of some of the latter at a home where a young mother and grandmother were caring for a new baby.

Happy chatter and laughter greeted me as I approached the open doorway of a half-dugout, dark within, but clean and neat. A girl of about fourteen, sitting on a blanket on the dirt floor, held a baby in her arms. An older woman, squatting near by, gave the baby a gentle pat and, glancing up at me, asked, "Papoose, you think good?"

"Very good," I assured the grandmother, "and very pretty. A perfect little girl." The mother didn't impress me as being a person who would give much thought to superstitions or taboos but if she hadn't observed them, how could she account for a perfect baby? She knew taboos, the older women had seen to that, so she must have remembered, the last few weeks before the baby came, to use a stick, not her fingers, to scratch her body. Somehow, she must have avoided hearing the cry of certain wild animals or the creature's spirit would have entered her child, causing it harm. There were other restrictions, but there in that close room I couldn't recall them, neither could I imagine this carefree young mother keeping them in mind.

The baby slept quietly, evidently feeling no pain from her recently pierced ears. According to tribal custom, the grandmother had pierced the ears in several places with a sharp thorn, inserting a thread to keep the wounds open, and rubbing in deer fat to prevent infection. When the little girl was old enough those ears would dangle bright strings of beads, numerous silver ornaments, or bright pieces of wood.

She was such a cunning little thing that I was relieved to learn she was not a twin. There was an old superstition that the souls of twins were in such close sympathy that whatever happened to one must, of necessity, happen to the other. Thus, if one suffered an accident, sickness or death, the other could not escape the same fate. For this reason, one twin was sometimes destroyed at birth. If the grandmother still clung to this superstition, and there had been a twin brother, it would have been her duty to dispose of the girl in order to free the boy of the dual handicap. For among a primitive people, even though men outnumbered the women, the girl would have stood small chance.

A cradleboard, padded with soft cloths, leaned against the wall. The grandmother laid it across her lap, put a blanket on it, then arranged the baby, hands snugly at its sides, body and legs straight. Wrapping the blanket about the infant, she bound her firmly in place. When strong enough to crawl, the child would be released from this confinement and allowed to propel herself about in the manner of all normal children, until she learned to walk. And this stage of development would put to the test the parents' observance of still another superstition. If either had killed a snake in recent months, their baby might be doomed to crawl, lacking the strength to stand erect and walk. When killed, a snake loses its spirit. Where else can it go but into the child? However, this baby's legs showed no signs of weakness.

Childhood days would be pleasant for this little girl. There was no "nap time" nor "meal time" for Havasupai children. They played until they tumbled over asleep, awakened when they felt like it. If they were not around when the pot of stew was taken from the fire, they filled their stomachs when they came home.

Children and grownups played together, and the stream was their playground. The little folks darted through the water as guiltless of clothing and as agile as small brown fish. The women frolicked, laughing and screaming, somewhat hindered by their long underslips, but missing none of the fun, while the men, enjoying more freedom in this sport as in other activities, wore only loincloths. They loved nothing better than to take a burro into a deep pool, piling children on his back until they submerged him to his nose. They would tip him over backward, holding him under much too long for his comfort, shouting with laughter when he came up sucking air into his lungs noisily and painfully. Yet the burro seemed to enjoy these bouts, entering the water willingly if not eagerly.

The intelligence used by the parents in training their children would set a worthy example for any race. A mother did not scold. Instead she taught her small daughter to play grownup, to weave baskets, sweep the floor, carry water and make fiber brooms. This training prepared the child to care for a home of her own. But, wisely, instruction went beyond material things, for the little girl was also taught to be kind to her husband's people. This early training was responsible, I think, for the harmony with which those related by marriage worked and played together.

Young boys must rise while it was "little light" and run swiftly toward the rising sun. This prepared them for the hunt and made them swift in capturing the enemy. They were indoctrinated in the ritual of the hunt which involved many superstitions and taboos. To ensure success, prayers must be offered at smokes or hunting shrines—appropriate pictographs on walls or stone. The ashes of deer droppings, sprinkled at specified times and places, made success more certain.

Physical punishment was seldom inflicted on a child. In all my experience I never saw an Indian parent strike a child. A whipped child loses courage, they said, and his soul withers and dwindles away until he dies, for the soul of a child is a tender thing and easily hurt.

However, the case of old Captain Burro was utterly at variance with this gentle philosophy. He seldom appeared at the school, spending his time among the villagers, where, as a rule, he was ignored or subjected to rude jesting. When a small boy he may have been an incorrigible thief or liar or he may have defied tribal superstitions or taboos for he had been subjected to the *jelka* punishment, and the ignominy of it went with him through life. One can well believe that this savage punishment would shrivel a child's soul, for the excrement of animals was used to make a smudge, over which the boy's head was held until he was limp from suffocation. It was not the physical torture that marked his soul, but the revolting form in which it was administered, accompanied by taunts and jeers. This he could not live down, nor could he escape the brand of liar and thief it put upon him. The bitter ridicule of men who loved nothing so well as a jest at another's expense would follow him until death.

His "withered soul" reminded me of Lily's crippled hand, and the Walapai's ridicule. The Indians had not learned to tolerate with sympathy those who did not conform to the established pattern, socially or physically.

Most beautiful of all, to me, was the instruction to children regarding the care of the aged. "When your grandparents are old and blind, lead them gently where they want to go. Break off chunks of the good corn bread baked in the ashes, and put them into their mouths. If they have no teeth, feed them the warm corn mush." I never saw any evidence that the old and helpless were neglected or turned out to die, as was so often the custom among the Walapai. One day, in fact, I came upon a wickiup housing four generations. They were all assembled in the yard that afternoon: blind great-grandfather, sprightly grandfather, father and son—talking and laughing, the older men smoking their pipes. Near by, a partially blind elderly woman, who had lost her husband, kept house for her grandchildren. Others, childless and too old to work, were living out their lives comfortably in the homes of relatives.

This village with its abundance of food and carefree atmosphere formed a strange contrast to the Walapai community, where hunger nibbled at the edges, and poverty and sickness stalked within. Contentment, even happiness permeated the village. Secure in their homes, crop failures unknown, storehouses filled, the People of the Blue Water very naturally remained loyal to their gods, who, from the Days of Old, had watched over the Havasupai families and provided for their welfare.

CHAPTER SEVENTEEN

The Frightened Shamans

CE Manakadja had come to my office on an official call. His linen duster and the derby hat perched atop his braids were special attire. These were the only ones I had seen, so I knew the occasion was important. After the exchange of greetings, tension eased a bit, and the chief reached into an inner recess of the duster and brought forth a thin slice of bone. It was a head-scratcher, made from the leg bone of a deer, eight inches long, flat and highly polished. It widened from its point to a broad end through which a hole had been drilled for the insertion of a buckskin thong. A louse, complete in every tiny detail, was tattooed on its point.

Fully appreciating the humor of his act, he illustrated how one stirred up the little fellows when they nipped too hard. He asked, "You savvy?" Then added, "You like 'em, two bits."

Necessity had devised this clever instrument, for even though we waged constant warfare against lice, and the Indians cleaned one another's heads, vermin were still a scourge. If one were too busy in his garden or at games to have a head-cleaning, the head-scratcher came into use. I occasionally picked up a louse or two myself during a conference or in a wickiup while working over the sick.

I bought the chief's headscratcher. It would convince my friends back home that I had lived among a primitive people. It still is one of my choice possessions.

But only a week or two later, Manakadja came to see me on a far more serious mission. His son Jasper was desperately ill.

The boy had developed a high fever; his flushed face and burning skin told me how sick he was when I visited him at his father's wickiup. There were drugs of all kinds in my office, requisitioned by one of my predecessors, but we had no one to administer them. Regardless of what happened to any of us, Indian or white, I had no authority to summon a physician nor funds with which to pay for his service. Jasper's parents and I did all we could to relieve the boy's suffering, but he seemed hopelessly ill, and none of us could determine the cause. I sent him crackers, canned fruit, tea, any food he could eat, but our supply, freighted out from Seligman and packed down the trail, was limited and the food expensive.

Manakadja had reverted in his distress to the primitive. Linen dusters and derby hats had no place in his life now. He told me frankly that he wanted to employ a medicine man. It was not until months later that I learned what a medicine man did to the sick, so I offered no objection. Usually when an Indian hired a medicine man, he kept the matter secret from the teachers, even to the point of denying it. This was due to his desire to protect his tribal customs from interference by officials who neither understood nor sympathized with them. Because we were instructed to discourage such practices, we usually did just that. Manakadja's candor was refreshing. I could not help the boy, so I told the chief to do whatever he thought best. I really hoped that I might see the medicine man at work and discover by what procedure he healed the sick.

We had three shamans—medicine men—in the tribe at that time, A'mal ("Sack"), Rock Jones and Bob. I knew all three, and thoroughly liked Bob. For years A'mal had been considered the most successful, his reputation firmly established by his spectacular healing of Lanoman, after other medicine men had failed. He was distrustful, I think, of white people who gave him no credit as a healer, and held himself aloof. Bob was a heavy-set man, a good mixer, jolly, with none of the defensive reserve and ostentation of the ordinary shaman. Rock Jones was a stolid, good-natured man. Both he and Bob occasionally rode up to the school for a social visit.

These two had a common distinction: each claimed that a dying shaman, a blood relative, had instructed him in the art of healing and had bequeathed to him his own shamanistic spirit, his songs, gourd rattles and the other paraphernalia he himself had used in his practice. This was the easiest and quickest way by which a man could acquire the knowledge and skill a medicine man must have. Otherwise, he must seek one of the animal spirits created by the mythic people of the Long Ago who had hidden it away in a world reached only through dreams. This took time and the result was uncertain, for if the spirit refused to enter his body, his ambition was never realized.

If an aspirant dreamed of hunting deer, it indicated his sha-manistic spirit was the deer spirit; or his dream might be of a wolf, coyote or some other animal. The animal that came in his dream was the one whose spirit he must own if he were to become a healer. Night after night he concentrated on wooing this spirit, discouraged when it coyly approached only to vanish, but continuing his efforts until he had it safely within his body. Then it was his to command. He could dispatch it on missions to ferret out information of an occult nature, things human beings could not learn for themselves, or he could send it scurrying through the body of the sick to discover the cause of the illness. While on such missions, the spirit could be heard talking to the shaman; when it returned, you could see the shaman gulp it down and hear it talk or sing, telling him all that it had seen or heard.

Those who had not inherited a dying shaman's songs must dream their own. First, a rattle was made by removing the pulp from a gourd, inserting pebbles, and attaching a wooden handle that would withstand vigorous use. This was placed within easy reach while the man slept. When a thread of song ran through his dreams, he roused quickly, seized his gourd and, rattling an accompaniment, sang the song over and over until he had memorized it.

A'mal must have qualified as a medicine man through the medium of dreams, which demanded the deep concentration that had given him such assurance and authority. In the past he never doubted his supernatural power, and his success had been phenomenal. Bob and Rock Jones took their practice less seriously. In fact, Bob often laughed at the suggestion that he possessed unnatural skill in healing. Bob's and Rock Jones's indifference probably was due to old Chief Navaho whose brutal acts had caused the shamans to doubt their own skill.

As was their custom, the Indians who were relatives or close friends visited Jasper, studied him for symptoms they had learned to recognize, and then pronounced their verdict—death! So when Manakadja asked A'mal to treat his sick boy, A'mal went through his ritual for a few nights, then refused to make further visits. The chief appealed to Bob, but he, like A'mal, was reluctant to put his skill to the test, especially since the Indians had predicted death for the boy. Bob was in a tight spot. He did not want to offend the head chief by refusing, neither did he want to comply since he was aware of the fate of healers who, too often, failed. So he asked me to give him the white man's medicine for Jasper. I was puzzled, not knowing what medicine to give him until I remembered that Jasper had a hard, dry cough. Believing it would relieve the boy, I gave Bob a small bottle of cough sirup. He accepted it gravely, carried it out to our gate, and leaning against a post, took a long draft of the sweet sirup. He replaced the cork, mounted his horse and rode away. That was the usual fate of our cough medicine. It seldom reached the patient, unless we took it to him.

Several days later the chief himself came, insisting on medicine supplied by the United States Government. He wanted to see me pour it from a bottle on the shelf. I gave him cough sirup. He held the bottle up to the light, peered through the sparkling red liquid, and asked anxiously, "Heap good? You think heap good?"

My first impulse was to tell him honestly, "No, I do not think heap good, but it is the only medicine on these shelves that I know how to give, except quinine and castor oil." But honesty would have destroyed the spark of hope his face still held, so I replied, "It will ease Jasper's cough, and I hope will help him to get well."

After he had gone, I looked upon the rows of bottles and tins with positive loathing; drugs enough to stock a drugstore, but useless to us. Most of the containers had never been opened. Who had requisitioned them? Why had such a requisition been honored when the school had never had a doctor nor a nurse nor anyone who was legally qualified to dispense drugs? A visiting official had exclaimed, "You have enough drugs to last the city of Chicago for ten years. What can you do with them?" The Indians asked for medicine only on rare occasions; their suspicion of the white man's drugs was greater than their doubt of their own medicine men's skill. Giving this no thought, I had sent medicine to Jasper. If they gave him a dose or two, and the boy died, it would be a matter of cause and effect, and the blame would be mine.

Two days later, Manakadja was back; hope had given way to despair. "You give 'em new uniform, bury my boy," he requested.

Surprised and shocked, I asked, "Is Jasper dead?"

"Pretty quick die," he said, his face tight and gray with suffering.

"Did you give him the medicine?" I asked, anxious to learn what had been done with the cough sirup.

He shook his head. "I taste. No good."

I was so relieved to learn that Jasper's relapse could not be laid to the cough sirup that I gave Manakadja a new school uniform without waiting to learn whether or not I had authority to issue government clothing for the dead.

It was the custom to gather about the sick and mourn, telling him of his approaching death. Immediately after death, the body was laid with the head toward the spirit land to the northwest, to which the soul would take its flight. It was lovingly washed, dressed in the best clothes obtainable, wrapped in a choice blanket, and the face painted. The body was then laid, face down, across a favorite pony for the trip to the burial ground.

They would hold a cry over Jasper while he was yet alive, and the child would know that he was entering an unfamiliar world. Thinking of this, I went to my stores and took a generous supply of food to send him. I had not given up hope, and the mere act of sending him food increased my confidence. The chief's face brightened as I loaded his arms. Even though he carried burial clothes, he was thinking of the food his boy would eat, instead of how soon he would die.

Saturday afternoon Bob came bustling into my office, his face beaming with excitement. "Big chief's boy no die!" he exclaimed. "Maybe get little better. Pretty quick, *toholwa* [sweat lodge]." So I went at once to Manakadja's place, arriving just in time to witness the sweat lodge ceremony for the healing of the sick.

The framework of the sweat lodge stood on a smooth patch of sand near the stream. Long poles, their butts thrust into the ground, their tips held together with bark or yucca leaves, formed a dome-shaped lodge about six feet in diameter and four feet high. A gap between two of the poles provided a low entrance. Long use had worn the floor of the lodge to a rounded depression. It was now thickly covered with fine willow twigs and leaves to make a soft bed.

Jasper's mother, one of Manakadja's two wives, came from her wickiup carrying Navaho blankets which she spread over the framework, several layers deep, making the interior as dark and airtight as possible. She went to the near-by fire and scattered live coals from the burning logs over the stones she was heating. Next she placed a pitch-smeared basket of cold water within the lodge and beside it laid some green twigs; then she was back at her fire, smothering the stones again with fresh coals.

Two men, wearing only breechcloths, emerged from the chief's larger wickiup, carrying the boy, limp and unconscious. Tenderly they eased him into the sweat lodge while another, as nearly nude as they, held aside the blanket that closed the doorway. The two men entered to administer the bath and to sing the songs of supplication and thanksgiving that are a part of the healing ceremony. Jasper's mother, using two heavy, green sticks, lifted hot stones from the fire, one by one, and placed them within the lodge. The blanket was lowered to close the opening.

The men in the lodge sang two songs in a loud, high chant, but I could not grasp the meaning. However, Mr. James had interpreted the songs that were sung when he had entered a *toholwa* as being repetitions of their god Tochopa's instructions in preparing the lodge and conducting the ceremony. After these minute instructions had been sung many times, the singer became a supplicant, praying to the heat to heal the head, the lungs, the feet, the ears, until each organ of the body of which he had any knowledge had been named many times. At the completion of the two songs, sung to wild, erratic music, the leader dipped the twigs into the water and sprinkled the heated stones. A biting, acrid steam filled the lodge, making the lungs ache with its fierce heat. More sizzling rocks were shoved inside, more water was sprinkled on them, more songs were sung.

I watched and listened, intent on learning all that I could of this ancient and sacred rite. Because they so heartily despised the white man's curiosity, his prying into their sacred ceremonies, I must be sympathetic in my effort to discover the deep truth back of it all. I must convince them that I believed, as they did, in the healing *toholwa* (sweat bath).

I knew they felt as I would feel if someone should enter my church and crane his neck and gawk, not with the hope of spiritual enrichment, but rather to observe the reactions of congregation and minister. I respected their sincerity. Tochopa was their benign god. He had taught Those of Old how to build the *toholwa*: the framework of poles, the covering of green boughs and mud sealing it tight so no heat might escape. But for some reason, the Indians no longer built those permanent, mud-covered structures; blanket-covered lodges such as this had replaced them.

In fifteen or twenty minutes the two men had completed the ceremony and emerged, carrying Jasper between them. They plunged him into the stream, laid him on a blanket which his mother had spread on the sand, and wrapped the blanket over him. All this time he had seemed unconscious, his eyes closed. But soon a warm glow suffused his skin, and the watching men and women stirred, murmuring happily; the boy was on the road to recovery. The healing ceremony of Those of Old had again done its work. A short time later Jasper was back in my classroom, a golden, red-cheeked boy, brimming with health.

While Jasper lay resting after his bath, Manakadja had gone to his older wife's house and returned with four hard ears of corn, presenting them to me as a token of his appreciation for my help in caring for his son. He was paying for what he had received, but there was more to it than that. Corn in the hand had the feel of warmth; it had life; and one could dicker for a long time in a trade by slowly adding grains to the buying price.

I could not use the corn, but in working with a people who were quick to anger and who punished with death, I stood in need of the things it denoted—the friendship and confidence of the tribe's head chief.

Jasper had recovered—without the magic cures of a medicine man. But why had the shamans, especially A'mal, whose reputation was unblemished, evaded the request of their head chief to hold a sing over his son? Navaho's influence, I learned, was still at work, although the former big chief had been dead for three years.

Indeed, not long after this, the Indians began talking more freely about Navaho's cruelty. One old man told me he had helped Navaho take a discredited medicine man up on a cliff, cut out his heart and toss his body over the precipice for the birds and the beasts to devour. He did not say what they did with the heart, but it must have been something significant, for the heart was the seat of the emotions, the symbol of life. The story was so startlingly akin to Old Testament accounts that it helped me to realize how many years of progress these people must in some miraculous way achieve before they could take their place in twentieth-century civilization.

Another medicine man fell by Navaho's hand, accused of sending his shamanistic spirit to make the people sick while posing as their healer. And the people, believing their chief was protecting them from evil, applauded.

Navaho was their Solomon. While I was with them they were still speaking with warm approval of the justice meted out to the young Apache man who escaped and sought sanctuary with the Havasupai while his tribe was being taken to San Carlos by government officials. Navaho heard the man's plea, then told him that by deserting he might cause his people to endure additional hardship at the hands of the white man. Therefore, he must return to his tribe. When the man replied that he would never return, Navaho, without speaking a word, struck the Apache dead. This was the type of justice the Havasupai understood. A tribesman did not seek safety at the expense of his own people.

Navaho was "Master of the House" to the Havasupai. He ruled with an iron will, but more justly—according to their sense of justice—than the people had ever been ruled before. He enforced the old customs and traditions: obedience to their gods, the *toholwa*, full granaries, the dance, the hunt, complete self-sufficiency of his people with no interference from the white man. At his death, the tribe lost its last great leader, a man respected for his strength and courage by both white men and Indians.

But his brutal handling of the medicine men had had a devastating effect. Every shaman in the village remembered and acted with caution. Each knew that a persuasive tongue could turn the people against a healer, that death was the penalty. No medicine man in the tribe, therefore, was willing to treat Jasper. The people, in a state of indecision, would have turned from healing by incantations to healing by diagnosis and medicine, but no medical doctor was available. Washington was too far away to recognize its opportunity to teach the Havasupai and their shamans a better and a safer way to cure illness.

The people themselves had not lost their peculiar intuition. They gathered about the sick and freely expressed their opinion. Sometimes it would be, "Pretty quick, die. Maybe sun go down." If they formed a favorable opinion, the announcement would be, "You get well, four, five suns."

When I was taken sick shortly after my arrival, I found comfort in the more cheering of the two verdicts.

I could not diagnose my ailment; even had I been able to do so I should not have known which drug of those we had on hand would be the proper remedy. Perhaps each twinge of pain was intensified by the knowledge that no matter how ill I became no doctor would come to help me. But the Indians came. News went through the village that Hico (white person) was sick, and they flocked to see me. They stood off a short distance from my bed, each uneasily making his careful scrutiny. They were looking for the sunken eyes, the pinched nostrils, the pallid skin—symptoms that had a special significance. They shifted their positions, pointed and gestured and talked in low voices, then the spokesman pronounced their opinion: "Pretty quick, get well. Indians sick all same, get well all right." They had not seen "the look of death" in my face. They filed out as silently as they had entered, and their visit did me as much good as one from a medical doctor. They had said I'd get well. And they usually were right about that "look of death."

Years after I left the canyon, the doubt Navaho had planted as to the shamans' integrity began to diminish. The medicine men took courage and resumed their calling. Men again placed gourd rattles by their beds and lay dreaming, avidly awaiting the coming of the spirit, the revelation of the songs. Some of these new seekers had been pupils of mine. Among them was a boy named Mark, who learned to rattle the gourd, to sing and to suck from the flesh the spirit that caused the sickness.

On the other hand, Bob lost faith in the shamanistic spirit he had inherited. When he himself became sick, and it failed to heal him, he ordered that at his death the tools he had used in his practice be destroyed. With scrupulous honesty he refused to bequeath his shamanistic spirit to another or to teach his songs to a tribesman. Like Those of Old, Bob was an uncompromising realist, and I have often thought that in his integrity he was unconsciously pointing the way to a brighter future for his people.

CHAPTER EIGHTEEN

Talking Stones

An evening with an old storyteller sitting by his outdoor fire, pipe in hand, means a tale worth remembering. In this setting, the old men passed on to the children the legends of the tribe's wanderings. Of course each narrator spiced his tale with a little of himself, his imagination, his whimsy or his logic. But the theme never varied: always the gods led the Havasupai. When memory grew dim, these storytellers need only tread again an ancient trail, peer into a long-abandoned cave, or read the messages on boulders and stone walls to recapture the story's flavor and sequence of events. Of these legends, one, at least, certainly had the ring of truth.

Evidence other than Indian lore indicates that, generations back, the Havasupai lived in the region of the Little Colorado River. They may have settled there after the god Tochopa, on account of the crowded conditions in Mattawedita Canyon, dispersed the tribes. However, this new location again placed the tribe within raiding distance of the savage Whajes (Apache), who relentlessly drove them from their cliff dwellings and gardens to wander in an unfriendly wilderness. The tribe crossed the desert to the San Francisco Mountains, but even here they could not live in peace, so again took the westward trail, seeking the home to which their gods would lead them. A canyon cut across their path. They worked their way down its rugged walls to the floor—an oasis of greenery cut by a rollicking stream of blue water.

Desert weary, they tarried by the stream, reluctant to leave a spot that had everything they so much desired, but their gods had not yet spoken. Discouraged, they began the long climb up to the plateau and westward. A child cried. The procession halted and the child's voice was stilled. Each effort to resume the journey brought that cry of protest. The wise men quickly issued their edict: "The gods speak to us through the voice of the child; this is the home to which they have led us."

Joyously the people unpacked their loads and began building houses and making gardens.

Handed down through many generations, this old tale expresses the Indians' desire to lay in the laps of the gods every problem that affects their lives. On the canyon rim overlooking a wide section of the floor, they found the god-spirit in two gigantic pillars of stone. So they built their houses on either side of the stream of blue water where the gods could watch over them night and day.

The Indians' accounts of the god-spirit residing in the two stones turned our attention to the walls of the gorge. Miss Goenawein, the only old-timer employed at the school, had visited every point of interest within walking distance, so she acted as guide.

From the Indians she had learned of the Black Man. After Sunday school she took Frances and me to a side canyon where we gazed up at the shiny, black form of a giant stone man, lying prone as if he had dropped down and fallen asleep. We stood in the hot sun, trying to discover what force had caught and held the black mineral while the red sandstone built its layers around it. Doubtless the old men had a tale about this phenomenon, had we asked them. But in the discomfort of the intense heat and the sunlight striking our faces as we gazed upward, our interest in the Black Man quickly vanished. So we wandered over to examine some pictographs on a boulder, beautiful primitive art that could hold one entranced indefinitely.

The boulder stood in the center of the canyon; the base, worn away on one side, left a projecting ledge some four feet above the ground. Stooping low, we crawled under the ledge, straining for a view of the ceiling. It had been polished smooth, then completely covered with pictures, doubtless the key to the tribe's history, the handwriting of Those of the Long Ago.

Several animals which we could not identify were artistically outlined; also done in outline was the buckskin-clad figure of an Indian. Two small right hands, evidently those of a child, had been placed palms down on the ceiling and outlined with white native paint. There were circles, divided into segments which contained symbols. We twisted our necks until they ached, tracing and studying, but the pictures were as meaningless to us as the written words of our language would have been to the people who placed them there. In various other parts of the canyon there were hieroglyphics in strategic places on stones or walls, some depicting the Great Serpent, which must have played an important part in tribal legends. The tribe's old men explained these paintings by saying that when the Apaches and other enemy tribes slipped in and drove the Havasupai out of the canyon, the Havasupai hastily placed them there as messages. These gave the direction the tribe was traveling and its destination for the guidance of those separated from the main body. That may have been true of some of the pictographs, but those on the under side of the boulder were the work of a painstaking artist, possibly created for a hunting shrine, where men offered prayers for success in the chase.

The sun had long since dropped below the rim and deep shadows filled the gorge. We had tramped six miles and were dreading the walk home. Then we saw an Indian pony nibbling at the sparse grass. It lifted its head, gave us a questioning look and came toward us. I took off my petticoat, tore it in strips which we tied in a rope. One of us rode while another led—the gods had been kind to us too! When we released the pony at the school he went running back to his pasture.

Our next exploring trip wasn't just a jaunt by three women; we had an escort, Mr. Burnett, the farmer, and his constant companion, a big yellow dog.

We had heard rumors of a secret crack in the canyon wall through which the Indians fled to the outside when pressed by enemy invaders. Immediately we planned to investigate. When Vesnor learned that we intended to go through the passage, he shook his head gravely and cautioned, "Indian moccasin walk trail all right. Think white man shoe no good." Before we were through with the experience we agreed with him.

After a walk of several miles, we stood in a side gorge and gazed up at a long triangular crevice that split the wall to an incredible height. A ledge of stone, fifty feet above the canyon floor, seemed to form the base from which the crack rose to an apex. We realized that this might prove a little more dangerous than some of our other ventures—but if the Indians went through, so could we. It would be worth the climb to stand under the open sky free from sharp, enclosing walls.

Two Indian ladders (logs on which crosspieces of heavy sticks were tied with leather thongs) took us up to the stone ledge. The loose rungs, giving under our feet, swayed the logs threatening to spill us. Shaky from our tussle with the ladders, we pulled ourselves up, single file, onto the stone ledge and faced the entrance to the crevice through which ran the old Indian trail. And behold! this was not the base of the crack at all, but its center—the fissure continued downward so deep into the earth that we could not see the point where its sides met. The trail, a mere edge of stone clinging to one of the close-set walls, ran through the narrow crevice midway between the top and the distant bottom.

Mr. Burnett took one look at the precarious trail, then scrambled down the ladders as fast as he dared to solid ground, where his dog anxiously awaited him. How deserted we felt when he left us to face the dark passage alone! I began to realize that we might encounter unsurmountable difficulties in that thin crack before it landed us somewhere "up above." We stood peering into its darkness, wondering what force had cut this vertical chasm through solid stone. Had a river come in from the plateau, carving its way through the sandstone wall, then disappeared? Or had an earth tremor split the stone apart? A few yards ahead the jagged walls seemed to reach across and touch, but the entrance was fairly wide. Rather than turn back, we started the climb.

The trail grew narrower as we advanced toward the earth's interior, the light from the entrance dimmer, the walls damper. Then, in the darkness, we came to that tricky section that is dreaded by those who use the trail. The ledge we followed disappeared. There were only rounded knobs on the wall for footholds, slippery with the slime and water that oozed over them. Oh, what a fall we might take! We did as the Indians must have done, leaned across the narrow chasm, pressing our hands against the opposite wall to brace ourselves, and cautiously stepped from knob to knob. We tried to keep our nerves steady by refusing to look down at the close-set, ragged walls which fell away to such terrifying depths. I wanted to get down and crawl, but the knobs were too small, spaced too far apart.

Vesnor had warned us, so we had put on shoes suitable for climbing, but I kept thinking of the moccasined feet that had worn this path, and the surer ease with which they walked. I knew that one misstep would plunge me to those sharp points far below, or farther down to the bottom of the slimy crevice.

After what seemed endless hours, a dim light appeared ahead. It grew brighter as we worked our way toward it. Presently we emerged in a deep, bowl-shaped depression, but a stone roof above the bowl shut out the sunlight.

Miss Goenawein used the Indians' footholds, while Frances and I boosted her up to the surface. Then she pulled and Frances boosted me out of the hole; together, we pulled Frances up. We were bent double under a boulder that would have completely covered the bowl from which we had just climbed, had not this section of its base been broken away. Crawling out into brilliant sunshine reflected from miles and miles of sparkling sand and red bluffs, we were careful not to stray far from this boulder that hid the mouth of the crevice, for there were thousands of others like it strewn over the barren land. We lacked the Indians' instinct to mark a spot so surely that it could never be lost.

Over at the rim, we looked down into the canyon we had so recently left, trying to locate the farmer and his dog, but they were not within sight. We stood about, discussing the Indians' frantic escapes through the crevice, and the fact that now it was a short cut for men who had a few ponies grazing on this level. Then one of the girls, just to hear the racket it would make, pushed a small boulder over the edge. Others followed. As they clattered over the wall, striking projections and bouncing far out into the canyon, the farmer came into view, running for his life, his dog leaping at his heels. We were as frightened as he, for we still could hear the falling stones crashing their way down, and knew that if one struck him, the blow would be fatal. We returned, as fast as the slippery crevice would permit and descended the wobbly ladders to the canyon floor.

The farmer confronted us with blazing eyes. "Those stones you rolled down would have killed me and my dog if we hadn't run with all our might," he exploded.

We tried to explain and apologized, but realized we could never again persuade him to accompany us on an exploring trip.

At our cottage, old Gentle Annie in her accustomed place at the foot of the cottonwood, waited for me. She wore a strawberry-red dress, my dress. She had wanted clothes, but could no longer see well enough to make them. So each time I came within reach, she grabbed my skirt and begged, "Dress, you give 'em." I was obligated, in a way: hadn't she shared her mescal slab with me? So I had given her the brightest dress I owned. She had been effusive in her appreciation, put it on over her other dress and walked proudly home. As I watched her, aged and tired, making her slow way down the path, I thought of the young wife she had been, standing by her man's side, fiercely defending their possessions, their home and her own body from the grasping hands of the enemy. One of these battles was particularly vivid in her memory.

In their younger days, Annie and her man had lived for a time in a cave high up on the canyon wall. In the dark hours of a summer morning, they were awakened by the soft scuff of moccasined feet.

Dimly they saw the hurrying forms of the enemy slipping stealthily past the mouth of their cave toward the village. Escaping through a rear opening, the young couple were working their way down the wall, leaping crevices, scrambling down cliffs, hurrying to warn their tribesmen, when, with a triumphant yell, the invaders gave chase. Gentle Annie and her man outran their pursuers and reached the village already alarmed by the commotion and frantically arming for defense.

At nightfall, when the thieving marauders retreated laden with booty, fighting their way up the trail, many dead, both enemy and tribesmen, lay on the canyon floor. Houses had been emptied of their dried corn, pumpkin and venison. Warm blankets were gone. Corrals held no ponies. Children had been orphaned. Bitterness was in the hearts of the Havasupai at the loss of their tribesmen, and the prospect of the almost impossible task of again providing against the cold winter.

In trying to describe the bitter fight, in the few English words at her command, Gentle Annie's knotted hands clenched and her dark eyes flashed with the violence of her emotions in living again the cruelty and hardship. "We work, we make—they take," was the simple statement that ended her story. The strawberry-red dress was a small gift but it had brought momentary happiness to an old woman in whom the fire of youth had not completely died.

On this visit, Gentle Annie was not thinking of wars; she had business to transact. She carried a little basket containing five fresh figs; offering them to me, she said, "Pigs, pive cent." I bought her figs, split them open and laid them on my window sill to dry. Within a few days they would be rich and sweet.

One day Miss Goenawein mentioned some small rooms or caves excavated in the sandstone wall beneath the gods, that held secrets of the tribe's exciting Days of the Long Ago. My old urge to explore flared. I wanted to learn what possible use the caves had been to these canyon dwellers. Were they granaries such as honeycombed the walls on either side of the village? Were their interiors brightened with pictographs recounting the tribe's turbulent past?

Were they carved there by Those of Old? A short trip might give the answer.

We scrambled up the talus on one of the steepest trails I had ever climbed, followed a ledge until we came to many openings in the face of the wall, each a tiny doorway. Stooping, we passed through one of the doorways, but could not stand erect under the low ceiling. The sandstone walls were bare. The floor beneath our feet gave a hollow sound for the caves were in tiers; a row of such cavities was immediately below the ones on this level. The ledge formed a path on which the occupants could pass from one cave to another.

We returned to the ledge and looked down on the peaceful scene so far below: the village, bathed in dazzling sunlight . . . men drying buckskin . . . women weaving baskets or gambling fiercely under their porch shelters . . . a wide pool, dark with the bodies of frolicking children. What need had these people for dome-shaped holes in their canyon wall, holes that bore no evidence of recent use? Yet across the canyon on a flat-topped bluff stood a fort; through the portholes in its masonry, the canyon could be defended from wall to wall—with help from these ledges.

With the battlefield a panorama below us it was easy to visualize the battles that had been fought on the canyon floor, Gentle Annie and others of her generation unwilling participants. In preparation, the Havasupai armor-bearers hastily scrambled into their armor—buckskin robes falling from their necks almost to the feet protecting the body front and rear, a wad of buckskin in the left hand to protect the face, a roll of it about the neck, the right hand free to wield hatchet or club. The shield-bearers, carrying strong wooden sticks from which buckskin aprons depended, accompanied the armor-bearers in the forefront of the battle or, in retreat, covered the rear. The shield-bearers were of particular importance, for the enemies' arrows clung to their buckskin shields or fell harmlessly from them. Armed men, crouched in the protection of these shields, sent their salvos against the enemy at every opportunity, while the armor-bearers clubbed and beat the invaders.

Fortunately, this tribe, unlike the roving Indians of the desert region, had never come in serious conflict with the United States Army. Had they done so, I am inclined to think the Havasupai may have won, at least the first bout. For an American soldier, confronted by enemy whose armor resembled buckskin nightshirts, and whose shields—their only protection from bullets—were tanned deerskins, would have been so convulsed with laughter that he could not fire a shot.

However, the Havasupai had one weapon that no enemy laughed off—their poisoned arrows. Juices extracted from the Jimson weed and other toxic plants, combined with the poison of scorpions and poisonous insects, cemented to the arrow tip with glue from roasted soapweed leaves, made a deadly weapon. They were expert marksmen, and if the flesh was penetrated by one of these poisoned arrows, there was no known antidote.

At the approach of the enemy, women and children scurried up the wall to their huge stores of food on a higher level, saved for just such an emergency. Men fought from their homes until driven from the canyon floor, some retreating to the fort to shoot arrows at the pursuers or to roll stones down upon them. Others took to the ledges along the walls, running ahead of the desert pirates, slaughtering them with poisoned arrows. But many, according to the Indians, retreated to this ledge with its little scooped-out rooms in which ammunition and food could be stored and the wounded cared for. Crossfire from the fort and this ledge could annihilate the invaders in this wider section of the canyon, which held the main part of the village. Protected by their armored men and their shield-bearers, the Havasupai warriors descended for hand-to-hand fighting, while archers slaughtered the fleeing enemy from stations along the walls.

By nightfall, the canyon was cleared. Women and children scrambled down from their high perches, joining the men in caring for the wounded, cleaning up the village, cremating the dead and repairing, as best they could, the damage. Then they held the victory dance, as bloodchilling as had been the conflict itself.

It was a gala occasion of feasting and dancing. Faces were grotesquely painted, costumes and ornaments were designed to heighten the emotional orgy. Enemy scalps, taken in the fight, were washed and cleaned by the old women, then tied to the tip of an upright pole. The people danced round and round the pole, patting their mouths, giving a more savage note to the victory song, working themselves into a frenzy while they harangued the scalps, blaming them for the raid. "We do not steal from your home. We stay here and make our gardens grow. You kill our people. You steal our food, our blankets, our horses, our women. Now you cannot eat. You cannot sleep warm at night. You are dead."

When Gentle Annie or any of the older Indians spoke of the victory dance, emotions ran deep, their eyes kindled with a fierce light. Again they were driving back the hated foe, running the scalping knife around the hairline of his abandoned dead, peeling off a scalp.

Eventually, the Great Father in Washington sent his soldiers to clear the canyon of all hostile Indians and settle for all time the matter of raids. We found the names of soldiers and those of army officers, including General Crook's carved on the canyon walls.

We retraced our steps down the trail feeling that, in those little rooms, we ourselves had lived their tribal wars. We crossed over to the fort that stood on an outjutting bluff, impregnable on three precipitous sides; on the fourth side, a narrow trail wound steeply to its top. At several points along the trail we found piles of stones left from their last battle, ready to be rolled down on an enemy. We picked up arrowheads, but could not determine whether they had been dropped there by the Havasupai or shot there by the enemy, nor if they had been smeared with the deadly poison. We peeped through the portholes, took pictures of the place and departed.

High up on the wall to our left were two lonely figures, the Buck and the Squaw. The Indians had told me the legend of their plight, so we stopped to see how closely the two stones resembled the figures of a man and a woman. At a time when the Apache had conquered and held all the land on one side of the stream, limiting the tribe to the strip on the other side of the Blue Water, an Apache man fell in love with a beautiful Havasupai woman. He crossed the stream, killed the woman's husband, and fled with her up the steep canyon wall. The Havasupai gave chase, but when the guilty couple had almost reached the rim of the inner canyon, the gods struck quickly, turning the pair to stone. There they remained through all the centuries, a grim reminder to all Havasupai women of the penalty of illicit love.

Such love affairs were not unknown in the village. When neighboring tribes came in to trade, a man would dole out the quantity of food he would pay for the transient affection of some woman of the visiting tribe: so many ears of corn, so many measures of beans. Some of the Havasupai women were capricious and took advantage of these occasions to live daringly. However, as a rule, the home seemed to be a stable institution in which man and wife maintained its integrity.

A slow walk through the village, stopping to talk to the people, accepting an ear of roasted sweet corn at one wickiup, a handful of crisp sunflower seed at another; then, with reluctance on my part, we started home. Somewhere in the canyon walls was a secret cave filled with tools and weapons such as were used by Those of Old. Vesnor, when a boy, had watched old men secrete this native handicraft and seal the cave, leaving no identifying mark. I knew I could never find it, and Vesnor refused to disclose its location. But how adequately those tools would reveal the ancient culture of an agricultural people such as the Havasupai!

We ate a pickup meal, then I sat in our old rocker to read my daily paper, published in Oklahoma City and a week old by the time it reached the canyon. The delay did not lessen the shock of the news of President McKinley's assassination. But the excitement, the hatred and fear aroused by his death could not reach us in our seclusion. We could not plunge into political intrigues and the turmoil of a world that seemed hardly to exist while we lived, vicariously, the adventures of a courageous people in discovering and defending a mysterious canyon.

CHAPTER NINETEEN

The Day the Mail Did Not Go

◖ At four o'clock one morning I was awakened by a loud pounding on my bedroom door. Miss Goenawein was calling excitedly, "Miss Gregg! Miss Gregg! Come here—hurry!"

I sprang out of bed, shoved my feet into slippers, pulled on a robe and ran to her room. There in the open doorway stood Spoonhead, the mail carrier, the mail pouch clutched in his hand. His long, queer head looked more than ever like the bowl of a spoon as I stared at him, wondering what mischief he had cooked up to get me out of bed at this hour.

His pony stood in the yard, bridle rein dangling. The saddle was decorated like a Christmas tree with Spoonhead's numerous bundles: food for himself and his horse, extra clothing for the cold nights on the mesa, and those mysterious knickknacks he took on such trips. I did not notice the absence of the large, red Navaho blanket he always carried neatly rolled and strapped to the back of his saddle, until he began gesticulating wildly and shouted, "My blanket! He steal 'em. He go there." He pointed to the base of the canyon wall.

There I saw a short, heavy-set Indian with a blanket thrown across his shoulders, crouched low, running stealthily from bush to bush, seeking cover for escape. In the dim light we caught only fleeting glimpses of the man. I could not understand why Spoonhead did not give chase and try to retrieve his property.

"Go after him and get your blanket!" I exclaimed, almost as excited as Spoonhead was.

He did not move. Instead he was watching me brightly, sure that the Hico would settle the difficulty; why else was she here? When he realized that I had no intention of chasing the thief, his elongated face grew inches longer.

"Tell me that man's name," I said. "You know who he is."

"Plenty dark. No can see," was his naïve reply.

Later, I learned his reason for evasion. If he betrayed the thief, he would betray himself. Spoonhead wanted his blanket but with no questions asked. He had no intention of catching the thief, and when he made up his mind that I had none, he said, "No take mail. No go. Got no blanket. Plenty cold up there." He dropped the mail pouch to the floor.

"Get on your horse. The mail must go," I told him. "I'll get you a blanket."

At that moment the thief dashed from behind a boulder to a mesquite bush, and I recognized him.

"That's Walapai Bill!" I exclaimed. "You knew all the time it was he. Find Vesnor and tell him to meet me at Walapai Bill's camp. You go there with him."

In the excitement I too was forgetting the sanctity of the United States mail and the tradition that come hell or high water nothing must interfere with its transportation.

The morning still held that drabness that precedes the dawn, and the usual thick fog hung just above the ground, so I went to my room to put on warm clothing.

Like a damp thread the narrow trail wound through dense underbrush so high that it met overhead, with every leaf and twig dripping water. Along the path I caught glimpses of watching eyes that moved through the brush as I moved, but drew back and vanished when I looked directly at them. The village was astir and palpitating with the news that an old feud had flared up anew. Like curious, impetuous children the Indians peeped from bushes and doorways, unwilling to miss an instant's excitement that could be caught and later exaggerated to entertain relatives and friends.

Walapai Bill's house was a low mound of earth with a door in one end. He was in the yard chopping brush in short lengths for his cooking fire.

"I want Spoonhead's blanket," I told him shortly. My patience was not improved by the fact that I was cold and soaking wet.

"Didn't see blanket," he said, his graying head bent over the wood. "You look my house, you no see blanket."

I pushed open the rickety board door that hung on leather hinges and entered. The dirt floor was worn to a saucerlike depression, the sides sloping to the flat circle in the center. A search did not reveal the blanket, which was too large and too vivid in color to be concealed easily. His wife also had disappeared. I went outside as Vesnor and Spoonhead rode up on their ponies.

With his usual astuteness, Vesnor knew exactly where to find the blanket. He pursed his lips and pointed to the canyon wall. "Over there, I think," he said. "Maybe wife hide 'em in storehouse."

"Bring the woman here," I told him, "and make her bring the blanket."

He sprang through the brush, climbed the talus, and followed a trail on a shelf of rock until trees and shrubs hid him from view. The Indians crowded in, forming a half-circle about the hut, eager to see the culprit brought in.

Vesnor returned, his hard right hand firmly grasping the woman's wrist. She followed, pulling back angrily with each step, the heavy blanket across her shoulder. Her lord and master had ordered her to hide his loot in their granary and she had had no choice but to obey.

I sent the Indians home except those actually involved in the theft. I told the women to give their children food and get them ready for school, then I investigated the affair.

Walapai Bill's cockiness melted rapidly when he was told that he could be sent to jail for theft, and that his interfering with the transportation of the United States mail was no light matter. His fat shoulders slumped and his bold daring changed to indecision. He prized above all else his freedom to go where and when he pleased, so built up his defense.

"Long time ago, I go on mesa. I hunt seeds, nuts; make good food. I hunt rabbits, deer. Gone long time, maybe so many"—he held up four fingers—"moons. Come home, door all break. Somebody go in house, take saddle blanket. Little one. I think Spoonhead steal 'em. That why I steal Spoonhead blanket. He steal me, I steal him. That way Indians do. Make play like little game; little mad, too."

Spoonhead angrily met the accusation, for not all of the truth had been told, and the blame had been shifted to him. "Long time, Walapai Bill, me, gamble. He lose. One dollar. He no pay. I take blanket. Little one. Worth maybe one dollar," he shouted.

Walapai Bill sheepishly admitted the truth of Spoonhead's statement. Each of them was entirely willing to return the other's blanket for they now realized the gravity of the situation. Spoonhead went to his camp and returned with the saddle blanket which he exchanged for his big Navaho. It remained only for Walapai Bill to pay his debt of honor to wipe out the long-standing feud. Unless this were paid, the good-natured pilfering would start all over again. I suggested that he take care of it. I was not sure that he had the money; if he had, where he kept it was a mystery.

He ducked through his doorway, very reluctantly lifted a rug from the center of the floor, dropped to his knees and began digging in the dirt with both hands. He clawed out the hard-packed soil, tossing the dirt back as a dog throws it when digging a burrow. I watched his queer antics in bewilderment, amused at the concentration with which he worked. Then his pudgy, brown fingers scratched metal and he drew from the hole a rusty baking powder can, with the word "Royal" still legible on its paper cover. He twisted and turned the lid until it came free; then, fumbling around inside, he took a silver dollar from the coins in the can. He handed the dollar to me, and the woebegone look on his face told how hard was the parting. I gave the money to Spoonhead, who stuck it in the pocket of his jeans, grunted loudly, mounted his horse and rode off. Now that he had his blanket, he would ride up the trail tomorrow and across the mesa to Seligman, the mail pouch tied to his saddle.

We settled our troubles as they came to us, so the Postmaster General never knew that a game of chance, played several years before, had that day delayed the delivery of the United States mail.

Walapai Bill took the matter seriously when he realized that his crime could have landed him behind bars, and was grateful for the settlement. He offered his hand in friendship, grinned broadly and said, "You ride my horse. I think good you ride him."

The big bay was in a brush corral near the house. His long bony head and long legs reminded me of that dash across the race track on our way to the Grand Canyon. I declined as graciously as possible, for the morning had taken on a new beauty and I wanted to walk home. The fog, that rose nightly from the stream, drifted upward between the red walls, trailing long streamers. The white clouds it formed sailed majestically eastward across the wide strip of blue sky above the village. Rills of sparkling water traced patterns from the stream to the thirsty gardens. The people were tilling the soil, irrigating their crops or eating their early meal.

Kate sat by her outdoor fire, eating toasted sunflower seed from a shallow basket. She grinned at me and I squatted by her fire; its warmth on my cold, wet clothing was something to appreciate. She did not permit my presence to interfere with her breakfast, but scooped up a handful of the crisp seeds, poured them into the right corner of her mouth, moved her jaws for a few seconds, then let an uninterrupted stream of hulls drop from the left corner. Repeatedly she scooped up more seeds, poured them into her mouth without disturbing the outward flow of hulls. It was as mechanical as a gristmill.

"How do you do it, Kate?" I asked, laughing.

She thrust out her tongue. "*It,*" she said, moving her tongue across her mouth from right to left. "You try," she invited, pushing the tray toward me.

I tried, but swallowed hulls with the meats, so gave it up.

Kate replenished her supply by pouring dried seed into her basket, scraping in live coals, and tossing them together with a rhythmic motion that kept seed and coals in a lively dance until the former were delicately browned. Changing the motion, she eliminated the coals as dexterously as a miner washes sand and dirt from his panned gold. Kate was ready to mill her second batch. Her ample body overlapping her fat legs called for a health talk on the dangers of overweight, but these carefree villagers had robbed me of the mood to lecture. Even to improve the health and the appearance of her body, I could not wipe that look of supreme enjoyment from Kate's pleasant face.

An older woman, bent over a basket she was weaving, sat on a blanket near the entrance to the house, her face lined with anxiety. In working out her design she was using the black bark of the devil's claw (two-pronged seed pod of the unicorn plant) against the white inner bark of the osier. There was something arresting about the woman's dejected posture and the wild, frightened look in her black eyes.

"Yunosi make new basket," Kate volunteered. She held up the basket she was using to show me its burned and broken condition. "I burn," she explained with a giggle. "Make new. I use."

Yunosi! That name explained the drawn muscles of the woman's face, the look of fright in her eyes. Only the previous week Bob had come to the office asking for medicine for Yunosi. His sister, he called her; but the terms sister, brother and cousin were loosely used to denote almost any blood relationship. From him I had learned her story.

As the wife of Chief Navaho's son, she had held an important position in the tribe. Her husband had been a good mixer; he had liked and befriended white men, and had learned enough English to converse intelligently, and from him Yunosi had learned many English expressions. A deep and lasting love blessed their union, so that after his death, she had more than the usual fear that his spirit would hover near her, unable to leave the one to whom he was so devoted.

Her fear became an obsession. She could not sleep, for she was haunted by visions of her husband returning in the darkness to be at her side. She would cry out to him, not in her native tongue, but in the English he had taught her, calling him by his English name, "Why you come, Tom, why you come?" She would point him out to others in the lodge and ask pitifully, "You no see? He there. Why you no see him?" Their inability to see him only increased her confusion. The hallucination tortured her night after weary night. And her repeated question as she stared and pointed crazily at the apparition no one else could see caused the Indians to give her the new name, "You No See," which soon was shortened to Yunosi. For this affliction Bob had asked me to prescribe medicine, but since cough sirup, castor oil or quinine offered no hope, I sent him away empty-handed.

When I saw how real her suffering was, I longed to help her find peace. As tactfully as I could I explained my belief about death, but she sat like a carved image, with terror in her eyes. Watching her weave her intricate design, I took comfort in the thought that in this tribe of too few women, Yunosi would be wooed again and in establishing a new home, the hallucinations would surely be forgotten.

Yet as I walked back along the trail, I could not shake the memory of Yunosi's terror. Childish feuds over trampled corn and stolen blankets were one thing, but this first encounter with a fear so deeply grounded in myth and superstition made me realize how much a part of their living culture it was; and it would become the heritage of our school children, unless counteracted by education.

But the sun's rays were creeping down the white cliffs. Before long Vesnor would be herding the children into the schoolhouse. I would need a more substantial breakfast than a few sunflower seed to fortify me against the further problems of a day in that crowded classroom.

CHAPTER TWENTY

The Peach Dance

As summer waned, the Indians' activities centered on the Peach Dance, their annual harvest festival, held in late August or early September to give thanks to Those Above for a bountiful crop and to petition for continued protection and care.

Men and boys hurried to complete a task at which they had worked indifferently for weeks—the clearing of brush and debris from the dance floor. Messengers rode up the trails to the east and to the west, carrying the knotted counting cord extending invitations to friendly tribes. The invited guests need only cut a knot from the cord each day, the last knot representing the day festivities would begin. These guests would bring news, and their presence would add zest and gayety to the celebration. Women left their games of chance and busied themselves at the grinding stones. Vegetables were brought in from the gardens; peaches, figs and apricots, either fresh or dried, were prepared for the big feast.

The Peach Dance was one of those age-old ceremonies revealing the true culture of the Havasupai. For centuries men and women of friendly tribes had flocked to the canyon to take part in the festivities and to trade Navaho blankets, ponies, saddles and silver ornaments for garden-grown vegetables, fruits and buckskin.

A few Walapai and several Hopi drifted in for the dance, and our hopes kindled that some of the white men and women who had previously attended this ceremony might make the trip into the canyon. Tourists always brought news from the outside—and how welcome that was! And, too, we caught some of their excitement in entering what was, to them, a wonderland. But, since my arrival, so few had come.

One hot summer day, three lads from Princeton, spending their summer vacation hiking across the United States, had walked out from Williams and climbed down the Lee Canyon trail. They were full of fun—and short on food, so we sold them what we could spare from our supplies. They took a quick look around, then went gaily up the Walapai trail to new adventures, leaving me with the feeling that, compared to them, I was very much encompassed by stone walls. Later, the wife of the Governor of Arizona came down with a party of friends to catalogue the flora of the canyon. They camped under the cottonwood, eating their meals from a boulder, quickly finished their work and departed. Their visit heightened our interest in the delicate plants tucked away in cool grottoes as well as in the more abundant hardier ones. And we had met a governor's wife who sacrificed physical comfort for the advancement of science.

Then there was the family from Chicago. They had driven their team across the desert, climbing down the zigzagging Walapai trail and stopped at our door to demand shelter. The frail wife and sick daughter sat their horses, wanting nothing in this world but a bed on which to lay their aching bodies. While I assembled the beds, they rewarded me with a description of the Pacific Ocean as they had seen it that summer, a sea of pale blue fire. Too many fish had perished in some catastrophe in the deep, causing the phosphorescent glow.

Then there had been George Wharton James's visit to the Indian village.

Each one had brought his bit of excitement and information, leaving us the richer for his coming. But now, when we longed only to see again a face from a world that was beginning to seem so remote, to hear what its people were doing, no one but Indians came down the trail.

After the sun had dropped in the west and the canyon walls had cooled somewhat, the Indians assembled at the dance ground, the space previously cleared and encircled by poles interwoven with green boughs. The song leader and the drummer took their stand near a pole in the center of the floor; the men formed a circle about them. Manakadja, as head chief, stood aloof; to him fell the responsibility of correcting any part of the ceremony that varied from ancient custom.

At a signal from the drummer, the men started to dance. The women broke the circle, separating the men, interlocking fingers with them. Shoulder to shoulder, the dancers moved slowly to the left with short, shuffling steps, knees slightly bent, bodies swaying to the rhythm. The dance was orderly, but the weird singing increased in volume until the pole had been circled three or four times, when Manakadja interrupted to harangue the crowd. After he had finished, the circle formed again and the dance continued.

The drum, on which the drummer thumped vigorously, was similar to one I had seen that summer, standing on end where the drummer had carelessly left it after a dance. It was a section of hollow cottonwood log with hide stretched over both ends. The drums of their forefathers had been pottery vessels, in which they poured a little water. The hide stretched over the mouth of the jar was moistened and made taut by upending the vessel. Such drums had naturally been quite common among a pottery-making people; and though there was now a strange absence of pottery, its production had obviously been discontinued only in the recent past. In many places in the canyon floor I had dug up broken clay vessels, whose worn surfaces showed the marks of long and hard usage. They were of a dull gray, crudely decorated in black, and lacked the artistic quality found in the exquisitely finished work of the modern pueblos. Why and how these people had lost the art of pottery-making is one of the mysteries of their changing culture.

The fantastic facial decorations, a band of paint across the eyes, or the face striped with many colors, made some of the dancers unrecognizable. Gala costumes were donned, with coyote or fox tails dangling at the back. The arms, legs and bodies of other dancers were painted white, or white with contrasting horizontal stripes. These grotesque figures added color to the dance and stirred the imagination with old-time fire.

In this dance, as in the Walapai mourning ceremony, the village crone had a unique part. Mr. James had told us of seeing women rush to the center pole during the Peach Dance, and, encircling it with their hands, whirl madly about it until they dropped from exhaustion. He had been present when several women darted into the center of the circle, screaming, dancing, foaming at the mouth and pulling their hair as they dashed against one another or against the central post, until they fell in a stupor.

If one of these prone creatures blocked the path of the circling dancers, she was dragged by the hair to one side where relatives cared for her until consciousness returned.

The men looked with tolerance on such hysteria but did not indulge in it. As a rule they were rather stern, self-disciplined, but jolly too.

This Havasupai dance may have included some of the ritual of the Ghost Dance, which at one time was the accepted religion of many tribes. It is said to have originated in 1870 based on the doctrines of a Paiute shaman, who claimed to have visited the dead in their far-off home, and learned from them that they would return to join the living. There seems to be very little information available as to the introduction of the cult at this early period or of its influence on the tribes who accepted its precepts. Its value to the cause lay in the fact that it paved the way for the revived Ghost Dance in 1890, which won converts among the Indians from the Sioux in the north to the tribes in California.

The Paiutes were responsible for both its origin and for its revival; the latter came about in a strange manner.

Wovoka, a Paiute, was a young lad when his father, described as a "dreamer," died. The boy, through his work among white people on a ranch, learned some English and gained a little knowledge of the white man's religion. When he was about thirty years old, there occurred a phenomenon that terrified the Paiutes, an eclipse of the sun. The Indians interpreted the eclipse as an attack by some ferocious monster on their god, the Sun. The darkened sun was a dying sun; fear plunged the tribe into wild demonstrations, shouting, the firing of guns, any act that would frighten the monster and force him to abandon his wicked purpose.

During this eclipse, Wovoka became unconscious—he is said to have been ill at the time—and was lifted up to the Other World. Here in a place of celestial beauty he saw all those who had died, happy and ageless in their faraway home. While here he was taught a dance which must be performed at stated intervals for five consecutive days. Wovoka returned to earth, recited his experiences among the dead and taught his people the dance, which became known as the Ghost Dance. He instilled in their minds the belief that by performing these dances as instructed, they would bring their dead back to dwell with the living in eternal happiness on a regenerated earth. This seems to have been an effort on his part to incorporate into his native religion the creed of the resurrection as he imperfectly understood it.

Disciples introduced the tenets of this strange religion to other tribes where the ritual of this cult, like that of the peyote, was made to conform to the will of the cult's tribal leader. In their determination to recall the dead, emotions ran high. In some tribes, men, women and children danced wildly, waving their arms, contorting their bodies, until emotional and physical exhaustion caused them to drop unconscious to the ground. While in this state they, too, entered the land of unearthly beauty and peace where they talked to dead friends and relatives.

In other tribes, the center pole held the "power" to transport a worshiper to the Other World. The Havasupai tied eagle feathers at its tip. To induce the trance, a man climbed to within reach of the feathers where he clung until he became unconscious and fell to the ground. When revived by the medicine man, the pole-climber was expected to relate what he had seen and heard in that far-off land.

To the primitive Indian, unconsciousness is "going dead for awhile." I learned this one day when I fainted in the classroom. The children ran from the room in terror, but later told me, "You went dead and we were afraid." The deduction was that one who "went dead for awhile" had most certainly entered the land of the departed and should have exciting experiences to relate.

However, the people were soon disillusioned. These emotional orgies did not bring back their dead. Even more discouraging, some of those who climbed the pole were said to have died within a short time. This gave the Havasupai their reason for discontinuing the dance. But more potent forces were at work. On some reservations the dances drew large crowds and the emotional demonstrations reached such extremes that soldiers were called in to restore order. One agent, at least, resorted to strategy by preparing a big feast for the day of the dance. Food would be plentiful, and free—but no dancing. The feast was well attended—the dance floor deserted. Within four or five years the demoralizing ceremony was entirely discontinued.

However, after the terrific excitement of the Ghost Dance, the older Havasupai women may have found their native Peach Dance a little slow, so resorted to hysterical demonstrations to enliven it.

The Peach Dance would end with feasting and horse racing. For the feast men and women were strictly segregated. The former, on one side of the race track, were discussing rules with Manakadja. Across the track, the women were busy with food under a long open-sided shelter.

The men served the food, placing it, according to custom, on green branches spread on the ground. As a matter of courtesy, visiting men were served first. Then men of the tribe. Women and children shared what was left. The feast over, the leaders took turns lecturing the crowd on proper conduct.

Up to this time neither men nor women had manifested much excitement. They had danced the previous night until long past midnight, and were tired and sleepy. The loud thump, thump of the dance drum had echoed and re-echoed up and down the canyon keeping us awake until weariness deadened the sound. But with the announcement of the first race, the people surged forward, crowding for a place near the track, laughing, shouting and betting on their favorite horses.

Walapai Bill's bay lined up with a dozen other horses for the first race. Had I cared to bet I would have placed my money on him, remembering my wild ride on that same mile-long track. Riderless horses, always betting favorites, were also trained for these races. They started on signal, kept their places in the race and—on occasion—won. No doubt one or more of them had been entered today for excitement was at a peak.

The signal was given, the race was on. Women rushed forward waving their *sutams* and screaming at the horse on which they had placed bets, "Win race! Win! Win!" Men tossed their hats into the air and shouted.

In the midst of the hullabaloo, I remembered the stack of letters that must be answered before the mail went out the next morning. Unlike the Indians I was not free to work only when it was "little light" and play when I felt like it. Unlike the Indians, too, I had no storehouses bursting with food. My subsistence depended on my efficiency. I had no choice but to leave the merrymaking at its height, but not before I'd had a chance to watch Walapai Bill's horse nose up inch by inch and win the race.

CHAPTER TWENTY-ONE

Trial by Water

◧ Whenever opportunity offered that hot summer, I slipped on an old dress in lieu of the bathing suit I did not have, and took a plunge in the wide pool only a few yards from our cottage. Completely screened by dense bushes and trees lining its banks, I floated lazily across its surface, catching enchanting visions of red walls and blue sky through the overhanging branches. God put something in running water and in trees that rests the soul; this secluded spot had that quieting touch. In its delicious coolness, I forgot the heat that beat back from the walls, the problems, the feuds, even the suffocating air in the crowded classroom. But duty refused to take a holiday, even in soaring temperatures, so the pool gave only momentary relief. One hope was left to us— the summer rains.

We knew that Arizona had a rainy season which broke the heat of its long, dry summers, but none of us realized that nature could react with a deluge out of all proportion to the need.

I doubt if anyone except the Indians knew what a flood would do to the canyon and to the houses and gardens on its floor. The Havasupai had an uncanny weather sense. If we had asked them, they would have interpreted the significance of the signs all about us and told us what to expect. But we didn't ask. The Indians must have been convinced that the Hicos knew everything worth knowing or we wouldn't be there trying to teach them, so they didn't bother to instruct us on the means of escaping from a water-filled canyon.

There was no letup in the heat. It was reflected from the walls in visible waves. Work in the classroom was almost unendurable. Heads nodded sleepily when the hot, still air in the low-ceilinged room became heavy with the smell of campfire smoke and sweat. There had been several sudden, pelting rains that passed quickly, leaving the air momentarily fresh and sweet and a little cooler. Now, we watched our narrow strip of sky for clouds, hoping for another shower. Even the occasional cool breeze that swept through the canyon lost its coolness when it came in contact with our torrid walls, so the nights, too, were hot.

Out under the cottonwood in our front yard, hung a weather-beaten hammock. Night after night Frances and I had tried to sleep in our poorly ventilated, sultry room; so one night I moved out under the tree. I found that making a bed in the tippy contraption was something out of my line, but managed to hold things down until I got in. It was like riding a bucking bronco; the more I struggled to maintain my balance, the more the bed tipped.

The commotion brought faint, squeaking protests from the tree; the small creatures that lived there resented the intrusion. We had amused ourselves many times trying to locate the bats sleeping among the leaves during the day, but I was to have a nocturnal view. At first, a thin squeaking line flew off into the darkness. Then the entire colony rose from the tree, soaring about on kitelike wings, to begin their nocturnal foraging. As if they had held a conference and agreed on the strategy, they swooped down, their bony wings brushing my face and hair. I was out-maneuvered and ran indoors.

The next day was a holiday, dry and hot as any day had been that summer. For a brief space in the afternoon the sunshine grew dim and watery; then, again, hot and bright. A change in weather was impending. We scanned our narrow strip of sky and hoped for one of those refreshing showers. There was only a hazy sky, and now again that peculiar misty sunlight.

Vera, one of the older schoolgirls, had come from the village to make a dress for herself on a school machine, and was hurrying to finish before dark. She was nervous about the weather, but wanted the new dress to wear to Sunday school, so went on with her work.

A hot wind blew through the canyon, bending the trees and swirling the sand about in clouds. Then came a breathless stillness. Vera threw her work aside, and ran out of doors. We followed. With a quick glance at the sky, the girl exclaimed, "Very bad storm up there, very bad!" Vera knew the canyon in all of its moods. She was terrified. So were we. Something sinister was brewing and our strip of sky did not tell us what to expect. If only we could see beyond the rim of that high canyon wall! Suddenly masses of black, heavy clouds boiled into view, rolling and tumbling ominously, the lower folds surging violently upward, those above shooting down in writhing, twisting masses. Through the blackness we caught occasional glimpses of a high greenish ceiling. What would the storm bring? If only wind, the walls would protect us; a hurricane could not negotiate so narrow a gorge; but if the clouds were loaded with water, we were in grave danger.

The topography of the surrounding country was against us; the plateau spread, like an open fan, to the south, the east and the west, forming a drainage area of hundreds of square miles which poured its water into our canyon. We didn't realize then that the indentations in the rimrock were old watercourses, which this drainage had cut through the outer limestone walls on its way to our chasm.

The stage was set for quick action. The clouds rolled and boiled, but in the canyon there was only stillness, pressing down. The big cottonwood leaves hung limp; the dead air warned of disaster. Then again came that inrush of hot air. The tension eased a little when big, misshapen drops hit the ground with vicious spats. The rain had come, but it was an unnatural rain that filled us with awe.

We retreated to the house and stood in the doorway watching the torrential downpour. Suddenly Vera burst into tears.

"Look! Look!" she cried, pointing to the high canyon wall back of the school building.

It was covered from top to bottom by a sheet of water. Vera knew what that meant. The canyon might fill to any depth, depending on the quantity of water that poured over the walls added to the amount that fell in the canyon. She wanted the security her own people could give her; they had weathered countless floods. We realized our helplessness, so put a coat about her shoulders and told her to run to the village. She flew down the trail like a frightened deer. Weather-wise as the Indians were, she may have sensed that a cloudburst or storm of destructive violence was imminent. She had barely time to reach the village when the clouds opened, pouring down water in a solid column.

The entire west wall as far up and down the canyon as we could see was now hidden behind a curtain of water. Then the east wall, only fifty feet away, was likewise hidden—more drainage from the mesa! Those curtains, hundreds of feet high, were pouring tons of water into our gorge each moment. The thundering noise made conversation impossible unless we shouted. The confusion bewildered us. We tried, hurriedly, to plan, but still held to the foolish hope that the water would drain off as fast as it came in.

Then came a new danger—something beyond our imagining. With startling suddenness, a full-grown river, boiling with sand and debris, leaped over the east wall with a force that shot it far out into the canyon and a roar that drowned the noise of the storm. We knew then that the plateau was pouring its accumulated drainage down on us. We realized the volume and strength of the current when a large evergreen tree rode its crest and fell, beaten and crumpled, almost at our feet. Nothing could stand against that roaring waterfall. It hurled a boulder over the rim, spun it crazily and smashed it on the ground with an impact that shook the canyon. Other rivers dropped over the rim. Surely the end was near. How long could the gardens, the houses and the people take such a beating? How long could our building stand? Would the sturdy old cottonwood go down?

Our stream of clear, blue water had disappeared. A maelstrom of dirty suds, tumbling stones along its bottom, swept down the

Havasu's bed, spreading across the canyon from wall to wall. Each moment its power was augmented by the increasing drainage from the mesa and by the river that roared down from the upper end of our canyon. We were convinced that the house would go, and could think of only one means of escape—the trails.

We hurriedly decided to try the Lee Canyon trail, fifteen miles long, but not so dangerously steep as the Walapai trail. The rain was coming now in wind-blown sheets. If the trail remained passable, we could reach the mesa. Miss Goenawein and Frances were rushing around preparing to leave, so I put on my raincoat. When we closed the door behind us, we were almost beaten down by the storm; I had the forlorn feeling that this was the end. The mouth of Lee Canyon was a long distance from the school; we would struggle against water and rolling stones just to reach the trail's lower end. After that, the climb to the outside. Any Indian could have told us that boulders and landslides would block both trails; that torrents would tear out their weaker parts, leaving sheer precipices. However, the Indians were looking after themselves; there was not one within sight. Even though the village stood in a wide section of the canyon where the water had room to spread out and would do less damage, the Indians were moving their possessions and their families to places of greater safety.

By keeping to the higher ground in the center of the canyon, we avoided the waterfalls plunging over the rim on either side. The water deepened as the gorge narrowed, but we pushed ahead. Not until we heard the roar did we remember the hazard of the Gap where the passage narrowed to fifty feet, thereby increasing the river's force. The Gap was filled with churning water ten feet deep, thick with mud and tumbling stones. The flood spumed out in front of us, divided into two streams that flanked the center ridge and rolled on to create more havoc below. There was no way to pass this barrier; we stood quite still, staring at it, beaten.

"The Walapai trail!" Francis shouted. "We can't stand here. Stones are cutting my legs."

So we retraced our steps, wading back to the mouth of the

Walapai Canyon, and followed the trail to the Corduroy Bridge over which our mounts had stepped so gingerly that July day, weeks before. Here too was a gap, narrower than the one that had just turned us back. The torrent leaped over the bridge to the ground, a fall of thirty feet. It cut off our last chance to escape by the trails. We had traveled in a circle, up to the Gap and back, only to meet defeat. Then Frances began climbing the talus of sand and stone banked at the foot of the canyon wall. Here was safety, within a few yards of our house! The talus took us above the flood water. We still got the full force of the storm, but soaked and bedraggled, we felt intense relief in being safe. Our greatest fear had been of being caught in that current, carried over the tremendous Havasu falls and dumped into the muddy Colorado. From this point, we watched the water plunging down the canyon bed, striking tree trunks, boulders or angled walls and shooting long streamers of spray high into the air. It surged against the buildings, ran up the walls, then fell back heavily. Fearful for their survival, we watched our sturdy cottonwoods twist and bend before the onslaught. If they went down, the buildings would go; the canyon would be swept clean.

Then quite suddenly, we sensed a change in the storm; the rain struck with less force. The clouds rolled away and never before had our strip of sky looked so serene, so blue, so beautiful!

We shivered in our wet clothing while the water subsided, which did not take long due to the sharp incline of the canyon floor. Frances began laughing and crying in hysterical relief. To divert her attention, I said, "Imagine how hungry you'd be, Frances, if we had climbed to the plateau; I didn't bring a thing but the clothes I have on."

"I know I brought food," she said. "I remember thinking we might be gone a long time, so crammed a lot of things that we'd need in my pockets."

She pulled a bunch of hairpins from one pocket and from another a few well-soaked slices of bread. All three of us shouted with laughter, released at once from the numbness of strain and fatigue.

We walked back to the buildings, admitting, with chagrin, that we would have been safer and drier had we never left them.

I took my camera and went out to get pictures of the rivers that still cascaded over the rim in five or six places between the school and the village. They were rapidly diminishing in size, but some of them drained in until late the following day.

The Indians' gardens and orchards that had been in the path of the main current were washed out and swept over the falls. The houses that stood on low ground were destroyed; however, the sagacity the Indians had acquired through long and bitter experience with floods enabled them to escape without the loss of a life, and with only minor losses of clothing. Each family had a crevice in the canyon walls that made a safe shelter. Here they set up temporary housekeeping.

I expected the children to appear for school Monday morning half-clothed, but only one pair of pants was missing. Six-year-old Dan, face clean, hair brushed and dripping wet, wore his uniform blouse, shoes and stockings, but no pants. He was a comical sight, but no one laughed.

The Indians warned us that nature would deal us another blow before we could settle down with our usual feeling of security— which wasn't very secure, after all. Many columns of stone stood out from the parent wall, separated from it by fissures in which water from rain or melting snow collected. Freezing weather turned the water into ice, increasing the pressure which widened the crack. This freezing and thawing, over a period of years, left the column unattached. A flood brought such sections tumbling down. This new danger was almost as exciting as the flood had been. It was always a gamble with us, not with the Indians, as to which section would topple over. The one directly back of the school building leaned out threateningly, but when I asked Bob for his opinion, he shook his head.

"Him no fall yet," he assured me, and since Vesnor agreed, we continued our school sessions. The men pointed out another pillar, farther down the canyon, that endangered neither school nor village, that would come down "four suns, maybe five."

From the day of the flood, falling boulders and landslides had kept us in an unsettled state, but on the fourth day, as the men had predicted, the big column fell. It leaned out from the wall, toppled crazily, its center buckling, and burst apart with a roar as if the gorge itself had split open and was shaking itself to pieces. A bedlam of sound struck the angled walls to be tossed back, echoing and re-echoing until it seemed there would never be an end to it. We hurried down to view the ruin, arriving before the dust had settled, while the stones were still sliding over one another, groaning and grinding as they shifted to a lower level.

The Indians patiently repaired their houses, dried out the furnishings, rebuilt fences, replanted gardens and orchards. How many times in the past had they undertaken this same task, I wondered. I wondered, too, at the leisurely way they worked, stopping to gamble a little, to visit and make merry for awhile, or to eat food some neighbor brought. If a task could not be done one way, try another; if it could not be done today, try it tomorrow. They had never worked by a clock, nor permitted time to become their master, so they, as a people, remained cheerful, unhurried.

Portions of the Walapai trail had been wiped out. The Indian men, using their native methods with brush and stones, soon had it passable but dangerous, so we were greatly surprised when several men rode down from the plateau and stopped at the school. One of them, Mr. Jacobs, an engineer in charge of a surveying party on the government reserve, expressed his surprise in finding us alive and the buildings standing. He said, "We watched the storm from our camp a few miles back on the mesa. From there, it looked as if a cloudburst hit right in this canyon. We expected to find this place swept clean as a whistle."

According to his report and that of his men, our danger was as real as it had seemed. But now that it was over, I was prepared.

The next time I was caught in a flood, I'd climb to a crevice and live like an Indian.

Several years later the canyon was again flooded, and this time the destruction was almost complete. The teacher and his wife, the only white people at the school, were no more prepared than we had been. They too had failed to learn from the Indians how to survive a deluge in comfort and safety, so they scrambled to the roof of their house—the same cottage in which we had lived—and climbed from that into the rugged old cottonwood. The old tree weathered the storm, saving their lives. They watched the maelstrom beat against the stone houses until they disintegrated like so many lumps of sugar. Today, the Indians can point out only one stone remaining on the site of the old buildings.

CHAPTER TWENTY-TWO

The Gods Speak Again

With shocking suddenness we learned that the Blue Water was to be commercialized. Mr. Ewing wrote that an Eastern firm had been granted authority to harness Mooney Falls to manufacture electrical power for distribution to cities in Arizona and neighboring states. Engineers, surveyors and workmen swarmed into the canyon where so few white men had ever ventured. Miners had once worked the ledges on the walls for silver, but never had the Indians' authority over the Blue Water or its canyon been questioned. These white men who were now tinkering with old Mooney Falls did not consult the Indians. They were authorized to complete the project, they explained to me, and, intent upon this, they kept pretty much to themselves. We sensed an intimation of things to come.

Did we owe this quick but orderly invasion to the visit of the Grand Canyon Forest Reserve supervisor that day he had accompanied us to Mooney Falls? Had he determined then the power which the falls could generate, and by his report encouraged this firm to speculate? While we pondered these questions and I protested to Mr. Ewing repeatedly, the men quietly but determinedly went on with their work.

The Indians realized now that, before they were through, these white people would fill the canyon. After the machinery was installed, men would remain to attend the plant; their families would come. To whom then would the canyon belong, and who would be forced to go? Who always went when the Indian had land that the white man coveted?

The white men had plenty of cash with which to allay the Havasupai's fears. They bought alfalfa from them for their horses, paying five dollars for the load a woman could carry suspended from a strap across her forehead. They gave a silver dollar to those who posed for a picture. But this proved little compensation for the Indians, who could only stand by and watch as heavy machinery rumbled in along the widened Lee Canyon trail, and old Mooney began to lose her wild timbered beauty. This trail, these falls, everything here had belonged to the Havasupai since the day the gods had led them into the canyon. Lanoman, gray-faced and angry, went about his duties. The foreign men were desecrating the "Mother of the Waters," sacred to his wife and those other dead whose spirits could sometimes be seen rising and falling through the heavy spray.

The Indians feared these invaders as they had never feared the Yavapai or the Apache. They could meet the latter and deal with them as they deserved, but these white men—working like ants, building roads, making permanent improvements—had taken possession without need of battle. Mr. Ewing wrote that the contract had been negotiated in Washington; he was powerless to interfere. And in increasing numbers the white men continued to come.

The Havasupai recalled the story the Navaho had told them of how the white men had elbowed them out of their ancient home. When, in retaliation, they killed those who had stolen their hunting ground, the Great Father in Washington sent soldiers with firesticks, who punished the Navaho, and took the guilty to some far place.

The people again gave thought to the warning of the Chemehuevi Indian who had come to them as an evangelist, reminding them of the old ways and warning them of the penalties of forgetting the customs of their ancestors. Mr. James, in *Indians of the Painted Desert Region*, recorded the Chemehuevi's impassioned appeal to the Havasupai at a dance where an agent from the Indian Office had appeared to persuade the Indians, by the offer of farming tools, to send their children to the Fort Mohave Indian School. At that time there was no school in the canyon. The Chemehuevi had been song leader at the dance, and made an eloquent appeal to the people to reject the agent's offer. He had cried:

Don't send your children to the school of the white man. If you do, they will grow up with the heart of the white man, and the place of the Havasupai will know them no more. Your tribe will be broken up, and then the white man will come and take possession of your canyon home where the stream ever flows and sings to the waving willows by its side. He will rob you of your corn fields and peach orchards. No longer will the place where the bodies of your ancestors were burned be sacred to you; your hunting grounds are now all occupied by him; the deer and the antelope have nearly disappeared before his rifle, and he is hungry to possess the few things you still have left. This offer is a secret plot against you. He thinks if he cannot drive you out he will seduce you out, and this school is the offer he makes to you, so that he can get your children into his hands. There he will teach them to make fun of you; to despise your method of living; your houses, your food, your dress, your customs, your dances will all be ridiculed by him, and so you will lose the favor of Those Above, and you yourselves will soon die and your name and tribe be forgotten.

And now the Havasupai believed that his prophecy was being fulfilled. The white men had come as predicted and taken over their canyon where the stream ever flowed. Soon they would be a homeless people.

Manakadja was deeply troubled. His tribesmen had elected him to his high office because he preached the doctrine that the white man and the Indian cannot live on the same ground; each must have his own, and there can be no encroaching, one on the other. The chief had decreed that no Havasupai blood should mingle with that of the white people, and never in the history of the tribe had there been such a marriage or mingling of blood.

But in the case of these intruders Manakadja was as helpless as any of us; so again the security of the People of the Blue Water rested in the laps of their gods.

And the gods spoke—through a storm cloud—deciding the issue with one swift blow. Work was progressing toward completion when a flood roared down the canyon, wiping out the widened, costly trail, demolishing the equipment that had disfigured Mooney Falls, and causing the firm such financial loss that the project was abandoned. The white men rode out, one afternoon, over the hastily repaired trail, leaving the canyon to the people to whom it rightfully belonged.

The power of the gods was manifest once more, renewing courage and inspiring the whole village with fresh vitality. The people worked in homes and gardens, their former cheerfulness restored by this assurance that the gods who had led them to the canyon and taught them the skills by which they had survived, were still able to defend them.

Their faith in their gods was so sincere, and they spoke of them with such candor, that I might easily have learned how much of their culture the Havasupai attributed to this source. To meet their spiritual needs, they had their god-given songs and dances. To care for their sick, the gods had taught them how to make the *toholwa* and the songs to be used in the healing ceremony. When they needed fire, the gods, through Coyote, had lighted the torch. These things I knew, but there was so much that I had failed to learn. They traced every skill to a time in the dim past when Those of Old were instructed by the deity. Now it was all too evident that some of these skills were falling into disuse.

They had been pottery makers but tin cans and lard pails had taken the place of clay utensils. Happily, baskets were still plentiful in every home. They were strong and somewhat coarse in order to stand up under the rough usage as toasting baskets, burden baskets, water bottles and general containers. However, the watertight cooking basket, used by their ancestors, into which heated stones were dropped to keep the contents boiling, was now a relic of the past. The imperfectness with which these cooked the food and the constant attention they demanded, doomed them to this fate. As the stones had cooled, they were replaced with others fresh from the bed of hot coals. Broken pieces of stone always had to be picked from the food. So these cumbersome vessels were discarded as soon as other containers were available. But the horn spoon, shaped from the horn of mountain sheep, was still in use. Making it was a tedious and lengthy process. The horn was soaked in water, then buried in moist sand until somewhat softened. The next steps —heating, oiling and fashioning the horn into a spoon or ladle— required the skill of long practice. Tin cups, obtained at the trader's store in Seligman, were gradually supplanting the horn spoon, and another skill would soon be forgotten.

In a report on conditions in the canyon for the year 1898, the acreage in cultivation and under fence was estimated at three hundred twenty-five. One thousand bushels of corn and fifty bushels of wheat were grown that year, in addition to an abundance of vegetables and fruits. And the tribe had a cash income of four thousand dollars. At that time, tribal affairs were managed almost wholly by the chief and head men, although the school had been in operation for three years. From the seeds their gods had given them, the Havasupai had reaped their independence.

They preferred their old system of barter and trade to a cash sale. The Navaho were silversmiths and weavers of warm blankets, while the friendly Hopi and Walapai had ponies or goods to trade. A Havasupai could measure out a small tray of beans and—after endless good-natured bargaining—exchange his beans for a fine Navaho blanket. Two spirals of their dried pumpkin or squash had the same value.

Every man of consequence kept a pony in his dooryard and sprang to its back to ride the short distance to a neighbor's wickiup. So horses were eagerly sought. A Hopi pony cost a large well-tanned buckskin or as much shelled corn as a large burden basket could hold. A man traded, or made gifts, for the girl he wished to marry, presenting her parents with ponies, blankets or grain to the value of about twenty dollars, if the girl was popular. Ten dollars in trade was a fair price for a lazy girl.

The men, of necessity, had developed skills. The tribe needed to move about and the obstacles of precipices and gorges could not stand in the way. They were ingenious in scaling walls, so the employees at the school merely widened the Indians' trails and used them. The men produced a superior quality of buckskin by a process of tanning with the roasted brains of deer and the marrow of the spinal cord. This was a tedious process of scraping, soaking, burying the skin in wet sand and rubbing it between the hands until soft and pliable. From these skins they had made moccasins and clothing for the entire family. But now, "store clothes" were becoming more and more common.

Even before the beginning of this century, the tribe's habits and customs were slowly yielding to the pressure of civilization. The clothes they wore, the food they ate, the language they spoke, their very thoughts were undergoing change. Instead of sitting at their grandfather's knee learning the tribe's history and the traditions that had molded the character of the people, their children were now bent over books in the classroom. At the Sunday services they were learning about a new and strange god.

But the loss that stirred the deepest resentment was that of their hunting grounds. In this their gods could do nothing. The superstitions and taboos to which a hunter must conform were now nullified by Arizona's game laws limiting the open season, which also restricted the use of charms to that brief period when deer were being slaughtered by the white man's guns. Even the prized calculus (a solid substance obtained from the paunch of a ruminant) carried by the hunter to charm the deer and make it an easy target, lost all value.

The restrictions on their hunting range were brought home to me forcibly the day a forest ranger stopped at my office and said, "I'd like to see the one in charge down here."

"I am in charge," I told him.

He regarded me coldly, then made his accusation: "You permit the Indians to kill deer out of season. It's against the law."

Someone had told. A picture flashed through my mind, one that I had acquired only a day or so previously. In the late afternoon, I was following the trail through the village when laughter and shouting broke the silence. At a home a short distance off the trail, Chickapanyegi, hot and tired, with headband askew, stood by his horse, unlashing from his saddle the carcass of a small deer. My first thought was of the violated game law. I said to him, "You know this is the closed season. Why did you kill that deer?"

He wiped the sweat from his face on his sleeve before he replied, "Indians, deer, here first. White man no here. Now white man make law. We got no meat. My family hungry."

"Eat your meat, now that you have it, but don't break the law again. I can't protect you. You will be taken away from your wife and children and sent to jail."

The crowd had grown while we talked, but they were silent, knowing well enough what was wrong and wanting to see what would be done about it.

They and the deer were here first; a close relationship existed between them. They killed only for food, and the deer spirit understood that. If one of them killed wastefully, the spirit that protected the deer would punish him with sickness and death.

I explained to the forest ranger the Indians' idea as to his ancient relationship to the deer and reminded him that the white man killed for sport, taking the legal limit and leaving to spoil the meat he could not carry away, while the Indian killed game for food and this was a sacred privilege. The ranger was as helpless as I. We both were obligated to demand respect for the law, regardless of our sympathy, but I wanted him to understand their idealistic attitude. The time would come when these Indians would need a friend at court.

"My sympathy is with the Indians too," he admitted, "but that will not keep them out of jail if they break the law."

So Vesnor and Lanoman went through the village, warning every man of the penalty of breaking the game laws.

Life among these people had taught me that we could not force them into an alien mold. We must teach them, lead them, give them time. Suspicion and superstition went hand in hand, controlling their actions. I realized that if, quite innocently, I made a decision or gave a dose of medicine and tragedy followed, I would face the same Indians, armed with the same knives and guns, who had demanded that a former teacher retract an order. Two hundred fifty against one was too great a hazard. The pleasure of working with these people had not dulled all thought of needful caution on my part. I still believed that it was better to be safe than sorry. Aside from this, I respected their deep-rooted traditions and primitive customs. So it was easy to make my administration one of give and take. I had violated an order by encouraging Manakadja to keep his two wives; my "take" had been his good will—a powerful influence in my favor.

Not long after I left the canyon, a decision by the man in charge of the tribe resulted, apparently, in the suicide of a young man. The Havasupai could not tolerate suicide. Murder—yes! What could a man do but kill to avenge a wrong? But a man should not destroy his own life. The body of a suicide could not be burned nor buried with those of their respected dead. Again they reasoned: cause and effect. And they proceeded to take action against the official who had made the decision. A hurried call to the outside for help quieted the rebellion. The old spirit of self-assertion had not yet been completely crushed, but again, as in times gone by, they felt the restraining hand of the white man's law.

All too well the Havasupai realized how government control had affected them and their way of life. Their right to kill game for the purposes of food and their freedom to roam would never be restored. One old man expressed the sentiments of all when he cried bitterly, "We are no longer men, but are little children who must *ask* when we go out or come in!"

CHAPTER TWENTY-THREE

Exodus

In November, Mr. Ewing and an inspector arrived. The matter of quarters became a problem, but we lodged the inspector in the dispensary, although he complained loudly of the odor of drugs, and Mr. Ewing shared the farmer's cottage.

Our first task was to count every item of government property from nails to buildings. While we were taking the inventory, Mr. Ewing told me that he was leaving Truxton. "How would you like to remain here in this position?" he asked. "The Indians want you to stay."

"I have just survived a flood—and falling stones," I countered. "Do you know what a flood is like down here?"

"I've heard. They're bad," he admitted.

"Well, I've learned how to escape floods. You simply scramble up to a crevice in the wall. But I'd like to return to my work at Truxton and transfer some of the older Havasupai children to that school. They are eager for the industrial training we could give them in the shops, and it would relieve the congestion in the school here."

The inspector's eyes twinkled when he said, "The truth is, Miss Gregg, the officials in the Indian Office are not sure that you have aged sufficiently to manage the larger school they have planned at Truxton. But don't worry. I have recommended that you be appointed."

I didn't worry, much. The Indian Office had kept me in this

canyon several months, instead of the one month originally planned, because they could not find a man with the necessary qualifications who would accept the superintendency at the salary paid. Educators were not clamoring for a chance to work in a canyon, isolated even from the privilege of buying from a grocery store.

Later my appointment as principal teacher of the Truxton Canyon Training School for the Walapai came through. What an imposing title for a new boarding school out in the middle of the desert! I knew that the Indian Office had combed the woods for a qualified man, for the responsibilities of this position were much greater than I had carried in the day school. I knew, too, that the inspector's recommendation had tipped the scales in my favor.

My reports and the school were ready to be turned over to my successor, but before I left the canyon I had a chance to witness the final event on the Havasupai calendar.

As jealously as the Havasupai guarded their canyon and as passionately as they loved it, the tang of autumn in the air turned their thoughts to a winter home on the mesa, and started them packing their possessions with a happy abandon. All summer they had planned for this—harvesting, preserving their food, and setting aside a portion to take with them.

Even though it was depressingly hot, the employees as well as the Indians were obliged to work harder through the summer, so that this winter outing might take place. I had taught at Truxton until school was dismissed for the summer vacation, and had quite naturally expected to be free from such duties during July and August. But no; here I must hold school through the summer and fall so that the Havasupai children's vacation might come in the winter. Nothing could be permitted to interfere with this jaunt to the outside.

The Indians used various arguments to prove the necessity for the migration. They claimed that there was not enough wood in the gorge for their cooking fires and to warm their houses. Yet they had wood to sell. They needed the wild seeds, fruits and roots that grew on top, they insisted. But, when I saw their childish delight as they made their departure, ponies loaded with cumbersome bundles, I knew that they were motivated by the very human desire for change, to get outside, where they could look about, with the full sweep of the vaulted sky above, with endless miles in which to wander.

Not an Indian who was physically able to ride but longed for this trip to the mesa. Only our policemen and the few persons needed to care for the sick and the aged stayed on through the winter.

It was a strange procession that finally departed up the trail. A single file of horses so encumbered by household equipment, clothing and food—all topped by a member of the family—that it looked like a train of bundles, walking off on four feet.

And what mysteries those bundles contained!

Near the village that fall I had watched a young woman glean the ripe fruit from a sprawling bed of prickly pear cacti by catching the fruit between two gathering sticks, and with a quick twist break it free. After removing the spines by swishing the pear with a fiber brush, she tossed the clean pear into the burden basket on her back. At home any remaining spines would be wiped off before the fruit was split and laid in the sun to dry. She had approached her task fully prepared with gathering sticks, brush and burden basket. Tied in those huge bundles that obscured their ponies, I knew, were the crude, homemade tools they would use in gathering the many edible wild plants that grew up above.

The pigweed on the mesa should be a luscious bush loaded with small rich seeds. Its leaves, boiled, were eaten as a vegetable; the ripe seeds were toasted, ground and cooked into a mush. Mormon tea would be gathered, dried and stored to be brewed in a refreshing drink. The dry pods of the mesquite were sweet and nourishing; they were chewed for their food value or, reduced to a powder and mixed with water, used as a drink. Fall ripened the fruit of the yucca, which was an important food. After frost, the Indians would comb the desert for the piñon nuts, oily and pungent, as they fell from the pine trees. The desert, which yielded its store of food to those who knew where to search for it, was ripe for the harvest.

Each day one or more groups climbed the trail, bound for Seligman to loaf about the trader's store, or for the pueblos of the Hopi or the scattered villages of the Walapai. They would denude the plateau of its food plants as they traveled. Laughing, shouting back merry good-bys to us, they climbed the trail. The canyon seemed full of empty houses.

From their talk I gathered a clear picture of their life on the upper level. They would kill an occasional deer or mountain sheep, if no white man were about; even without these there would be meat, for rabbits were plentiful. They satisfied their need for sweets by robbing bees' nests hidden in clefts in walls or in hollow trees. Long ago they had found a cave in a distant cliff that contained more rock salt than they could use. So with vegetables, meat, salt and honey in addition to the supplies they took with them, their needs would be satisfied.

When harsh winter set in, they would retire to their small, tight winter houses in the cedar thickets and live off their stored foods. One of the most delicious of these was the corn that had been roasted in the husk, while fresh and green, dried somewhat and stored. They would cook the ears in boiling water and the grains would have the sweetness of fresh corn.

Those who had not bothered to bring cooking pots, drew on the desert's reserve by burning the spines from a section of barrel cactus, removing the center pulp, and using the cavity for the old-time method of stone boiling. Accustomed to making the most of the things at hand in the desert, on the mountains, or wherever they might be, the women cooked mush and boiled vegetables or meat in this unique container, giving no thought to the hardship involved.

Melting snows and swelling buds would start the wanderers leisurely homeward, pausing on the way to reap a rich harvest from the agave, commonly called the mescal plant. Families worked in groups, first testing the plants for ripeness by thrusting a sharpened stick into their hearts. If they were soft and juicy, the harvest was on. With a wooden wedge the women pried the entire plant from the soil, cut away the outer leaves and tossed the fibrous pulp into their burden baskets. A large pit was dug, wood put in, set on fire and covered with stones. Someone accustomed to the task piled the hearts into the heated pit, using a cross layer to separate the mescal belonging to one family from that of another. These tasks were performed with high good humor. When the pit was filled to a depth of four or five feet, the mescal was covered with a layer of grass and leaves, on which dirt was piled to hold the heat. At the end of two days, the hearts were soft and brown. Each woman took her share, spread it on a wide stone surface, and pounded it into a thin sheet three feet wide and twice as long. This was quickly dried in the hot sun, then folded into a slab for convenient storing.

The mescal pit yielded the brown paint about which Carl had told me at Truxton. The stones on which the plants rested in the roasting pit were heavily coated with the burned juice. This was either scraped from the stones or soaked in water which was later evaporated by boiling. When the right consistency was reached, red mineral paint was added to thicken it to a putty-like substance of the desired shade for facial decoration.

My successor finally arrived. He was young, friendly, quick to co-operate, and his wife was charming. They were a bit shaken from the descent of the trail, and appalled at finding themselves in so deep a gorge, but quickly made their adjustment, and were eager to begin work. I remained for a few days to help them get acquainted with conditions and to check the government property, which I would turn over to him.

Again I fitted my things into the clumsy packsaddles, this time for the trip out. As I packed, the remark made by an Indian lad to a lazy boy who refused to work, ran through my mind: "Well, what are you going to do—just stand there and breathe?" With the Indians out on the mesa, and no school to teach, perhaps the new man would have time to do just that. I envied him. Yet I knew that this was his first association with the Indian people, and he would need the time to become acquainted with those remaining in the village and to understand the Indians' slow transition from primitive life to the complexities of modern civilization.

On the day of my departure the few friends who were still in the village came up to say good-by. Vesnor and Lanoman, Walapai Bill, old Captain Gabe came—and precious, old, Gentle Annie, wearing my strawberry-red dress, much dimmed by constant washing in the stream and exposure to sun. We shook hands. Questions were asked, "Why you go? You no come back?" Gentle Annie's gnarled fingers clung to my hand. "You no go," she insisted. "Pretty good you stay."

They were anxious about the future. The one in charge of the reservation could assume almost any authority over them that he pleased; and strong men that they were, they resented being told when they might "go out or come in."

Few farewells have been so difficult for me.

At Hilltop that night we cooked our supper on a stove that had been set up in the warehouse for use during inclement weather. We ate outside in the frosty air, only a few yards from that bowl-shaped abyss which had so filled me with awe the last time I stood on its rim. I had been uncertain then as to what I might find at the end of the trail. Now I knew that there were floods, and falling columns of stone; that the thermometer soared to one hundred and seventeen degrees and forgot to come down. But I knew also that a kindly, trusting people lived there—a people gifted with native wisdom, warm with laughter and carefree play; and children who needed an uncrowded school, offering better opportunities for adjustment to the alien culture we were thrusting upon them. And there were canyon walls with their guarded secrets—one of them a sealed cave filled with the ancient arms and tools of Those of Old.

I climbed to the wagon seat for the two-day drive to Seligman, facing the painful fact that my exodus, unlike that of the People of the Blue Water, would be final. When the snow melted, and the old cottonwoods felt the touch of the warm sun, the wanderers would return. I had a pang of regret in realizing that my successor would have the fun of hearing the exciting stories of the winter's exodus and witnessing their eagerness to work again in their gardens while it was "little light." Yet I found consolation in the thought that a larger field of service awaited me at Truxton where some of the older Havasupai children would join us to share the greater opportunities.

PART THREE

Back to Truxton Canyon

CHAPTER TWENTY-FOUR

The Circling Year

Truxton and the Walapai at last! It was a sunny day in late November—only a few days from December's wintry winds—when the porter swung my luggage down to the sand, then helped me alight. The wide canyon with its long stretches of sparkling sand encircled by familiar mountains and mesas, the greetings of teachers and pupils, made me feel immediately at home again.

From the usual crowd of boys waiting to see who got off the train, Sam, with his old infectious grin, came forward to welcome me. He took my traveling bags and asked, "We going to have school now, Miss Gregg?"

I remembered how impatient many of the children had been to escape from school, so eager for a summer free from restraint. "Are you anxious for school to start?" I laughed.

"We've been out a long time. Not much to do around here," he answered.

The children now lived at the school. The older boys and girls had been working in the industrial departments all fall, but the classroom work awaited my return; they had had too much idle time on their hands. I too was eager to get started, for we had missed three months of the school year and the work somehow must be made up during the winter and spring. Pupils had been brought in from remote parts of the enormous Walapai Reservation, children for whom we had not had room in the old day school. We would have a busy year.

I soon learned how completely things had changed during my stay in Supai. Mr. Ewing had been removed from office and had gone to his farm somewhere out in the desert. I never learned the exact charges against him. He had bitter enemies—cattlemen and ranchers he had forced off the Indians' land, and others who accused him of being arrogant, rejoicing to see how the mighty had fallen. He also had staunch friends. No jury would convict him, but he died a broken and disillusioned man.

Dr. Perkins, who had been employed as physician at the Chilocco Indian School in Oklahoma, was now superintendent of our new boarding school. He was also medical doctor for the Walapai tribe, the school children and the employees. By putting the duties of two positions on one man, the Indian Office realized a saving in salaries, but it made a very busy man of Dr. Perkins. Frequently he was called to attend a sick Indian on a distant part of the reservation while we had sick children at the school, and his duties as administrator piled up in the office.

The Doctor's young, attractive wife was also employed. We loved her at once, and she became affectionately known as "Perkie" among those of us who were her close friends.

At dinner, the night of my return to Truxton, I was introduced to Daisy Rice, a willowy girl, with abundant brown hair, who was adept at making people laugh. But those in trouble soon learned the warmth of her kindness and sympathy. I discovered that her clowning was camouflage. Daisy's thoughts were constantly of her twin sister, who had recently died, and for whom she wore mourning year after year. Another sister, Sara, small, fair and eternally blushing at Daisy's pranks, was the primary teacher. The girls claimed one-sixteenth Sioux blood, which we never would have suspected had they not told us.

Some of our new pupils would be Walapai children from the Kingman Day School, so we expected their arrival—but not in the way it occurred.

One bright afternoon shortly before school was to open, a freight train stopped where our dirt road crossed the track. (We and the train crews referred to this spot as Truxton Station.) Perkie and Daisy, standing in the front entrance of the main building, watched, puzzled, for no freight was being unloaded. Suddenly bright sunbonnets popped over the side of a freight car; the sunbonnets and long, striped-shirting dresses scrambled down the sides and tumbled to the ground. The girls of the Kingman school had arrived by freight! Led by their matron, they marched in formation to the girls' building, while Perkie and Daisy doubled up with laughter. We knew then that all we had heard about the severe discipline at the Kingman school was true. Could we have put large gaudy sunbonnets on *our* girls? I think not; anyway, we didn't try. The Truxton children had a sense of independence and a love of the hot sunshine on their black heads that we respected. Our pupils giggled and tittered every time a sunbonnet came into view, until Perkie finally banished them.

The principal of the Kingman school was an exacting man who had precise methods of teaching. When reciting, the pupils read in unison in monotonous, loud voices that became a roar. Mr. Ewing had told us that the people of Kingman, hearing them, would laugh and say, "The Indians down at the school are reading their lessons."

However, the pupils reacted to the strict discipline somewhat as did the Pilgrim fathers. It developed sturdy, hard-working, reliable children. So when I learned that the man who had been principal there had made a determined fight to secure the principal-ship at Truxton, I was convinced that his work at Kingman might have won him the position I now held had not those sunbonnets been his undoing. Perhaps one of the several inspectors, who traveled from school to school to evaluate the work, couldn't tolerate the idea of sunbonnets on the unwilling heads of desert Indian girls.

Twenty children came from Supai, partly to relieve the conges-tion in the Havasupai school, but also, the children wanted the industrial training we now could offer with our new equipment. They were timid by nature and, in a strange environment, became discouragingly self-effacing. When one of them stood to read, his voice dwindled to a whisper. Then one of the Kingman pupils would yell his way through his reading assignment winning the wide-eyed admiration of the Truxton and the Havasupai children.

The school became a melting pot: three groups tossed in with the expectation that they would fuse and come out a perfect whole. Although the Walapai children from Kingman, those from Truxton and the Havasupai children were all of the same blood, environment had cast each group into a different mold. However, it worked out to the advantage of all; each group acquired some of the virtues of the other two. When Miss Estella Reel, Supervisor of Education for Indian schools, paid her official visit, she congratulated us on the way each pupil read in a clear, distinct voice and the speed and accuracy with which the children solved difficult problems. The melting pot had toned down the Kingman children and boosted the morale of the Havasupai: we had a good school.

Miss Reel shocked some old-timers in the Service by declaring that Indians had a natural appreciation of beauty developed through their closeness to nature. To prove it, she ordered attractive percale prints to replace the ugly shirting from which the girls' dresses were made. It was such a drastic, unheard-of change that many doubted her wisdom until they saw the pride that the girls took in keeping their pretty new dresses clean. Miss Reel also insisted on a more varied diet for the children, refusing to accept the time-honored excuse that the food served in the schools was better than that available in the children's homes.

In this new boarding school the boys were instructed in engineering, carpentry, painting and masonry. The girls were trained in the skills of homemaking. The principle of industrial training had been introduced in the first Indian schools, established by the Quakers, for the purpose of preparing the children to become self-supporting. When the government took over Indian education, the schools were patterned on this very successful method.

Our school was on a remote reservation, so we were not permitted to teach high-school subjects, but transferred our graduates to the Phoenix Indian School or one of the other large schools.

By changing to a boarding school we had unwittingly increased our problems. The warm fall days added to them. The children always resented confinement; they wanted to mount their ponies and gallop up the mountains or across the mesas to secret places they knew, where nature was lavish and completely wild. High in the mountains were meadows with bubbling streams, thickets in which the crested quail gathered at nightfall, and rocky heights, sheltering wild burros to be lassoed. Confined to quarters, the children grew moody; and a moody Indian means trouble. To ease them over this period of adjustment, we allowed them to return to the village, which was across a low hill to the west, whenever work or school duties did not interfere. Some were permitted to remain at home over the week end—until we learned what sometimes happened there. Dot, a primary pupil, failed to return after one of these visits.

Dot was a short, dumpling-like girl of twelve, as full of play as a kitten, and yet her hair was as gray as that of a very old woman. No one, not even the Indians, could explain Dot's hair, but its grayness had no subduing effect on her personality.

After a week's absence Dot returned. When questioned she ducked her head, giggled and said she had been sick. As usual, the primary pupils, who knew all and told all, had the answer. Their teacher had asked her class why Dot was absent. Piping up in a chorus, they explained that the Indians had performed over Dot the ceremony that changes a child into a marriageable woman. (The one word they used to describe her illness is a bit too graphic for print.)

Dot had reached the age of puberty and during her absence from school, the Indians had put her through an ancient ritual. She had been bathed with soap from the yucca plant, her hair washed, her face and body painted, then she was placed on a bed of heated stones and warmly covered. By her side sat an old woman, monotonously instructing her in what would now be her duties as wife and homemaker. She should be industrious, gather wild seeds, grind them into meal, that her family might have good food. Each domestic task was named and eulogized and tied in with the duty of serving her man. Aside from her household tasks, there was little that even an old woman could teach to a girl of Dot's age; life was lived openly in a small house of one room.

The child was not permitted to sleep but must listen all night to the old woman squatted at her bedside. At dawn, Dot rose and ran swiftly toward the rising sun, allowing no one to overtake her, to prove her fleetness and strength.

After conforming to this exhausting ritual, repeated many times in the four-day ceremony, we expected Dot to be minus some of her avoirdupois and giggle. But she had lost neither. She was the same fat, gray-haired Dot, only her cheeks had a new glow and her eyes a knowing sparkle, of which the boys took notice.

Dot's experience had a disturbing effect on our girls, reminding them of the old tribal ceremonies in which they longed to participate. They became restless, increasing the problem of discipline. One Saturday evening Daisy and I were in Dr. Perkins' office, working on quarterly reports, when the door opened and one of the older girls solemnly announced, "Mab is dead." We hurried to the dormitory.

Mab lay on her bed, apparently unconscious. A group of girls stood anxiously about. One of them said in an awed voice, "I not hit hard. She just go dead." She was the other participant in a quarrel that had ended in a fight. When the odds had gone against Mab, she eliminated herself from the unequal contest by falling on the bed in this form of hysteria to which Walapai women resorted when caught in a tight place. Such scenes were not new to Dr. Perkins; one quick slap brought Mab back to consciousness with astonishing suddenness.

However, the girls' loneliness in the foreign atmosphere of the boarding school had one effect that delighted us: each of the older girls "adopted" a smaller one, trying to take the place of the child's mother. She combed her hair, dressed her and comforted her when she was homesick.

In their own homes, the girls had been kept under a watchful parental eye, and we were careful to give them even better protection. The building and the campus had a dividing line: the east half belonged to the girls; the west half to the boys. But whereas the girls were restricted to their section, the boys were allowed to roam the near-by country. We took the girls on frequent long walks, either for a visit to their village or to some point of interest on the desert, but the restlessness engendered by the confinement of boarding school life and the sudden close association of three different groups of children was bound to explode in some way.

I was in my room one evening, writing letters home, when I heard running feet on the stairs; someone knocked sharply. My door was pushed open, and Daisy said, "You're needed in the dining room. The girls are acting crazy."

I had made out the detail that placed those twenty girls in the dining room, so felt responsible for their behavior. Their duties were simple. They set the tables and placed the food on them. After the meal, they carried the dishes to the kitchen, cleaned the tables, swept the floor and reset the tables for breakfast. But what I saw when I entered the dining hall was shocking.

The twenty girls moved about with a dazed look on their faces, some with arms outstretched, hands groping. Their eyes had the wild glitter and the inability to focus that sometimes characterize the eyes of the insane. The color had drained from their faces. Habit asserted itself, and some of the girls went about their usual task, trying to remove the dishes from the tables. Their dazed minds could not estimate distances; their shaking hands groped for the dishes, trying to grasp those beyond reach. Bertha, a tall, thin girl, daughter of a chief, carried her dishes to the kitchen sink, washed them, reset the table, then immediately picked up the dishes and went through the same performance, repeating it several times. Dot ran about the dining hall lunging at imaginary mice, then baffled, stared at her empty, trembling hands. Mabel, in a daze, went from one girl to another under the delusion she was picking lice from their heads and cracking them between her teeth as she had seen a few of the older women do. The matron was frantically trying to learn the cause of the girls' behavior.

Don, Seth and Sam silently entered the dining room, but stood back, watching intently. We asked them for an explanation, for since the girls had not had access to the school dispensary, they almost certainly were under the influence of some drug known to the Indians. The boys only shook their heads.

Someone had sent for Dr. Perkins. He gave the situation a quick glance. "Stramonium," he diagnosed. "They found a patch of Jimson weed, and are suffering from poison." He ordered an emetic. The girls drank the distasteful concoction, although we were almost certain it was too late to be of benefit. It took effect immediately, and after we had put the sick girls in bed, an investigation began.

We learned that when the dining room girls had finished their work and were dismissed after the noon meal, they went to the base of the mountain east of the school to play. Somewhere in that wasteland they found a patch of tall, big-leaved Jimson weeds. The girls knew what the plant was, and that if they ate it they would "go crazy." They knew that Fred, a boy in my classroom, had been given Jimson weed by the medicine man to induce the hallucinations through which the shamanistic spirit is acquired. The tribe needed more medicine men, and the shaman was teaching Fred the mysteries of his cult. But the drug had dulled the boy's mind, and had left him weak and physically ill. He was considered unfit material for a medicine man; his training was discontinued. There was not much anyone could do for Fred; he was unable to comprehend the classroom work, and not strong enough to work in a shop. Knowing these facts, the girls had eaten both leaves and seeds of the plant.

Miss Calfee and I spent that night caring for the sick. Dot, who had so recently arrived at womanhood, spent the night catching grasshoppers, instead of the mice she had chased in the dining hall. To her drugged mind the air was full of them; the hallucination was so frightful that she was unable to sleep for thirty-six hours. Bertha Tokespeta lay in a state of shock, eyes staring, until her dreams became too horrible to be endured, then she would call in a frantic whisper, "Miss Gregg! Miss Gregg!" When I went to her, she clung to my hand for a few minutes, then sank back into her dreams. We knew of no magic way to mitigate the effect of the drug, so kept the girls in bed until they became normal, which wearied all of us with nights and days of constant nursing.

The patch of Jimson weeds was destroyed, but that did not end the menace, for scattered here and there were other plants. We could not hope to strip the desert. If we passed the matter off as unimportant, our little folks would be experimenting with the poisonous weed, and there would be no end to the harm done. They were daring, and even though their parents had warned them of its effect, they would learn in their own way. So we pitted Solomon's wisdom against that of the Walapai, who abhorred punishment of children for any reason whatsoever. The girls were deprived of the privilege of attending the weekly dance, denied trips to the village and other social pleasures.

The next Saturday afternoon six of the older girls hunted over the grounds east of the school until they found a few plants, and learned by experience what the weed would do to them. But they were more cautious than the dining room girls had been, and only their unsteady movements and the wild look in their eyes betrayed them. By this time we had begun to suspect that we might be in for a Jimson weed epidemic, for each would experiment for himself unless we could find something more effective than punishment and our talks to prevent them.

Even so, it came as a terrific shock when a group of our older boys, including Don, Seth and Jim, boys we had found trustworthy and dependable in every emergency, went on a Jimson weed debauch. When they were sufficiently recovered to talk, they could give no explanation for their act except that they wanted to see how it felt to "get drunk" like the other children. However, one of them admitted that they ate the Jimson weed because they were not allowed to hunt rabbits and quail, to climb mountains and to ride their ponies when they pleased. When confused or angry, the Walapai turned to trickery; the children missed the complete freedom they had enjoyed at home, and this form of revolt gave them a peculiar satisfaction.

None of us sympathized with Don and Seth. They had helped us instruct the younger children as to the dangers of the drug, and the pupils looked to them as examples in good behavior.

But with Jim it was a different matter.

Our hearts ached when we realized that his mind might never recover from the effect of the stramonium. For a long time he was desperately ill, making little progress toward recovery. When he returned to the classroom, he was no longer the first to complete the problems in fractions or percentage, but stood at the blackboard with a pained expression on his once bright and handsome face, trying to force his dull mind to perform tasks to which it was no longer equal. The children were so shocked at the change the weed had made in Jim that they had no desire to experiment further. They even forgot their resentment at the loss of their freedom and helped destroy every Jimson weed that could be found.

Except for the lingering effect on Jim, the stramonium episode was rarely mentioned by the time Christmas came that year.

We were in the midst of a cold winter. Snow and biting winds made us huddle in our wraps when we went out of doors. A white Christmas was not unusual in this section of Arizona, and the shimmering expanse made a beautiful picture. The colorful sands lay under a thin white blanket, each desert bush bowed under a white cap, and mountains and mesas wore ermine robes. But brilliant sunshine all too soon restored the vivid color to our familiar landscape, leaving no mud, just moist sand that gave pleasantly under the feet.

We celebrated the holiday in the children's dining hall. A magnificent evergreen, ceiling high, was brought in from the mountains and Miss Calfee loaded it with gifts that had been donated by friends in the East. There were bags of candy, nuts and fruit bought with school funds. It was an old-fashioned Sunday school Christmas celebration, and took me back to those that had been so dear to me in my childhood. We sang Christmas carols, the children repeated verses from the Scriptures, and Miss Calfee offered a prayer. After the gifts were distributed, a Christmas dinner was served, trimmings and all. A few of the parents from the village had attended the religious service. Those who wished— which was every one of them—remained to share the children's dinner of roast pork, mashed potatoes, candied sweet potatoes, vegetable, fresh baked bread, pie and coffee. Old Indians who never before had sat with their feet under a table, laughed and chatted noisily over this unaccustomed feast.

Lengthening days and gentle rains soon indicated a changing rhythm and our long cozy evening gatherings began to take on a monotony. Suddenly—overnight it seemed—a thin green carpet spread over the desert and the orchards bloomed. Another spring had come to Truxton Canyon, and we looked forward to the adventures the outdoor months would bring.

CHAPTER TWENTY-FIVE

Donkeys Pay Dividends

⬤ Warm sunny days and a restlessness that a magazine or the latest book could not satisfy, took Daisy and me down to the Indian village on our free Saturday and Sunday afternoons. Wandering from wickiup to wickiup visiting with the people, we often found a burro or two browsing near a home. Children climbed on their backs and laughing and shouting, rode down to the wash or sent the animals scrambling up a slope to a side gorge. That gave us an idea—we must own burros. We had visions of riding gaily off to one of the ranches farther up the canyon for a refreshing chat with people who were as isolated, socially, as we. Or a trip to a mountain canyon watered by a lively stream and, at this time of the year, gay with delicate flowers.

Whatever Daisy did she did with vigor. She dashed about, greeting the people as if they were lifelong friends, making comments that brought shouts of laughter. When she had everyone in a jolly mood, she broached the subject of burros. In our rounds we eventually came upon a lovely tan donkey standing in the scant shade of a wickiup.

"Let's buy him!" Daisy exclaimed, delighted. Her long black skirts swishing, she walked to him, stepped astride his back and lifted her feet, expecting to ride. The animal did not move. A ripple of laughter ran through the group that had gathered. Daisy dismounted, a procedure which took little effort; her feet had been practically on the ground.

We were near Suja's home, and he came out to exercise his inalienable right to handle the situation.

When Daisy told him that we wanted to buy the burro, he pointed with his lips to Grace's small home at the base of a cliff.

Grace was sitting on a blanket in the yard playing with her baby, who ran happily about, his entire body exposed to the warm sunshine. We asked for Boots. "He work mine," she told us, a worried look on her face. Quickly her hands went up, she blew in the open palms and with a sweeping gesture brought them down over her face and body, as Boots had once done. It was the Walapai's way of saying, "Blow away, evil spirit! Blow away!" Boots had returned to his work at the mine. She was remembering the accident that had happened there and was trying to shield him from harm.

When we asked if she would sell the burro, she replied, "I sell, five dollar. Boots want burro, catch plenty on mountain."

Daisy urged me to buy saying she would find another as good. Five dollars and the burro changed owners with no loss of time.

Later, after a good deal of dickering, we found another—a skinny, slate-gray animal whose stubbornness shone in her eyes.

We led the burros down to the road early Saturday afternoon planning to take a short ride up toward Crozier. But they refused to budge.

"He no go! He no go!" Suja, who had come to see the take-off, cackled. One old Indian called, "Use spur. Burro savvy spur." In lieu of spurs, we dug our heels in the burros' flanks. They turned melancholy eyes to question our motives. When we used a switch, they merely wiggled their tails. By the middle of the afternoon Daisy and I gave up. We turned them loose near a pile of tin cans where they began polishing labels.

The Indians continued instructing us in the management of Jack and Jill, but we lacked their skill in handling burros. Our donkey-riding days were brief—their wills being stronger than ours. Sam drove the team and we took the little scamps up in the mountains turning them loose to join the wild herd in which we had decided they belonged.

We were driving slowly back to the school when Sam pointed to a canyon, and said, "That's Cottonwood Canyon. Some Indians have gardens up there." We were more delighted with Sam's improvement in the use of English than with the information. In their native tongue, the Indians expressed their thoughts in names and action words. For an Indian, Sam was loquacious. However, we wanted to see the Walapai farther out on the reservation who lived as they pleased, beyond the influence of the white man, so drove up the canyon to its dead end. Here a stream of clear water fell from a high cliff flowing down over a satiny face of tilted stone into a pool fringed with spring flowers.

With Sam leading, we scrambled up the canyon wall, using footholds and handholds the Indians had made, until we reached the top of the falls. A wide mountain valley dotted with pine trees and flanked by sharp peaks spread out in front of us. Shaded by giant cottonwoods and willows, the snug log houses of several Indian families sat close to the grassy banks of the stream. Horses were grazing in their dooryards; dogs ran out to bark at us, and the commotion set flocks of crested quail on the wing. The Indians, irrigating or cultivating their crops, glanced up inquiringly, then went on with their work. I understood, now, why the Indians in the village near the school had lost their childlike happiness. They, the Tall Pine People, had come from homes like these to the parched desert to build shelters from scraps, to carry loads of water a long distance, to be buffeted and beaten by sand-laden winds.

We were obligated to Jack and Jill, the little nuisances, for this glimpse of the Walapai, living in abundance, game plentiful, gardens luxurious, in an isolated valley not yet claimed by the white man. But this did not end our obligation to Jack and Jill for they were instrumental in giving us another unusual adventure.

While we owned them, the two donkeys had often disappeared from the school grounds to browse about in the Indian village.

The people took a lively interest in helping us locate them, for being donkey riders brought us to their level. Daisy and I took advantage of this pleasant relationship to learn as much as we could of the things the Indians believed but spoke of only among themselves.

That is how we learned of the mysterious cave.

From several of the Indians we had heard strange stories of a cavern in the rimrock of a distant mesa. Only a medicine man could enter it and remain alive. Ghosts made it their home, and those who came in contact with ghosts, sickened and died. There were many rooms in the cave, some extending far back into the mesa. No one had ever gone the entire length of them; the bones of two Indian men who had tried to explore them lay in some unknown recess or tunnel. So, of course, we promptly organized an expedition; Daisy, her sister Sara, Frances, who had been transferred from Supai to Truxton, and I determined to see the cavern for ourselves—and return alive.

This, we argued, would help free the Indians from at least one superstition; in those days we gave much thought to freeing the Indians from any inhibition that hindered their progress toward the white man's civilization. We also looked eagerly forward to a pleasant jaunt to the outside. We couldn't miss that.

First, we secured Dr. Perkins' permission to use one of the school teams and a spring wagon. It would be useless to ask any man of the village to drive to the cave, so we tried to persuade some of the older schoolboys to drive the team. No one would go. Even the offer of cash did not tempt them. When we had given up hope, Ben, the tallest, thinnest boy in the school, offered. We chose a holiday for the trip. Then two inspectors arrived and we faced a dilemma: to go and let them form what opinion they would of our work or stay and make an impression. We decided to go. If we gave up the trip now, after conquering so many obstacles, we would never make it.

We packed a good hearty lunch for five people and were ready for the great adventure early in the morning. The inspectors came to the wagon to see us off, looked through the basket of lunch and almost decided to accompany us; the fare was tempting. They commented on the trimmed and filled lantern we were taking to explore the cavern's darkest passages and reminded us, jestingly, that this was the final journey, the one from which we would not return.

For five long miles we jolted over the rocky, washed-out road; then, surprisingly, we were out of our canyon. So long as I live I shall not forget the exaltation of that moment. Each of us felt it. No enclosing walls to shut out the sky and distant views! Even Ben felt the same joyous reaction. We laughed, sang and shouted listening to the echo from distant cliffs, our exuberance unbounded. I realized now how our school children felt when they gazed with dreamy eyes at the far heights looming above our canyon rim. This was their playground. Here in the harmony of sun and wind and space they were in tune with their surroundings.

We drove miles and miles across the roadless desert to the base of a broad, lonely mesa. There we left the team and wagon. It was a two-mile climb up to the cave.

Its enormous mouth, seventy-five feet high and about half as wide, had the imposing dignity of an old cathedral entrance. Yet, as we stood at the mesa's base gazing up at that shadowed opening, we felt strangely sad.

The main room, about fifty feet long but very wide, arched up to an incredibly high ceiling. We paused at the entrance, sensing the mystery within when two owls floated out of the darkness and drifted slowly over our heads to the outside. Bats followed, a cloud of them, squeaking faintly. Trails worn deep by the feet of many animals led from the desert, across this room, to the mouths of side caverns.

We lighted the lantern and started to explore to the very end of the farthest cavern, but soon discovered that the small openings leading into them were almost closed by deep deposits of animal droppings, stones that had fallen from the walls, and dry powdery dust. If we were to free the Indians of their superstitious fears, we must do more than take a look around and leave. There were low openings through which, we could tell by the spoor, large animals entered their secluded lairs by crawling through on their bellies. We kept our dignity and left belly-crawling to the big cats.

But we did find a deep crack in one rubble-choked entrance that led back to a large room into which our lantern threw a feeble beam. I worked through and over the filthy debris until the aperture almost pinched out. I could go no farther without crawling on my hands and knees through the dehydrated excrement and thick dust. My teacherish qualms as to sanitation prevailed over my explorer's urge; the big cats could have this room too so far as I was concerned.

The cavern was filled with that intense, weird silence of dead places: dead walls, dead rooms, dead dust—and, outside, the too quiet desert. Yet, through the silence, from distant caverns came whispering sounds. Moving feet? Slow, drifting wings? Angry, swishing tails? We could not tell. Undoubtedly mountain lions, possibly wildcats and coyotes lived and bred in the inner caves. I was wondering what we would do if one sprang at us from an opening when Daisy exclaimed, "Ghosts or no ghosts, let's go down and eat. I could devour every bite in the basket." She walked out of the cave, swinging the lantern as she went, and started down the slope.

Suddenly we were more interested in the lunch basket than in musty old caves or Indian superstitions, so rushed out after her and raced down the side of the mesa. Ben fed the team while we spread the lunch on newspapers, then the five of us ate very leisurely, sitting on the sand in the wagon's shade; quite unaccountably, everything seemed tremendously funny. It was fun to be out on the desert with no other person within miles and miles; it was fun to have nothing to do but have fun. But after lunch, we discovered our tiredness; the musty cave dirt was in our hair, on our clothing, and in our nostrils. The roadless desert, reaching out in every direction, brush-studded, punctuated by high cliffs, had lost its illusion of freedom and become a dry waste of land, lonely and desolate. We drove back to the school, arriving at eight o'clock that night.

We lost no time in assuring the inspectors that we *had* returned alive, then raided the pantry in a way that made a deep impression on the mess cook when she came down to prepare breakfast the next morning.

The village Indians looked with ill favor on our expedition. Ben was gently chided by the old men, but even they realized that tribal traditions were losing their hold; the wisdom of the old men could not compete with the "paper learning" their children gleaned from the books they read in the school.

Daisy and I were forgiven for entering their ghost-inhabited cave. They had not forgotten that we had been donkey owners; we were friends, not just teachers at the school. Our investment in donkeys had paid satisfactory dividends.

School closed for vacation in June—the hottest month of the year, the children had decided one day in the geography class. July and August would bring the summer rains, but now heat rose in waves from the hot sand wilting vegetation and human beings alike. The gray-green desert shrubs grew dull and colorless under their coat of fine dust. The Indians lost no time in deserting their shacks on the windy slope for timbered mountains or shaded streams. I thought of Cottonwood Canyon, high, cool, hedged in by stony peaks—an inviting spot for a summer outing. I could understand the Indians' haste to seek these old familiar haunts.

I had been granted educational leave to attend the National Education Association in Minneapolis to be followed by my annual vacation at home. My month with the family seemed far too short. Long before I felt ready to leave, I was at the Edmond station boarding a train once more for Truxton Canyon.

CHAPTER TWENTY-SIX

Smallpox and Sen-Sen

In late August, Indian wagons streamed in over the sandy road bringing the children back to school. The men sat importantly on the spring seats while the women bounced over the rough terrain in the wagon bed, their gay dresses and the men's gaudy shirts making bright splashes of color.

At the edge of the school grounds, the wagons disgorged their human load and an assortment of bags and bundles. Cooking fires were lighted. In a jiffy savory pots were simmering and thin bread was baking on heated stones. These cooking fires became the mecca of the children who had previously returned and were living at the school. They were drawn by the tantalizing odor of familiar foods and the mystery of unopened bundles. Daisy and I could not miss this excitement, and went from camp to camp to see which children had returned, even tasting unidentifiable foods.

We were eating the crisp, thin sheets of corn bread the women peeled from their baking stones when one of the men asked suddenly, "Where burros?"

We told him we had turned them loose in a grassy meadow. He pondered this for a frowning moment, then grinning, exclaimed, "I go catch. Maybe sell you, five dollar!" So we were again established as donkey riders! Our Walapai friends remembered!

Sara, the primary teacher, and I opened school that fall with crowded classrooms, even putting chairs in the aisles to accommodate the overflow until Miss Kenderdine, the recently appointed kindergarten teacher, should arrive. Day after day, expecting her, we watched the trains but each night brought disappointment. Finally, one blustery November evening when we were at dinner, the train slid to a stop a short distance beyond the house.

Perkie laughed and exclaimed, "Oh, my goodness, there's the new teacher—on a night like this!" I thought of my own arrival— alone and bewildered in the deep railroad cut. I, at least, had had daylight! This girl was alone on a dark, stormy night. Perkie left her dinner, lighted a lantern, and ran out to the track.

In the darkness, she heard a girl cry out, "What shall I do? What shall I do?"

The reassuring voice of the conductor answered, "Oh, you'll be all right. Someone will come for you."

The girl, catching sight of Perkie and her bobbing lantern, called with evident relief, "There comes someone with a lantern!" The train rolled away in the darkness and Perkie brought the new teacher down to the dining room.

Miss Kenderdine was a slender, quiet, reserved brunette, a typical Eastern girl. More than the miles she had traveled separated Pennsylvania from Arizona. The barrenness of the land must have shocked one accustomed to verdant hills and tilled fields. The lack of churches, clubs, social organizations and neighbors gave a newcomer a forlorn, lonely feeling, but she took her place in the school activities with the grace of an old-timer. The kindergarten was organized, relieving the other classrooms of the most disturbing element, the little folks, full of chatter in their own tongue, unable to make their wants known in English.

Our object in adding the kindergarten department was to give the small children better care and more nourishing food than the homes provided. Also, supervised play, learning songs and games, helped them forget homesickness and acquainted them with the routine of school life. The Indians were beginning to realize that the boarding school provided good food, warm clothing and comfortable surroundings for the children, so brought them in willingly.

With Perkie's help, we planned a gay social winter—after two stagnant years. The young people of Hackberry drove out to our dances and parties; when they arrived the fun began. Even a few outsiders livened things up wonderfully. In return we attended the Hackberry dances. Some of the cowboys were shy at first about dancing with "schoolmarms" until they learned that we were not averse to stamping feet, enthusiastic yips and yells, or to their trick of lifting a girl off her feet and swinging her round, and round, and round.

But our fun ended suddenly and in an unexpected way.

Early in December, a few of the children developed chicken pox, brought to the school by a new pupil. Soon others came down with it. Dr. Perkins suspected that one or two of these cases might be smallpox; it was almost impossible to differentiate one disease from the other.

The sick children were isolated, and we hoped to escape an epidemic. Two weeks later, one of my boys smiled at me brightly and said, "I got a bellyache. I want to go to sleep."

Doctor pronounced it smallpox. Then we knew there would be no Christmas for us that year, for the boy had exposed others, and down they came until the beds were full. One afternoon Dr. Perkins came to my classroom and said, "I want you to see an interesting case. It's smallpox, a good old-fashioned case of it, so you should take precautions."

I slipped on a long-sleeved apron that came down to my feet and followed him to the room where Fanny lay sick. I stood by her bed and stared in dismay at the purple lumps, as large as plums, that distorted her flesh. She looked almost blue-black. Dr. Perkins had ordered cloths, saturated with a preparation he had given the temporary nurse, kept on the faces of those he suspected of having smallpox, so no one was disfigured. The nurse replaced the gauze on Fanny's swollen face and lowered the shades. I left the room, removed the apron, doused my hair with alcohol, washed my face and hands, and returned to the classroom, convinced that I would have smallpox—a conviction that failed to materialize.

Christmas slipped by almost unnoticed, something that came and passed, leaving us staggering with weariness. Classrooms were closed, and the whole institution became a hospital. The teachers, the laundress and the seamstress helped with the nursing, the cooking or wherever we were needed, until the children recovered.

The parents complicated our problems by crowding onto the porches—entreating us to let them visit their sick children. Had we granted their requests, the contagion would have swept the reservation. We realized that it was a trying time for them as well as for us and eased their anxiety by giving each parent as complete a report as possible on his child's improvement. The news that a child ate food, brought the exclamation, *"Hanaga! Hanaga!* (Good! Good!)"*, and a contented parent returned to his home.

Within a few weeks the sick were well. The school again functioned as usual. On sunny days ball games sprouted like mushrooms on the playground. Both boys and girls had played baseball for years, but now the boys were organized in teams, and practiced as they never had before. In February they accepted a challenge from the team at the Mohave Indian School for a game to be played in Needles. The boys practiced every spare moment, for it was their first opportunity to test their skill against another school. They were as ignorant as babes as to what that meant. Frankly, we were a little troubled about this trip, wondering what ideas our boys might pick up from the more sophisticated Mohave young people. Certainly there would be aftereffects to deal with.

To boost their morale, Dr. and Mrs. Perkins, Daisy and I accompanied them to Needles. Engine trouble developed, so we spent most of the night on the road, arriving before daylight Saturday morning only to learn that there was not an available room in any of the three hotels. Each of us wanted a bath and a bed more than anything else we could think of. We sat in the hotel lounge until dawn, when a few early risers crawled out of their beds and we crawled in to sleep until noon.

Our boys had been invited as guests at the Mohave Indian

School during our stay in Needles. The invitation had been accepted with the hope that by becoming acquainted with the Mohave children and meeting the opposing team, our boys might feel at home in this foreign atmosphere—their timidity had always kept them on the outskirts of towns and cities. There was a chance, too, that by mingling with these more assured young people, they might gain confidence in their own ability to win.

After lunch, we went to the ball game. The moment I saw Don, I knew our hopes had been in vain. When the captain is depressed every boy on the team reacts to his mood. The very confident Mohave boys had completely crushed our team's enthusiasm.

The wind came up from the southwest tossing plumes of sand so dense that we could hardly distinguish the players. The Mohave boys were cocky and sure. Our boys were timid and discouraged. They were confused by trying to play on a new field and the sandstorm obstructed their vision, making their eyes smart. They lost the game.

We had planned to do the town of Needles, seeing everything it had to offer, on Sunday, but the sandstorm and our sleepless night changed our plans. We took the evening train home.

The following Monday my classroom was filled with the overwhelming odor of Sen-Sen. All forty pupils were munching it. I reminded the children that chewing gum had been outlawed in the classrooms and that the same rule applied to Sen-Sen. Their response was greater secrecy in its use. Since this was its first appearance in our school, I suspected that the boys who had played in Needles were responsible for its sudden popularity, so asked Don for an explanation.

He said, "Those Mohave boys beat our team because they eat Sen-Sen."

I explained that the Mohave boys won because they had had more practice, better coaching, and were playing on their home field; that Sen-Sen had no more influence on the game than chewing gum or candy would have had.

His reply was: "I asked the captain of their team what made

them play better than we did; he said they ate Sen-Sen and it made them strong. Now we eat Sen-Sen. Next time we'll beat."

I had to be factual, even though I knew it would hurt. If our boys were to go out into the world and mingle with other young people, they must not be so gullible. I told him that they had been kidded by the Mohave captain, that he and his team would laugh at them if our team took his statement seriously. The boys were very reluctant to accept this view of the matter, and felt deep resentment against the perpetrators of the joke. However, Sen-Sen no longer attended classes.

Throughout the winter the Santa Fe had kept us informed on weather conditions on the outside. When a train flew by with snow piled high on its coaches, we knew that the people in the Rockies were piling anthracite into their base-burners. The quick flash we had of men and women reading, playing games or just looking at us through the train windows left us a bit envious, for they seemed so comfortable and completely contented.

We were at dinner one cold, cloudy evening when we heard a grinding crash. We drove up the wash to see if the Santa Fe had contributed something toward the enrichment of our fare. Once a derailed car had scattered oranges over the sand, providing the Indians and us with a wonderful treat. This time it was ice! Huge cakes of it. We felt terribly cheated until someone suggested ice cream. The train crew laughingly told us to help ourselves; they couldn't gather up broken cakes of ice. So we took home enough to supply us for several days with a seldom-tasted dessert.

When we unloaded the ice at our kitchen, we suddenly realized that we had no freezer. Perkie solved our difficulty with a large pail and a small one that would fit inside, but one of us had to turn pails and stir until the mixture was frozen. We huddled near the dining room stove to eat our ice cream, but that didn't lessen our enjoyment, nor did our quick dashes to the back porch to refill our dishes. In fact, eating ice cream in weather so cold that our teeth chattered, stimulated our sense of humor. Our party was more fun than we had had in a long time.

Late in the afternoon of March 22, 1903, a broken axle landed unexpected guests on our grounds and gave the Indians—and us— a glimpse of affluence that really impressed us. A passenger train rounded the shoulder above the school, and with a loud banging and pounding, came to a stop. We hurried out to see what had happened; some of the Indian children followed. An elderly man— John D. Rockefeller—strolled out on the platform of the last car, watching the train crew who were examining the axle.

A young man descended from the coach and assisted a girl to alight. In a flash I knew their identity—John D. Rockefeller, Jr. and his wife! The society columns of my daily had given the itinerary of their trip to the West Coast. Suddenly I became painfully conscious of the impression we must make on them—dozens of Indian children mingled with a few sun-tanned, desert-hardened, not-too-well-dressed teachers, frankly staring at them. The signal was given, the young couple climbed aboard, and the train moved off, leaving the damaged coach standing on the track.

After dinner that evening, the porter conducted four of us through the coach. We were duly impressed by the bedrooms with their silk quilts and fine linens; the drawing room's diminutive fireplace and comfortable chairs made us feel smug—our desert world shut out.

Through the early twilight, we walked slowly back to our cottage, newly conscious of the barrenness of our Indian school quarters. When I opened the door to my room, I was shocked by the cheapness of the fishnet curtains that I had so proudly hung at my windows; the green rug was not velvet; the sheets were not linen nor the quilts silk; but we had fun here, and the room seemed cosy and cheerful when the crowd gathered of evenings for games and a cup of tea and cookies.

But life among the Walapai was so full that we gave little thought to the absence of luxuries. There were still interesting places to explore in the environment of our canyon; the Indians still held ancient ceremonies of which we had learned all too little. One of these Daisy and I were to witness, the secret, religious ritual of healing—something few white people have ever seen.

CHAPTER TWENTY-SEVEN

A Medicine Man at Work

◨ Across the low hill to the west of our teachers' cottage a gourd was rattling with unabated fury; voices of men rose in hoarse shouts; and above this, came the high, staccato voice of one man. The noise, coming through the open window by my bed, awakened me. It was ten or perhaps eleven o'clock; the night was dark and cold. A sharp wind drew through the pass where the Indians' low wickiups huddled. I leaned my elbows on the window sill and sat in my nightgown listening, trying to figure out, if I could, what was taking place among the Indians in the village. The savage shouting and singing, the gourd rattling, continued hour after hour. Finally, I went back to bed.

A few nights later, I heard it again; again I listened and watched. The bright moonlight revealed only the hillside, now white with snow, the sharp, outcropping rocks desolate against it. Faint shadows marked the wide trail leading from the school through a slight dip and up the slope of the hill beyond which lay the village. There was nothing to indicate the cause of the disturbance.

But I didn't give up. Bill, my faithful choreboy, was dusting erasers as usual one evening after school, when I asked, "Who rattles a gourd and shouts at night in the village?"

He replied slowly: "Pete sick. Medicine man too old, he not walk in snow to Pete's house, so Pete's papa wrap him in blanket and carry him medicine man house. Medicine man sing for Pete all night."

So the medicine man was at work just across the low hill.

I wanted to see what he did to the sick, for I could not condemn him, as I had been doing, if it were possible for me to witness his method of healing and I failed to do so. The Indians talked of miraculous cures he had wrought; they also admitted his failures. Pete's father and the medicine man argued that the presence of a white person would inhibit the shamanistic spirit, without which the old man would be helpless, so none of us was permitted to witness the ceremony. A few days later, Pete died.

This Walapai shaman was a very old man. He seldom came near the school although, a few years previously, he had allowed the superintendent to take a snapshot of him rattling his gourd over a man lying on the ground, wrapped in a blanket. How artificial this pose was did not impress me until I had seen the old healer perform in good faith over the sick.

So far as I had been able to learn, any Havasupai boy or man might become a shaman by inheriting the shamanistic spirit of a dying medicine man or by his own effort through dreams. The Walapai shaman on the other hand selected his disciples, choosing young boys, whom he trained in the mysteries of his cult while he administered a Jimson weed (stramonium) brew to induce the necessary hallucinations. This was an old practice among the Walapai. When Bourke visited the tribe between 1870 and 1874, he found the medicine men indulging in a beverage made of the leaves, stems and roots of stramonium, thereby inducing a state of exhilaration in which they uttered prophecies.

Bourke also states that the shamans of the tribe claimed power over the forces of nature, and that they renewed this power occasionally by rubbing their bodies against certain sacred stones near Beale Springs.

This Walapai shaman cut flesh, but I had seen no indication among the Havasupai that their healers resorted to this means of providing escape for the spirit that caused sickness. I first learned of this Walapai shaman's method of healing by incisions from Mike Metathanya. Mike, a young man in one of my classes, developed rheumatism, and complained of pain in his forehead. His enlarged joints, flabby flesh and indifference to class activities were symptoms of ill health. At that time we were in the day school, and had neither doctor nor nurse, so there was nothing we could do for him. Finally he dropped out of school and was gone for several weeks. When he returned he had a number of vertical white scars on his forehead. The incisions were entirely healed but the scars stood out prominently against his very dark skin. Those scars were no accident; each cut had been precisely placed. When I questioned Mike as to the cause, he was embarrassed, so I didn't press the matter. I appealed to my reliable informant, Bill. He said that Mike had been treated by the medicine man who declared that the pain in Mike's forehead was caused by an evil spirit imprisoned there. The medicine man had made the cuts to enable it to escape. I could understand Mike's reluctance to tell me of his experience, for he knew that I did not approve of the shaman's practice. However, anything I said against their medicine man was refuted by the fact that Mike was now well.

I doubt if I should ever have witnessed the old shaman's healing ceremony had Charley not taken three "wives" out in the desert one cold, blustery night. Like other coeducational institutions, we had our problems which were multiplied by housing boys and girls in one large building. In order to give the girls protection in any emergency, the matron occupied a room opening off their large second-story dormitory, and at night locked all the exits, keeping the keys within reach of her hand. These facts discouraged the other boys—but not Charley. He was the wishy-washy boy of the school, always unsure, sliding out of difficulties with an abashed grin, but what he did was too risky for the sturdier boys to attempt. It took careful planning and the certainty that he would not be betrayed.

His dormitory was not locked at night, so he had every opportunity to make his arrangements. He located a ladder and, sometime during the night, placed it under a window of the girls' dormitory. We did not learn how many girls he had invited to join him; if he expected only one, he must have had a surprise when three climbed down the ladder. They ran with him to his hideout somewhere in the desert.

The matron discovered the absence of her girls and when they tried to slip back into the building, before dawn, confronted them. They readily admitted their part in the escapade.

When brought to account, Charley hung his head and said with a sheepish grin, "I just took my three wives out for a little while."

The adventure had its repercussions. Mab, one of the three girls, developed a bad cough, the result of exposure. Tuberculosis followed. She failed rapidly and begged to be taken home. Her father demanded his right to take her, even though he had only a one-room shack. Since the school had neither hospital nor nurse, not even a room where the child could be isolated and given proper care, he was allowed to move her to his place. At least, she would be more contented there.

Weeks later, I heard the medicine gourd again. Many voices joined in the shouting, loud, excited voices. Mab's father, Sakawema, had called in the medicine man.

One day when Sakawema came to the school on an errand, I inquired about Mab, and asked if I might come to his home to see what the medicine man did to make her well. He hesitated, then whirled and walked off, muttering to himself. The following day he was back to tell us that Mab could not eat the Indian food, but wanted oranges. I gave him the few I had, then repeated my request. This time he muttered, "I think you come, no good." Abruptly he walked away.

On his next visit, his face was haggard. "My girl heap sick, maybe die," he said. "I pay medicine man. He come, work hard, no get better." Then he added, "You bring oranges, sugady [sugar], crackers, you come Sat'day night. See what he do."

I bought the food and persuaded Daisy to help me carry the packages to his home. We heard the commotion before we left our cottage. It grew louder and more insistent as we climbed the slope of the hill and walked down into the village to Sakawema's home

—a shack constructed of old boards and railroad ties. Hot, steaming air poured out when I lifted the blanket from the doorway. There was no other opening except a smoke vent in the roof.

The place had been tidied up for the occasion. The dirt floor had been swept; the few dishes, tin pails and cans in which Sakawema cooked were washed and stacked in a box nailed to the wall. The only light in the room came from a fire burning in the center of the floor.

Men and women of various ages sat in a crowded circle on the floor. Not a head turned when we slipped inside the room, not an eye wavered from its fixed gaze at the wizened old shaman who crouched by Mab's head. We were completely ignored. Don, Mab's brother, sat by his father near the center of the circle. He was one of my most advanced pupils, a large husky lad, fully grown. I saw his face freeze in an expression of hostility. He was a leader at the school and an officer in charge of a company of boys, but, while he conformed to the white man's regulations at the school, he obviously resented any prying on our part into the Indian's way of life. He knew that we had come to witness a ceremony in which we had no confidence. And I knew, that whatever happened, we would not dare speak in protest.

No one took our packages so we set them in the box with the dishes, then slid quietly into the vacant space by the entrance, which had been left for us.

This cold reception from those with whom we had been so closely associated surprised and disturbed us. Old Suja and his wife were in the circle; Grace sat with her back to the wall, eyes staring to the front. No one can so completely ignore a person he does not wish to see as an Indian. Lieutenant Ives discovered this fact, to his astonishment, when he met a band of Walapai at Diamond Creek in his cross-country trip in 1858.

He and his party were quite sure that these Indians had never seen a white face, and anticipated a definite reaction. He writes of his chagrin when a hideous old squaw, staggering under a load of wood, stalked by with several companions, not giving the white men so much as a glance. I had frequently witnessed this blithe ignoring of persons or things that a Walapai did not care to see. But this night it seemed peculiarly frightening.

The medicine man's whole ritual was based on the theory that sickness came when a mysterious spirit entered the body for the purpose of torturing it. It might be the spirit of the dead, returning to avenge some real or fancied wrong, or the guardian spirit of an animal—Wolf, Coyote or Deer. One man admitted that he had killed deer wastefully and thrown the flesh away. That gave his shaman a perfect clue. He explained that the guardian spirit of the deer had entered the man's body to punish him for his wastefulness, and caused him to cough and spit blood.

A shaman is expected to determine which spirit is present, why it is there, and coax, suck or drive it from the body of the sick. We did not learn what spirit he accused of causing Mab's illness, but the prospect of watching this old conjurer put his theories to the test was tremendously exciting.

This was the second sing the medicine man had held over Mab; he had agreed to sing for six nights. When we saw the procedure by which he would attempt to heal the girl, we were fearful that she could not survive four more treatments, even though they were not given on consecutive nights.

She lay on a blanket on the dirt floor, her head close to the fire. Squatted on his haunches on a folded blanket by her head was the shaman. He wore only a loincloth. Trickles of sweat ran in crooked rills down the brown, wrinkled body. At the moment we entered, he clutched his medicine gourd in his right hand, shaking it with all his strength; with his left fist he struck his chest resounding blows while his body twisted slowly from side to side, each movement perfectly timed to his staccato singing and gourd rattling. Then, suddenly, he began the drama on which the Indians pinned their hope for a cure.

The sickness was in Mab's chest, so this was his point of attack. In a tense silence while his audience leaned forward in breathless suspense, the shaman bent over the girl, pressed his mouth hard against her bare chest and held it there. His taut muscles, the tenseness of his posture, reacted on the Indians—and on us. We were witnessing something beyond our known world. He was sending his own shamanistic spirit into the girl's chest, cajoling and instructing it to scurry about and find the little white puffs that looked like clouds, the round pieces that looked like hailstones, the slender white things that resembled worms, for these were the forms assumed by the spirits that caused sickness.

Suddenly his attitude changed; his whole body grew rigid with effort. He pressed his thin lips hard against the girl's flesh, making coaxing noises; from his throat came gurgling sounds as if he was swallowing something he had drawn from her emaciated body.

We were watching an ancient and exotic performance—a shaman withdrawing his shamanistic spirit from the body of the sick where he had sent it to explore. Now it was re-entering his own body. He was gulping it down. But it had not found the things for which it searched.

The circle of Indians leaned toward him, anxious, groaning.

He worked himself into a frenzy, his brown body bathed in sweat, his eyes aflame. The girl was not improving; the sickness would not yield. His own shaman spirit could not find the cause. He lifted his grizzled old head, and turning his seamed, stony face toward the hills, shouted to the *quigete* (harmful spirit) to take from this girl the sickness it had sent.

His audience echoed his demand, some moaning, others shouting.

He used his own ventriloquist's voice to hurl back from the hills the *quigete's* defiant refusal. Beat and torture himself as he would, the *quigete* would not yield. Again and again he screamed to the hills; again and again came defiance. The Indians, tense, perspiring, moaned in an agony of defeat, not realizing that it was the old shaman's voice that shouted back.

Suddenly the medicine man leaned over and beat his tight fists on Mab's sunken chest. Continuously he beat with the rhythm of a drummer. He sucked and gurgled. Mab lay there, eyes closed, her head turning restlessly from side to side, uttering low moans. Our hearts ached for the child but we dared not interfere.

The old shaman screamed to the circle of watchers—a cry of desperation: "Help me! Do not leave all this to me! Work with me, work hard! Drive out these things that make her sick! It is hard, very hard. I cannot do it alone."

The excited crowd, without rising, pressed toward him, eyes flaming, perspiring faces flushed, and shouted back: "We are with you. We are your brother. We help. Work! Work hard!"

We could not understand much of the excited shouting, but a plump middle-aged Indian sitting on our left, possibly one of those six Walapai who had traveled with the Barnum and Bailey show, for he spoke English easily, leaned over and whispered the interpretation.

Then Suja, the philosopher, who had dispensed wisdom while he puffed smoke rings from his stubby pipe, half-rose, and with upraised, clenched fists, shouted: "Sing! Sing loud! Sing! Make rattle plenty! We help. All Indians help. Make girl well! *Hanaga! Hanaga!*" The excited circle echoed his cry.

Our interpreter, eager as any Indian present, had half-risen from his place on the floor to shout with the others. Then he settled back and told us in a whisper what they had shouted. He added, "Old man gets sleepy as hell. We yell loud to keep him awake."

I glanced at Don. The muscles of his face were drawn in tight ridges, sweat rolled down his cheeks and dripped from his chin; his eyes were those of an Indian, a fanatical Indian, straining with all that was in him to lay hands on that magic power. He would support with the last breath of his life that thin, mummified zealot that sucked and gurgled and screamed in a wild frenzy. And I wondered: *Tomorrow will he stand in front of his company at school and give his commands to his boys? Will he sit at the head of his table in the dining room and help serve the younger children? Tonight he is steeped in Indian tradition. Can he change by the time the breakfast bell rings in the morning?*

Mab lay very still, completely relaxed; she breathed the thick, hot air with difficulty. Nothing they could do to her now could cause suffering. She was beyond the reach of pain. I felt dizzy—and frightened. These Indians that I had known so well were no longer the same people. They were possessed by a fury that was beyond my comprehension. In that hot, tense atmosphere, I began to realize the folly of two girls placing themselves in the position we were in. This old shaman, more than any other I had known, feared and avoided the white man, recognizing in him an enemy of his conjurer's tricks. If his antics failed to heal the girl, he would need an alibi, for the Walapai, like the Havasupai, were not tolerant of those who posed as healers, but failed to heal. If he instilled the thought in the minds of those highly excited Indians that we had defeated his efforts, he would divert their attention from the fact of his failure to the fact that we were present; that we had confused him and prevented his shamanistic spirit from finding the cause of Mab's illness. We had planned to stay until the medicine man left, sometime after daybreak, but now, at 3:00 A.M. after witnessing several repetitions of the ceremony, we wanted just one thing, escape.

I lifted a corner of the blanket that closed the entrance. Not a head turned nor an eye wavered. Without rising, I eased my body through the doorway until I was out under the familiar stars and the silvery moon. Daisy followed. The night wind brought clean, sweet air from the mountaintops. We stood a moment, a little dazed, and still frightened.

I whispered, "Hurry!" After those soul-shaking hours, I could not get away fast enough. I wanted to run.

She laid a detaining hand on my arm. "Walk slowly until we are on the other side of the hill," she whispered. We walked slowly, not looking back, and were soon in our own comfortable rooms.

For hours I tried vainly to forget the scene I had witnessed, and get some sleep, then my door opened silently, and Daisy, with her pillow in her arms, crossed the room.

"I can't sleep. Get over." she whispered. "If only I could stop hearing that jangling gourd and the shouts and the groans of the Indians!"

"You are worrying about Mab," I answered.

"Yes. And so are you or you'd sleep in spite of the din."

Now that another human being was in the room the noise from across the hill seemed less weird. I felt the black waves of sleep washing me into oblivion, until Daisy exclaimed: "Are you awake? I've just thought of something. Do you know who'll eat all the food we carried over there? The medicine man! That explains why he allowed us to come—the old fox!"

That made everything clear. Sakawema wanted the shaman to cure Mab, but he couldn't pay the price. So I paid the price. But I didn't feel cheated. For a long time I had wanted to see this healing ceremony, the complete ritual, taught to the shaman of old by their gods.

"I suppose he'll be sucking sweet oranges for days," I said, "and eating more sugar than he ever saw before in his life, and nibbling crackers, but I hope Sakawema kept some for Mab."

The next morning, Don, red-eyed and weary, sat at the head of his table at breakfast.

The memory of the things that were done that night stayed with me like a terrifying dream. It was intensified each time I heard the gourd rattling and voices shouting on the other side of the hill. I knew now what the sick lived through—if they lived. What could be done to counteract the influence of the medicine man, to put a stop to such needless torture? Force could not do it; that only antagonized. In the past we had used too much compulsion and too little understanding in approaching the Indians' problems. There was only one solution: give the Indians hospitals, doctors and nurses, let them experience the healing power of modern medical practice and they themselves would put the medicine man out of business.

Later, hospitals were built on the Indian reservations and staffed with nurses, but Mab and many others died before these things were provided.

CHAPTER TWENTY-EIGHT

The Walapai Surprise Santa

When school opened the next fall I discovered that the small boys' matron had joined her husband on their ranch, so while planning our classroom work for the year, I also took over her duties. Quite a number of kindergarten boys had been brought to the school during the late summer, leaving their parents free to roam. In caring for these little chaps, I tried to help them make their adjustment to conditions at the school and ease them over this period of homesickness.

They were mere babies and timid as wild animals. At home they had gathered about the cooking pot, eating food by the handful. When we placed them on stools at tables covered with white cloths and white enameled dishes, they were literally paralyzed. One little fellow worried us by not tasting food for three days. The high beds frightened them—what if they fell off? Some took their blankets, after lights were out, and slept on the floor. Their hardened little bodies had dashed about in shirt tails, or unhampered by any garment, for all the summers they could remember, so new underwear, wool uniforms, stockings and shoes were pure torture. The shower bath was another terror. Everywhere they went, things they had never seen before startled and frightened them.

The pleasantest hour of the day for me was immediately after supper when the boys put on their nightshirts, gathered around me to listen to stories or to sing until time for their prayers, then scrambled into bed. No matter how many songs we sang, they always begged for more. Teddy, a little man of five, knew only one phrase in English, the one he heard repeated countless times during meals in the dining hall. When we had finished a song, he would pipe up, "More bread, please, more bread!" Meaning, of course, that he wanted to sing another song, even though his singing consisted of funny squeals.

A new school building was ready for occupancy that fall. Desks and chairs were in place for the teachers, slate blackboards were on the walls, and desks for the pupils needed only to be screwed down. Dr. Perkins suggested that I go with him to inspect the furnishings. A new employee had arrived, the industrial teacher. He and his detail of boys were waiting for us in the classroom. The boys already had the desks firmly screwed to the floor.

Mr. Iliff and I were introduced.

At that moment I saw only desks screwed where I did not want them.

"But I want the desks placed so the light will fall from the left," I protested, looking to Dr. Perkins for support. He had scented trouble and vanished.

"I'm sorry, but to change them will leave holes in your floor," Mr. Iliff replied. "You were on vacation. Dr. Perkins thought you would want them as they are."

I was convinced I was in for a long argument, so was agreeably surprised when he laughed and said, "All right, boys, let's take them up and change them."

We talked for a while, discovered that his home was not far from our old home in eastern Kansas where we had lived before we moved to Oklahoma. When we learned that our ancestors had been neighbors (his from the Isle of Man, mine from Scotland), we felt like old friends.

Then, quite unexpectedly, Miss Calfee resigned, and that brought the problem of Christmas to the fore. Miss Calfee had been Christmas—she and the Massachusetts Indian Association. Who would inherit the task of providing the program and gifts for the children? I thought I knew—and felt sure I could never manage, for I had no organization back of me to supply the gifts. But even such weighty problems are temporarily forgotten when one finds adventure in trivial things. Soon after we had returned from our vacation Daisy took up a hobby that was intensely exciting but I was not able to join her.

Early the previous spring, one of the workmen who roamed the desert in his leisure time had discovered a rattlesnake den some miles from the school. He told of finding snakes on a hillside, twined and intertwined in ropelike masses, basking in the hot sunshine. What puzzled him, he said, was that there were snakes other than rattlers in some of the twisted masses. His discovery explained the source of the many mountain rattlers that appeared at the school.

One dark night as I walked from our back door to get some clothes I had hung on the line, I noticed a long, thick stick lying by the path. When I passed within inches of it, the stick slowly formed a coil. I called for help, and one of the men shot an ancient rattler that had wandered close to the house and stopped to rest awhile.

They were everywhere. We warned the children to watch for them, even on the school grounds, for we had no certain antidote for their poison. However, one small boy, while climbing among the rocks, was struck in the leg. He was very sick by the time the older boys got him back to the school. Dr. Perkins worked over him, trying every known remedy, but the boy's leg swelled to the size of a stovepipe and turned black. His father hovered over him and begged Doctor to let him take his son home, but when Doctor explained the child's critical condition, and the danger of discontinuing the treatment, the father made one last plea.

"Doctor, let me stay here, sit by my boy, sing all night," he begged.

His request was granted on condition he keep his voice low so that he would not disturb the children and the employees who slept in the building. All night the frantic "sing" went on, a low ardent plea to the spirits, possibly the snake spirit, to come out of the boy and cease torturing him. The child recovered. Of course there was one disturbing factor: Doctor never knew whether his remedies or the father's "sing" had neutralized the snakes' poison. He had hoped to make this a test case.

It wasn't possible for Daisy to hear all this snake talk without reacting in her characteristic way. She asked Mr. Iliff to make her a forked stick; she would free the desert of these dangerous rattlers and make it safe for our children to play where they pleased. One night at dinner he appeared with a long pole, forked at one end. The following Saturday afternoon Daisy urged me to comb the desert with her in search of the quarry. But in the back of my mind was the memory of Professor Allen's zoology class in Central State Normal at Edmond. In assigning laboratory work, he had asked me to capture, skin and dissect a snake. I performed the experiment, but when I was through with it, I never wanted to see another snake.

I felt like a deserter when I let Daisy start on her hunt alone but that was one adventure I could not share, even after she returned to recount the thrills of the chase and triumphantly exhibit the kill.

Our staff had been increased by a lovely, slender brunette from New York, Goldie Cole. She was young, not over eighteen, I think, and literally sparkling with fun. Her vivaciousness infected those of us who were ready for anything—except snakes.

In October, a teacher for our intermediate grades, Miss Catherine Finnegan, arrived, and November brought Miss Katharine Speirs for the primary department. Miss Speirs was young, jolly and a typical Westerner. She owned an interest in an Alaska gold mine, and had made the trip by boat to visit her property and get first-hand information from the miners, which was a bit unusual for a woman of her education and culture.

Now that we had our full corps of permanent teachers, Christmas again became the theme of our discussions. I was not wrong about the inheritance; it was mine. It made me responsible not only for the entertainment program, but for gifts for about two hundred children, since we intended to include the little folks in the village.

Miss Speirs's primary pupils prepared a gaily costumed Mother Goose Christmas play; Miss Finnegan's learned songs and recitations; I selected a play for my grades. No child in school had ever seen a play staged, but how they clamored for the chance to appear in one! When the characters were assigned, the pupils chosen were angrily scolded by those who failed to get a part. Sam had the male lead. He memorized his lines quickly, and I congratulated myself on the wisdom of my choice.

But November was almost gone and no one could suggest a source for gifts. I'd never been so frustrated in meeting a need. Mr. Iliff kept reminding me, "Christmas without gifts will be worse than no Christmas at all. You'd better get busy."

While our troubles were piling up, Daisy resigned. Her work would fall to the rest of us, in addition to our holiday rush.

As usual, the train would be flagged at the point where the dirt road crossed the track, so teachers and children congregated there to see her off. We knew how sorely we should miss her, and were gloomy enough. In an effort to cheer us with a little comedy, Katharine Speirs stepped on a rail and delivered a eulogy on the activities of a certain Republican candidate. At the conclusion of her flowery speech, she waited for the expected applause. None came. Katharine cocked an eyebrow and exclaimed, "What? No applause for all my oratory?"

Sam sat on his haunches near the track, his arms hugging his knees. He turned a solemn face up to her and said, "We're all Democrats here."

That brought the expected laugh, dearer to Sam, the mimic, than anything else. It eased the tension too, and we made Daisy's departure as gay as she had expressed the wish that it might be.

We returned to quarters, and to our obsession: gifts, hundreds and hundreds of them, for each child must have two or three; it had been that way on the few Christmas celebrations held at the school.

At last, Perkie, always helpful, offered a suggestion. "The large mail-order houses put aside shopworn and imperfect merchandise to help out in worthy causes," she said. "Why not write some of the firms with whom we place orders?"

That was a chance. Since we bought our supplies from them and I had helped the children prepare orders for things pictured in their catalogs, I offered to take some of this unmarketable merchandise off their hands, explaining our need. I even offered to pay the freight from my salary.

Their replies were prompt and generous. They would be happy to contribute to the Indian children's Christmas, and since this was their gift, they reserved the right to pay the freight.

Now that our most important problem was settled, Dr. Perkins frequently remarked, as he had done the previous years, "Christmas belongs to the children." We did not suspect his meaning until he added, "This year we'll have Santa Claus."

"Who can play Santa Claus?" I protested. Santa Claus was a new feature; there never had been one. All that the children knew of the good Saint Nicholas they had gleaned from their schoolbooks; the few Christmas entertainments held at the school had been strictly religious, and certainly the Indian lore did not include Santa Claus.

Dr. Perkins was economical with words, a habit formed from dealing with Indians who better understood English if shorn of all verbiage. He said, "Ask Joe Iliff. Get whatever he needs. Order a mask."

"I'll ask him," I replied. "We'll need a lot of things—red flannel—cotton bats—"

"Make out a list," he said, and was gone.

Bringing Santa to the Walapai seemed as simple to him as had been the appearance of the good saint at the celebrations he remembered from his childhood. But he, like the rest of us, was to learn that a people's background and culture can account for un-expected reactions.

By this time Mr. Iliff had endeared himself to all of us by his cheerfulness and his willingness to help wherever needed. The group of teachers who sometimes gathered about the piano in the school auditorium for an hour of singing or assembled in one of our rooms for a party, had dropped formality; among ourselves we called him Joe.

When Joe and I took our usual walk after I had conducted the evening hour of supervised study that we had added to our schedule, I broke the news to him by saying, "We've chosen our Santa Claus."

"Who is the unlucky chap?" he inquired.

"By name, Joe Iliff," I said.

"Well," he hesitated, "I'm willing to help, of course."

Joe made a game of it, raveled yards of rope which we sewed to his cap to make long white hair that fell about his shoulders. The mask arrived from Los Angeles. It would be fun if we could so disguise him that the Indians would not suspect he was the in-dustrial teacher, the man they called by a Walapai name meaning "Suspenders-crossed-in-the-back."

We concluded later that we had overdone the matter of dis-guise, but while we were planning it, it was such fun that our enthusiasm caused us to seek perfection.

We spared no effort to arouse the children's anticipations; we intended to give them and their parents a Christmas so full of surprises and happiness that they could never forget it. But you can't do that with an Indian unless you prepare him for it. So we had some of the older boys, including Don, Seth, and Sam open the enormous boxes shipped us from the mail-order houses. Then we had groups of older boys and girls help us sort and tag the gifts. The whole school took on a festive air. The matrons had their girls make candy bags, boys and girls filled them. Joe took his boys twenty miles back in the mountains to get the big, perfect evergreen that sat grandly on the stage. Everywhere there was laughter and hurry and excitement.

Dr. Perkins went about the school grounds, hands in pockets, a smile quirking the corners of his mouth, asking the parents when they came in from their reservation homes, "You savvy Santa Claus?"

"No savvy," was the invariable reply.

The superintendent would hold up his fingers and say: "Look. This many suns, you come. See Santa Claus. Get presents."

This conversation was repeated again and again and the news traveled. The Indians rode ten, fifteen miles over rough desert just to ask the question, "San Claw—how many suns—he come?" And Dr. Perkins replied with fewer and fewer fingers.

"How look?" they asked, brows wrinkled with perplexity. "He *man*? Maybe ghost? You think Coyote send him?" Then came the last reluctant suggestion, "Maybe *quigete*?" They wanted to pin the superintendent down to a description that would give them a clear picture, take away fear.

Doctor would grin and say: "No. Santa comes to bring good, not harm." He would give them a description of a man, bundled in red coat, coming down from the land of ice and snow. But their questions continued; curiosity boiled. Still, it did not occur to us that our explanations did not give the Indians a clear picture of Santa Claus. So we laughed and continued to build up the great moment of Santa's arrival.

On December twenty-fourth the air was electric with expectancy. This was the great night—Christmas program, gifts, and Santa Claus.

The officers of the several school classes marched their companies into the auditorium. We seated the little folks in small seats immediately in front of the stage. Their feet swung in excitement, brown fingers pointed out toys on the loaded tree while they whispered and squirmed. The other companies were seated according to size with the largest pupils in the rear. The parents filled the remaining seats and packed the aisles to the rear doors.

We kept the passage free to the entrance directly in front of the audience, for Santa would enter there at the proper time.

Our program lasted for more than an hour. The Indians beamed their pride in their children's achievement. Sam handled his part in the play beautifully until his thoughts switched from his lines to the possibility that the strange figure of Santa Claus might burst through the near-by door at any moment. He began giggling and forgot his lines. I prompted, Sam giggled, but somehow we got through the scene and that ended the program.

Suddenly in a tense silence there came the jingle of sleigh bells, a loud pounding on the front door and a demand for admittance. Every eye focused on the entrance. No one stirred or seemed to breathe until the door was thrown open and old Santa, with a monstrous pack on his back, bounded in. Not an Indian in the hall had ever in his life seen anything that resembled that apparition. The ruddy-complexioned, bewhiskered mask, the long white hair, the red coat with its white cotton trim, and the high rubber boots made a bewildering combination.

The children took one look, then the older ones sprang to the tops of their desks, waved their arms and shouted, "Hurrah! Hurrah!" We had said this was Santa Claus, the bringer of gifts. They believed us. They also bewildered us, for never before had a child thought of standing on one of our new desks. Excitement held them rigid, gaping, rules and procedures completely forgotten. But the reaction of the older Indians, too, was something we had not counted on, and it upset the whole program.

Suja, the tribe's old philosopher, his face blazing with emotion, eyes wild with fright, sprang to his feet and, waving his arms, screamed a warning. The camp Indians recovered from their stunned silence with a hoarse, frightened cry, "*Quigete! Quigete!*" and stampeded through the rear doors. Pandemonium broke loose among the children. Their parents' word stood above all else with them. We had said "Santa Claus" but their parents had said "*quigete.*" So *quigete* it was. Our kindergarten pupils ran to the teachers who happened to be near and clung to us, tears rolling down their fat cheeks while they sobbed, "No good! No good!" One thin little chap buried his face in Dr. Perkins' trouser leg, where he clung with icy hands, his skin as blue as indigo.

Some of the children followed their parents to the yard, others stayed in their seats, eyes popping, but unwilling to miss any of the excitement. We sent Jim Fielding, the Indian policeman, to tell those in the yard that this was Santa Claus, who had come to bring the gifts. He persuaded them to come back inside and be seated. We released the clinging fingers from our clothes and got our kindergarten pupils back into their places. The other children resumed their seats, but they were too alert, eyes too brightly shining.

Don, Seth, Sam, and a few of the older boys who were taking training in carpentry had volunteered to distribute the presents, but they did not recognize their teacher in his disguise and refused to go near him. The audience was quiet while Santa told of his home in the North and of his long drive over ice and snow to bring gifts to the children at Truxton. While he talked, some of our small girls leaned forward, intently peering up under the front of his long, red-flannel coat, whispering. The peeping and the whispering spread from the small children to the older ones. Santa was betrayed. They had seen three sofa pillows pinned to his suspenders to make his stomach look plump and round as it looked in the pictures we had shown them of Saint Nicholas. They recognized the cushions. They had seen those cushions many times on a certain couch at the school. That planted suspicion in the minds of Don and Seth, so they listened to Santa's voice. Suddenly one of them exclaimed, "Mr. Iliff!" and the tension eased. They spoke Joe's Walapai name to the older Indians; all repeated it. They knew "Suspenders-crossed-in-the-back" and were not afraid.

But nerves that had been so tightly wound were still taut. When Santa took the gifts from the tree and the boys distributed them, pandemonium broke loose again. The little folks tried out their new horns, just short toots to prove the horns were real; the bird whistles—there were dozens of them—trilled for the same reason; toy drums rolled to add to the bedlam. The older boys and girls with their gifts of handkerchiefs, beads, books, knives, games, neckties, dolls, and ribbons were as excited as the younger ones.

Santa called for order but the Indians were too excited to listen, so we stopped the distribution of gifts and that settled them down. The next whistles, horns and drums distributed started the commotion again. So I went to the stage and tapped the bell for silence. There never had been a time before when I could not easily control these pupils. There never had been a time when a tap of the bell failed to bring instant quiet. But their wild emotions were too deeply stirred now; there was no stemming the hysterical outburst through which they were finding release. The laughter, the shouting, the tooting, whistling, and drumming were deafening.

Under ordinary circumstances the Walapai were masters of themselves, calm, poised, even stolid. But under that crust of stolidity lay dynamic emotions that, suddenly aroused, released unpredictable power. If this uproar continued, anything could happen, even violence. It was my duty to get control. I made another effort; my voice was lost in the bedlam. Jim Fielding had a powerful voice, so I told him to shout to them; the parents needed taming more than the children, for they, too, were hilarious, thumping drums and blowing horns. Jim roared at them to sit down, to be quiet. They paid no attention whatever. The Indians had taken over!

Then I thought of candy.

"Jim, show them the bags of candy, nuts, and oranges," I said. "Tell them they will each get a bag when they are in their seats and quiet."

Jim picked up a handful of candy bags and held them high above his head while he bellowed the information. The calmer ones pushed the others into seats. All over the room there hissed a loud "sh-sh-sh!" as they settled down. Quickly we distributed the candy bags. Before the commotion could start again, we helped the officers line up the companies and march the children to the dormitories, each child struggling with his load of toys. We had to help the little ones; the matter of transportation was too much for their small hands.

The parents, laughing, talking in loud voices, munching candy, returned to the village. They were still excited but no longer bewildered about "San Claw." He was "Suspenders-crossed-in-the-back" who had brought them their candy bags, containing unaccustomed luxuries.

So far as the children were concerned, we had merely transferred the excitement from the school building to the dormitories. The matrons were frantic until they had each child's toys in his locker and the children in bed. But long after lights were out the chatter went on until nerves relaxed and everyone fell asleep.

Joe helped me lock the auditorium, then we went to the teachers' cottage to stand by the stove in the living room awhile talking over and laughing about the unexpected turn the Indians had given our celebration. The high plane of excitement on which we had spent the last few hours had had its effect on us, too.

"The Indians are educating me," I told him. "I didn't know it was possible for them to lose completely that poise and indifference they so cherish. They came tonight quiet, dignified; then suddenly the shell cracked and out tumbled a lot of frightened human beings. Emotions can do strange things to us."

"I had no thought of frightening them," he said, laughing. "Old Sakawema, Whatahomige, and Mapata! Those men come to the shop every day to talk to the boys and watch them work, but they were as frightened as the most ignorant men present."

"The women were even worse," I replied, remembering the jammed doorway, "crowding and shoving to get out, especially those with babies strapped on their backs."

"Let's forget about the Indians for a while. I want to talk about us," he said, reaching out his hand to draw me to him. "How would you like to marry Santa Claus?"

"I'd like it," I told him. For a few minutes we were absorbed in discussing our plans for a happy future. But the hour was late. We had been through an exhausting day. I went to my room knowing that a bright path lay ahead for Joe and me.

The next day we served the children the usual bountiful dinner. And the most exciting Christmas Truxton had ever known—one that surprised us as much as the Indians—came at last to an end.

CHAPTER TWENTY-NINE

An Indian Investigating Committee

Our depleted staff was reinforced that term by two new arrivals—a blessing in the light of later events, for before the winter ended, all of us were called upon to meet unexpected and almost overwhelming emergencies.

From Yuma, Arizona, came Nell White, a girl of such charm and beauty that we doubted if she could stand the hard steady grind of work in an Indian school. But in her position as matron, Nell mothered the small folks under her care and also very efficiently assisted Doctor in the operating room and in the care of the sick.

The next arrival was a tall blonde girl, Miss Johnson, the new seamstress from Kansas who, unannounced, stepped down from a Santa Fe train and walked up to the school, as I had done. The evening of her arrival we assembled in the living room of our cottage after dinner; we wanted to get acquainted with her, and she was eager to learn about this particular spot in the desert and to meet those with whom she would work.

She may have been somewhat homesick, for she talked of her father's big farm, of her brothers and the many young men and women who were her friends. We broke the news to her that eligible young men were our scarcest item, and the conversation turned to banter. Had she, we asked, brought one of those young men along?

Her hearty laugh rang out, and we knew then that the homesickness had worn off; she was glad to be with us.

"No-o," she said, "not unless one is in that big telescope bag the porter unloaded instead of my own luggage. It's big enough. Could be."

"Open it!" we chorused. We were in a vivacious mood. Seeing a new face was stimulating. We liked Miss Johnson.

She went to the hall where the telescope bag had been left when the boys brought it up from the train, set the heavy, worn bag on a chair, and loosened the straps. She lifted the top section and we gazed in dumb astonishment at a pair of badly worn, high-heeled cowboy boots that topped the pile. Beneath were the worn clothes of a ranch hand, old and almost threadbare. They were pathetic, but we shouted with laughter.

"You brought his clothes, now produce the man," someone managed to gasp.

"Really, are there no young men here?" she asked in surprise. "At home they were all over the place."

"We proudly exhibit one eligible," Katharine answered, laughing, as she gave me a roguish glance, "but don't depend on him. Plenty of handsome cowboys working on ranches—but shy—you'll need a cow pony to catch 'em. You'd better hang on to those old clothes; they're about as romantic as anything you'll find at an Indian school. Married men and engaged men—" she ended with a yawn.

We knew that Miss Johnson had had her romances. She came West because, like the Blue Water People, like Indian people and white people everywhere, she wanted a change.

The bag was sent to the station in Hackberry, and in time Miss Johnson received her luggage, but our spontaneous laughter had established a feeling of comradeship with this newcomer that proved to be lasting.

Our troubles began late one February afternoon when Joe and I were returning from a walk. We noticed a bright fire burning on a hillside some distance away; in the midst of the flames stood a small boy. Joe ran to the child, cut and tore away his blazing garments and carried him, badly burned and completely naked, to Dr. Perkins in the dispensary.

From his companions we got the story. They had found a tin can containing gunpowder. To keep the teachers from interfering with their experiment, they had taken the gunpowder up the slope and touched a match to it; this boy had held the lighted match. Instantly he was enveloped in flames. His companions had tried to remove his clothing; when his flaming undergarments and pants caught on his shoe, which they could not unlace, they walked off a short distance and left him to work out his own salvation. If we had not seen the flames, the boy would have burned to death, with his small and bewildered friends watching. The burns were deep and covered so much surface that it took weeks of patient care by Dr. Perkins and Nell to restore the boy to health.

This happened on February 9, and by the twenty-fifth of that month one-half of the school was down with influenza, followed by measles. My classroom and Miss Finnegan's were closed, and we nursed the sick. Fortunately I had had the measles, and escaped the influenza. Miss Speirs kept the primary room functioning for a time, but the sewing room was closed, and Miss Johnson took charge of the children's kitchen. She was young and strong and an experienced cook as well as an excellent seamstress.

Again we were caught up in an epidemic—no hospital, no nurse, and a very busy doctor. By March 8, every employee but Perkie, Nell, Katharine Speirs, the engineer and me was in bed with a severe case of influenza. One hundred seven of the children were desperately ill. Since his student helpers were all sick, the engineer had all he could do to keep the heating, water and light plants going. Katharine took charge of the sick employees, and Perkie, Nell and I nursed the sick children. There were so few of us able to work, and there was so much more to do than we could possibly accomplish, that by night of each day we had stored up enough fatigue to last for months.

Finally two emergency employees were secured to help us

through the siege, a night nurse from Kingman, and a cook for our mess. We carried the same load through the day, but the cook prepared our meals, and at night we were free to go to our rooms. Within a few days Doctor Perkins recovered and took over the care of the sick.

The fruit trees burst into bloom very early that March; the desert growth took on a new green, and in favored spots flowers appeared to brighten the landscape, but there was no relief from our strenuous duties; each day they grew heavier and anxiety deepened. Many of those sick with measles developed pneumonia, and one case turned into spinal meningitis.

Then one Wednesday night we lost a pneumonia patient. The following night another boy died of pneumonia. The whole staff was tense with an almost desperate determination to save the rest of these children at any sacrifice on our part. Saturday night we lost another boy; then the little fellow with spinal meningitis died. It was heartbreaking to be unable to help those patient, undemanding children, so terribly ill, but medicine seemed futile in these critical cases. We could only work and hope.

Twenty-three boys suffering from pneumonia were in the large dormitory on the second floor, and I was detailed as their day nurse, on twelve hour duty. Miss Finnegan had been in charge of this room, but she had reached the point of complete exhaustion. I took temperatures, kept charts, administered the medicine, but had several older boys to assist me, for no amount of persuading could induce even the smallest boy to use a bedpan if I took it to him, and the older boys would have been scandalized. For such personal service, they wanted their own people, and their own sex. The boys also served meals to those who were on a soft diet, but I took care of whatever nourishment Doctor prescribed for the very ill. One small boy had been given beef tea for so long that when I approached his bed with a tray, he'd lift his head to give it an expectant look; when he'd see another cup of beef tea, his head would drop back on the pillow, silent tears rolling down his baby face. That silent, bitter disappointment was hard to witness day after day, and no amount of explaining convinced him that he was not well enough to eat the beans and beef stew for which he hungered. However, he was making a slow but satisfactory recovery. It was those who lingered on the border, those who might slip across at any moment, that gave us real concern.

Dave was a thin child of about thirteen, and his was one of those stubborn cases that refused to yield to treatment. He lay with his eyes closed, moaning softly. But at a definite time each day his muscles would begin twitching and jerking, while his temperature shot up to one hundred five degrees. Various remedies were tried, but the cycle continued. Finally Doctor said, "The next time his temperature shoots up, we'll take immediate action."

Doctor spent from four to eight hours each day with the sick, in addition to his other duties, so he was even more overworked than the rest of us. However, when Dave's temperature began to climb the next day, I sent for him and helped him give the boy a treatment that was new to me, but which resulted in almost instant relief.

Doctor ordered clean sheets and a tub of the coldest water obtainable. We dipped the sheets into the water, gave them a slight wring, and spread them on the bed, then lifted the boy onto the dripping sheets and folded them over his hot body. The immediate reaction was such violent twisting and jerking of shocked muscles that I was sure we had subjected him to needless suffering. Then his muscles relaxed, his breathing became smooth and even, and he slept quietly. Doctor hurried away to his other patients, but I stayed with Dave, marveling at the miracle wrought by a simple cold compress.

There were those who could not be relieved by cold compresses or cured by any remedy at our disposal, and it was almost more than we could bear to see them face death, knowing that it was death, with such calm stoicism. Teddy, whose English at first had been limited to "More bread, please, more bread!" had developed into a chubby, red-cheeked, bright-eyed little fellow who had acquired a better vocabulary in a few months than some of the children had learned in years. Because he was bright and attractive, the older boys had taken him in charge, taught him to play ball and included him on hikes. Teddy had influenza, then pneumonia. When Doctor was convinced that there was no hope for his recovery, he allowed the parents to take their boy home, but he visited him at his father's shack. Late one evening he stopped at the wickiup and stooped down to examine the sick child. Teddy caught Doctor's hand in his and said, "Doctor, I know, tonight I die." That night Teddy died. Perhaps the Indians had seen "the look of death" in his face, and prepared him for the inevitable; we never knew.

Finally our sick were well with the exception of those who must be nursed back to strength through weeks of patient care. We began the task of restoring the building to its usual brightness. The children helped us wash walls, polish floors and set up beds with fresh bedding, for they were beginning to understand a little about the need of sanitation when dealing with communicable diseases. Classes and work in the industrial departments were resumed. But neither the children nor we could push into the background the memory of those who were no longer with us. The long hard siege had left its scars. There were toys that must not be used, clothing that must not be worn, names that must not be spoken.

Not until spring warmed our canyon, turning the white and pink orchard blossoms into small green fruit, and arousing the wanderlust in the children, did we return to anything like normalcy. Our troubles seemed at last to have come to an end.

Then the Indians' Investigating Committee arrived. These were the tribe's old men: knotted fingers, rheumatic knees, long, thick braids of grizzled hair. They were the wise elders who knew the truths and traditions that had guided the Walapai from the days of Kathathanave. They would test the white man's innovations by old tribal standards to determine which had caused the children to sicken and die as they had never done before.

Led by old Chief Wilatouse, they approached hesitantly, chattering in their native tongue. They hobbled up the steps and entered the main building in which the children lived and which housed Doctor's office. From the very beginning the Indians had looked askance at this new building. The white walls, the showers, the latrines, the radiators were incomprehensible to them.

Because they had suffered, Doctor was patient and kind. Because they were old and bewildered, he explained that the radiators, like their own campfires, kept the children warm. He demonstrated the showers, even though they could not understand how water sprouted from a wall. He let them blunder from room to room, upstairs and down, dim eyes peering suspiciously, heavy canes thumping, while they examined minutely and discussed their findings. The *quigete* could conceal itself as easily in any of these strange contraptions as it could hide out in the hills or among the rocks.

The old men went into a huddle, pointing, wrangling, gesticulating, but they reached a decision and filed into the office to make their report to Doctor. They had determined the cause of the sickness and the deaths—the hard white finish on the walls!

It may have been done to put their troubled minds at ease, or their verdict may have had nothing to do with it, but that glaring finish received a coat of paint, to the relief of everyone. So far as we were concerned, there was no *quigete* in the white plaster, but it reflected light and we did not like the glare.

That April was one of the most beautiful I remember seeing in Truxton Canyon. But we were all too shocked and fatigued by the winter's crises to respond with our usual exuberance. I little realized that these were to be my last weeks among the Walapai.

CHAPTER THIRTY

The Return

◖ I was busy preparing the pupils for their final examinations and making arrangements for my vacation at home, when a telegram came from my brother: "Mother sick. Come at once."

Friends helped me with my trunk—the trunk Mother had lovingly packed, sending me off on the adventures for which she herself had longed. Miss Speirs offered to take over my duties until I returned and Joe came to express his sympathy and make plans to see me during his vacation.

When I arrived home, Mother was gone. In our loneliness we grieved for her, but were comforted by the thought that she had embarked on the greatest of all adventures and that she had joined our father. My two small sisters needed my care. So I gave up all thought of returning to Truxton, all hope of ever again seeing the People of the Blue Water, tendered my resignation, and taught that year in the Edmond schools.

The following summer Joe and I were married. We established a business and a home for ourselves and my sisters and started our family of two sons and a daughter. But we had not given due consideration to the hold the kindly Indian people had taken on our lives. Back we went into the Indian work, this time in the nonreservation boarding schools.

Our work took us to the Chilocco Indian School at Chilocco, Oklahoma, one of the largest in the United States. Here the children of white employees attended public school. The free schooling granted Indian children was not available to those of white blood. Joe held the position of superintendent of industries, planning and supervising the work of the instructors in the various shops in which painting, carpentry, masonry, plastering, shoe and harness making, engineering and printing were taught the boys. There also were courses in dairying, stock raising, agriculture and gardening. Open for the girls were excellent courses in home economics and nursing. A student had the privilege of selecting the course in which he or she would specialize.

Indians who were financially able were required to pay the actual cost of their children's food, clothing and education in these non-reservation schools. After working among the Walapai and the Havasupai, who had so little, the wealth of some of these oil-rich Indians seemed beyond belief. I remember seeing a father, after paying his son's expenses for the year, drop a dozen ten dollar bills on the superintendent's desk, saying, "I got plenty money. My boy can buy anything he wants."

The superintendent brushed the money aside and quietly explained that each child was limited to a small quarterly allowance for spending money; his son was no exception.

Our next move was to the beautiful Indian school at Chemawa, Oregon, where Joe was again superintendent of industries, directing the teaching staff in the many shops the school maintained for the boys' training. I was principal of the academic department, which employed a large corps of teachers, including a librarian. Students who finished our tenth grade—we were permitted to carry only two years of high school work—were housed and boarded at Chemawa while they completed the eleventh and twelfth grades in the high school at Salem, the state capital, traveling back and forth by interurban.

Many of our students married and established homes of their own. A few entered universities to complete their education; one boy earned his degree and became a practicing attorney. Another taught printing in a state university. Many of them worked in factories or railroad shops, several rising to the position of foreman. Girls graduated in home economics, or took hospital training and became graduate nurses, completing their training in Los Angeles hospitals. Alaskan girls, with the teacher training we gave them, returned home to establish schools for the children of their tribes. Of course, the greater number of our students followed less glamorous paths, the girls as factory workers, salesgirls, cooks or maids in homes; the boys earning their living in the mechanical trades they had learned in the school.

Social, religious, industrial and academic training in these large schools made the little we had offered the People of the Blue Water seem small indeed. But from these small schools the ambitious pupils were transferred to the better-equipped large schools, so we were feeling, actually, the reverberations of our earlier work.

At Chemawa, both Protestants and Catholics had a resident missionary. There were YMCA and YWCA organizations, debating clubs, literary societies, glee clubs, choirs, basketball, baseball and football teams. Each spring we closed the school year with a grand finale of teas, dinners, graduation exercises, ending with an operetta for the entertainment of the school, neighboring towns and the countryside. We worked to the point of exhaustion, I'll admit, but the children's enthusiastic participation made it worth while. Adding the responsibilities of home and church to those of a modern school lengthened our hours on duty, but the school offered the all-round education these students would need in competing with young people who had enjoyed the advantages of home, church and public school training.

After long years in the large Indian schools, Joe and I retired and built our own home in pleasant California. Then, in November, 1941, we decided to spend Thanksgiving with my sister in Arizona. By swinging to the north on our return, the highway would take us through the school ground at Truxton. We decided to see what changes the years had wrought.

A winding mountain road led us up to Prescott. When we had breakfast the next morning at dawn, the town was disappointingly quiet; I wanted to turn time back to the days when life in Prescott held the recklessness and the thrills of its untamed early days.

In Seligman, some of the businessmen gave us news of the People of the Blue Water, "the Supais," as they now called them. One even offered to take us down to the Indian village, saying, "Shucks, that trip, now, ain't nothing at all! Used to be a hair-raiser." We didn't have time to make the trip, but my mind was filled with questions. Now, after forty years, would I be able to recognize my former pupils? They would be men and women, busy with their children or their grandchildren. Would they recognize in the gray-haired woman I had become, the lively young teacher who had so keenly enjoyed life in their canyon? Many teachers had come and gone, some staying a few weeks, others a few months; any impression that I had made had doubtless been lost in the motley pattern.

I knew that a flood had destroyed the old school plant and new buildings had been erected a mile downstream at the edge of the village, on ground that greatly reduced the danger from floods. A principal and two classroom teachers were appointed and a nurse came to look after the health of the Indians. New screened cottages were built, provided with running water, light and refrigeration. Strange contrast to our old stone house!

Other changes have been made. The trails have been widened, their treacherous kinks and angles straightened, making the trip down a pleasant but still exhilarating experience. Tourists need not camp under an old cottonwood tree unless they prefer the out-of-door life; accommodations are now available at the school. A letter to the Agent in Charge, Supai, Arizona, will bring all needed information as to accommodations and arrangements for an Indian guide and horses for the trip down. Automobiles may be driven to the upper end of either trail but both trails are too rugged for driving.

There is one thought the tourist will do well to keep in mind; the official in charge of the reservation is responsible for the behavior of guests. A considerate visitor will leave his little brown jug at home when he visits an Indian reserve.

A visitor will not see Vesnor's wife swishing about in her colorful *sutam*, nor Billy's wife, her delicate beauty enhanced by eye shadow and painted cheeks and chin, for *sutams* and Indian cosmetics belong to a generation that is gone. The People of the Blue Water are accepting the customs and traditions of a foreign world, a world that was almost completely ignorant of their existence prior to April 12, 1948.

On that day, a great, man-made bird floated over the rugged canyon walls and settled in the village. It was a helicopter carrying sections of metal that could not be brought in over the narrow trails—pieces of a Quonset hut, material for a house of worship. Officials of the Protestant Episcopal Church and news reporters were flown in. Messages describing the ceremony of laying the cornerstone were flashed across the nation from coast to coast. News items and magazine articles, beautifully illustrated with color photographs, followed. At last the Havasupai, hidden in their isolated, precipitous canyon, had attracted the attention of the outside world.

The last half-century has brought bewildering experiences to the People of the Blue Water. The church and the school are weaning them from the customs and traditions of Those of Old. The imperative voices of Coyote and Deer must reach but dimly ears attuned to sound movies and the telephone. To a people learning to place their faith in the Christians' God, the gods who protected their canyon home—the two giant stone columns on the rim—will soon become mere pillars of stone. The dedication of the St. Andrew's Missionary Chapel is significant of these Indians' changing world. The man who represented the tribe in this service was Chief Dudley Manakadja, son of former Chief Manakadja, who had declared that the white man and the Indian could not live on the same soil, their bloodstreams should never mingle.

We were tempted to linger, hoping to meet some of the Indians

—Spoonhead, for instance, riding in with the mail. But lack of time hurried us on to Truxton.

A new policy in the Indian Office had abolished the Truxton Canyon Training School, just as it had closed many other boarding schools, placing the pupils in small day schools scattered over the reservation. Even the name of the post office and the station had been changed from Truxton to Valentine in honor of a former Commissioner of Indian Affairs. So we were prepared for the empty, dust-covered buildings, buildings that had almost burst at the seams in accommodating the eager young life they had housed when we had seen them last.

We stopped at the administration office. The agent and his staff were eager to talk to people who had helped to establish the school. But with memories brought so poignantly alive by the sight of the old buildings, we could not discuss the school's early history, and asked permission to walk about the grounds.

We peered through dusty windows into empty buildings. What a shattering of illusions! The gigantic task of building the boarding school which Mr. Ewing had promised the Walapai for their children, had taken years. A stroke of a pen had reduced it to a useless mass of wood and stone.

It was a short walk down the slope to the big orchard, so vividly associated with memories of the old day school. Across the wash loomed old Mountain-lying-down. There it stood, unmoved by the tragedy of empty buildings that should be sheltering children and preparing them to live in an unaccustomed world. We, too, became serene. The knowledge the children had acquired at school, had gone on with them into their homes. They had the skill to build better houses, to increase the production of their land, to give their stock intelligent care instead of abuse. The men and women of the Walapai tribe and of the People of the Blue Water, who had attended school, could read and write; they could buy and sell, knowing values. The Walapai were now living in homes of their choice on the reservation. Tribal-owned herds of cattle promised a brighter future for these people.

While Joe and I lingered under the spell of those far-off days, I thought of the cave in the rimrock of a distant mesa that Daisy, Frances, Sara, Ben and I had visited. Again I felt the thrill we had experienced the day of our adventure. But had the Indians learned the sequel to that trip, they would reaffirm their belief that those who entered the cave died of the dreaded "lung sickness." They knew that Ben, who had driven the team, died of it within a few months. They did not know that, a short time later, Sara and Daisy had also died of tuberculosis, which they doubtless had in an incipient stage at the time we made the trip. Frances too is gone. I should like to hear some very old Indian, who is yet able to commune with Coyote, explain why four were taken and one left, when all were equally guilty.

In Kingman we learned the fate of Sam Swaskegame who had served in World War I, but had not returned at the war's end. The American Legion had named its Kingman Post "Swaskegame Post No. 14," honoring Sam, who had volunteered to swim a river at Chateau Thierry and enter the enemy position. While swimming toward the enemy, Sam was shot and killed. We thought of slim, eager Sam, the natural mimic—Sam, the American soldier, bravely facing death.

I recalled the scene in my classroom, brown faces bent over books, and, looking up to grin at me, Sam, his heel withdrawn from his low shoe. And I remembered my vagrant thought: *The Indian's heel trying to escape the white man's shoe.* Sam's heel had not escaped.

Many Indian boys died in World War I, but few were so honored as Sam. Three memorial services were held for him: one by the Methodist Church, one by the American Legion, but the one that no man who heard it can ever forget was the tribal ceremony conducted by Swaskegame, Sam's father. The grieving old man paid tribute to Sam the American soldier, while his lonely heart mourned for his Indian son.

We came home by way of Hoover Dam, and felt dwarfed by the monumental works of man. What would the People of the

Blue Water think if they could stand where we stood and see old Hackataia, "Roaring Noise," harnessed by the white man and made to work for him. Their own Havasu stream flowed into the muddy Colorado. The Blue Water was here in Lake Meade too, not leaping and singing and sparkling blue, yet holding for me images of the People of the Blue Water: Billy's wife, fiercely defending the memory of her dead sister; Gentle Annie, wearing the strawberry-red dress, recounting her experiences in bloody wars; Vesnor, telling me how he had been healed by the greatest Healer the world has ever known, yet still living in close touch with those strange animal spirits, Coyote, Deer and Bear, and with the god-spirit manifested in the Stones, the Water, the Sun.

The many years that I spent with the Indians had proved to be more than an adventure; they were an education. They had taught me the beauty of unquestioning faith, of dignity and a tranquil mind. An Indian, standing with face uplifted to the morning light, communing with his gods, has become to me a symbol—a symbol of oneness with the spiritual world.

The white man, also, in these tense days, is seeking complete harmony with the Supreme Being. Perhaps, if we develop the listening ear, the serenity and the unquestioning faith that are the primitive Indian's heritage, we may become more receptive to the guiding voice of that Unseen Power.